BRITISH MILITARY OPERATIONS

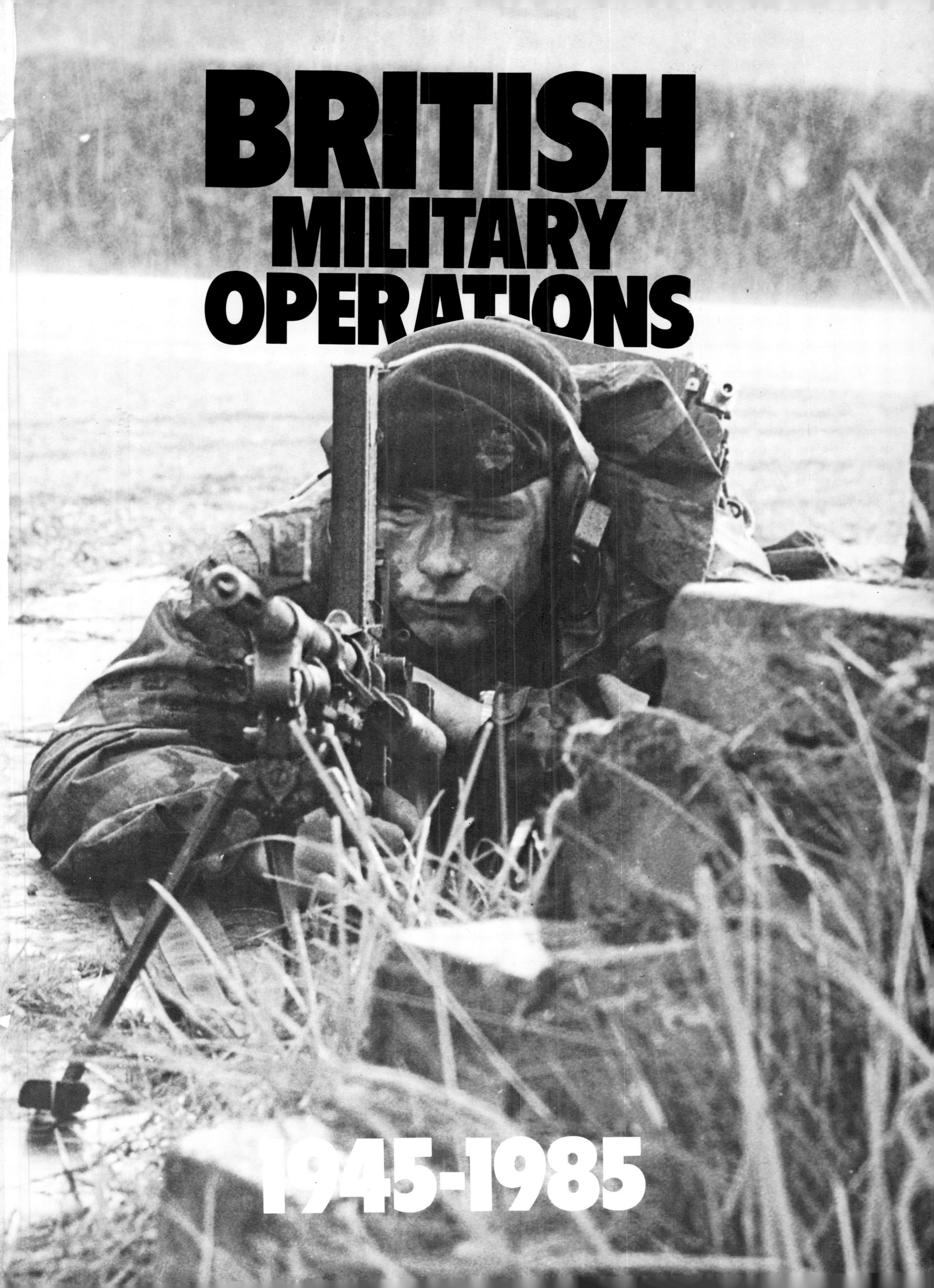

1945-1985

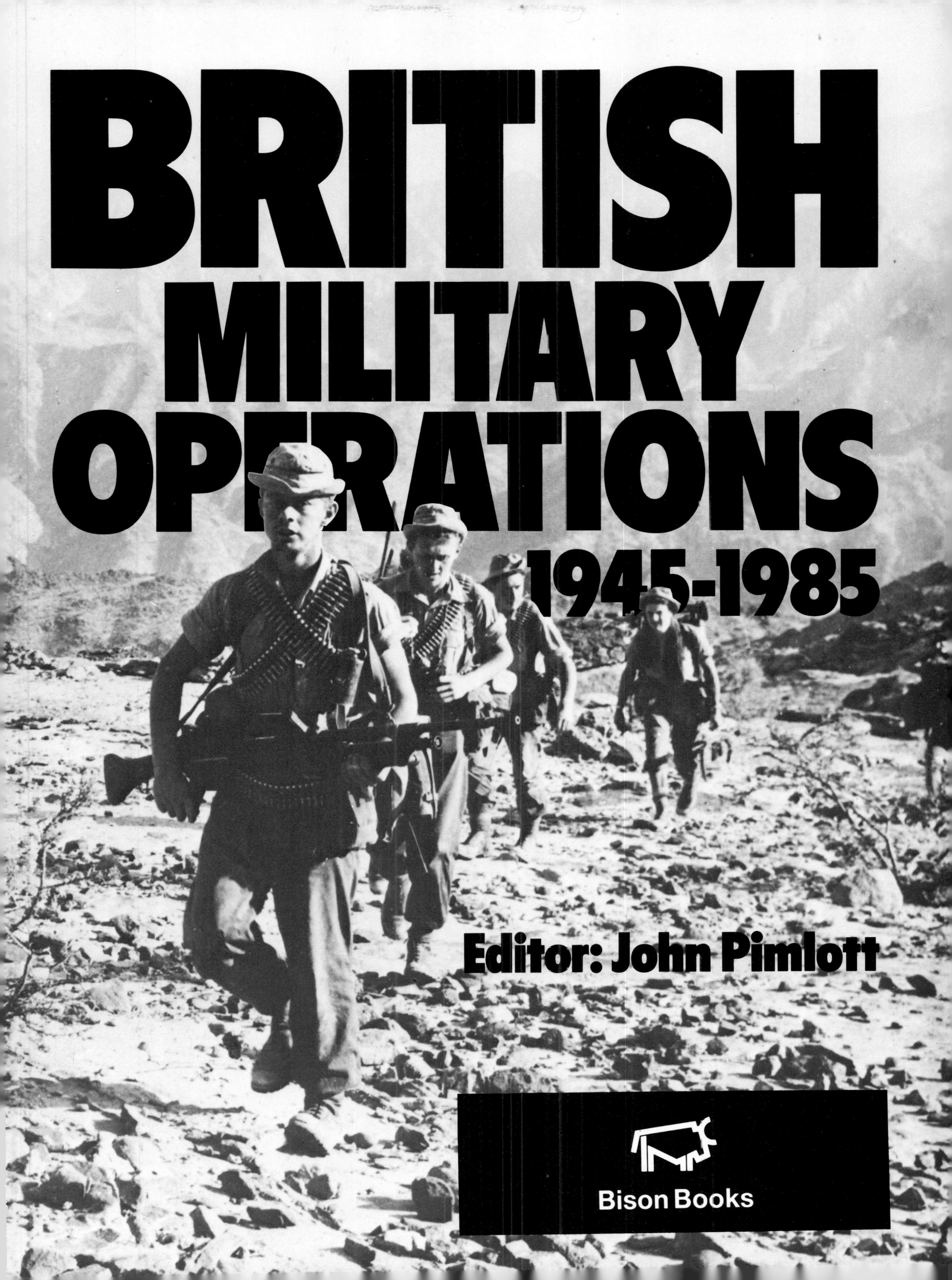

BRITISH MILITARY OPERATIONS 1945-1985

Editor: John Pimlott

Bison Books

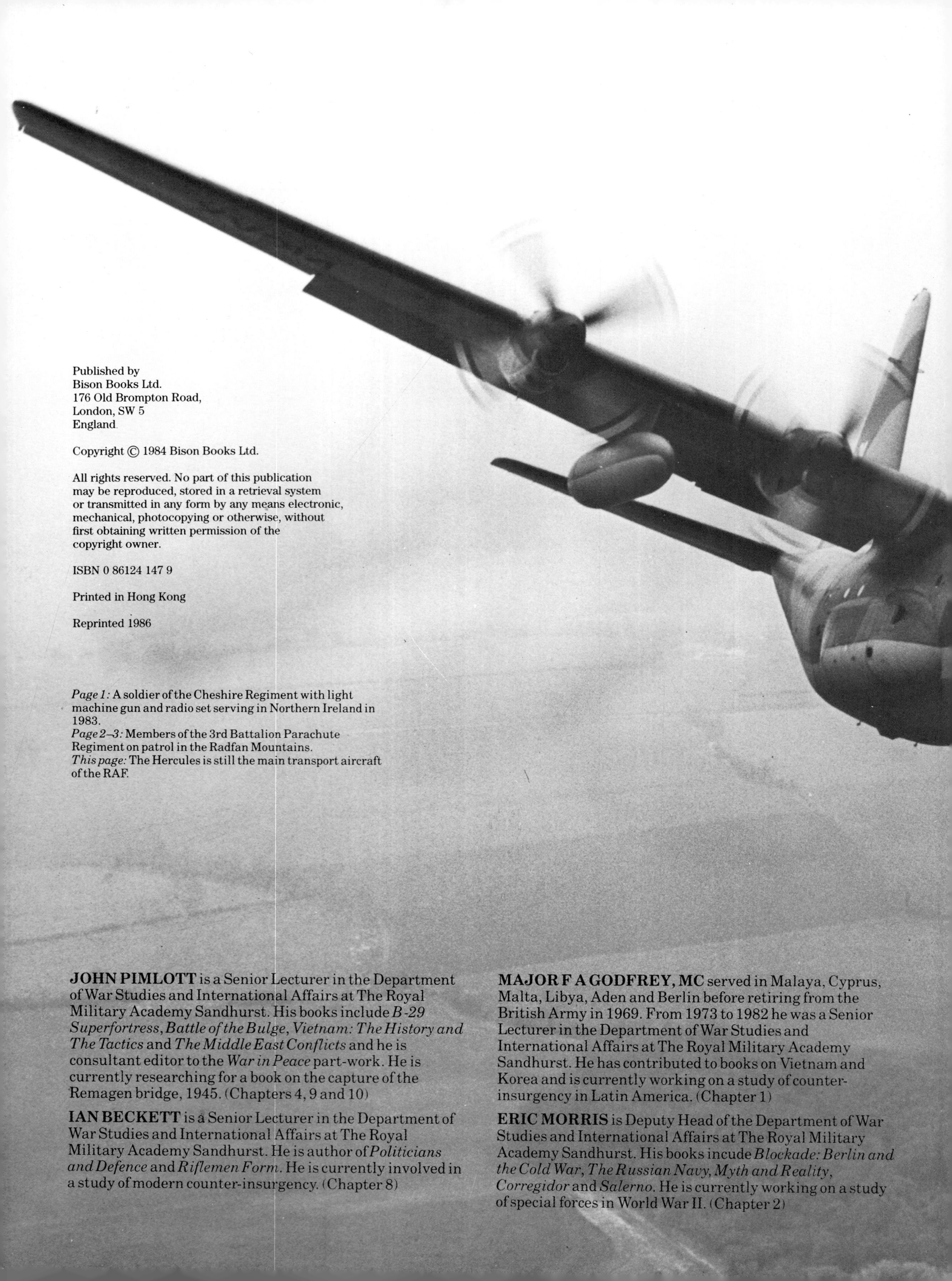

Published by
Bison Books Ltd.
176 Old Brompton Road,
London, SW 5
England

ISBN 0 86124 147 9

Printed in Hong Kong

Reprinted 1986

Page 1: A soldier of the Cheshire Regiment with light machine gun and radio set serving in Northern Ireland in 1983.
Page 2–3: Members of the 3rd Battalion Parachute Regiment on patrol in the Radfan Mountains.
This page: The Hercules is still the main transport aircraft of the RAF.

JOHN PIMLOTT is a Senior Lecturer in the Department of War Studies and International Affairs at The Royal Military Academy Sandhurst. His books include *B-29 Superfortress*, *Battle of the Bulge*, *Vietnam: The History and The Tactics* and *The Middle East Conflicts* and he is consultant editor to the *War in Peace* part-work. He is currently researching for a book on the capture of the Remagen bridge, 1945. (Chapters 4, 9 and 10)

IAN BECKETT is a Senior Lecturer in the Department of War Studies and International Affairs at The Royal Military Academy Sandhurst. He is author of *Politicians and Defence* and *Riflemen Form*. He is currently involved in a study of modern counter-insurgency. (Chapter 8)

MAJOR F A GODFREY, MC served in Malaya, Cyprus, Malta, Libya, Aden and Berlin before retiring from the British Army in 1969. From 1973 to 1982 he was a Senior Lecturer in the Department of War Studies and International Affairs at The Royal Military Academy Sandhurst. He has contributed to books on Vietnam and Korea and is currently working on a study of counter-insurgency in Latin America. (Chapter 1)

ERIC MORRIS is Deputy Head of the Department of War Studies and International Affairs at The Royal Military Academy Sandhurst. His books incude *Blockade: Berlin and the Cold War*, *The Russian Navy, Myth and Reality*, *Corregidor* and *Salerno*. He is currently working on a study of special forces in World War II. (Chapter 2)

CONTENTS

MICHAEL ORR is a Senior Lecturer in the Soviet Studies Research Group at The Royal Military Academy Sandhurst. He has written widely on modern military topics and is currently engaged on a study of Soviet counter-insurgency techniques in Afghanistan. (Chapter 6)

KEITH SIMPSON is a Senior Lecturer in the Department of War Studies and International Affairs at The Royal Military Academy Sandhurst. His previous publications include *The Old Contemptibles*. At present he is working on a book about the German Army. (Chapter 3)

FRANCIS TOASE is a Senior Lecturer in the Department of War Studies and International Affairs at The Royal Military Academy Sandhurst. He has written several articles on modern conflict and is currently preparing a contribution to a forthcoming book on counter-insurgency. (Chapter 5)

PETER REED was educated at a British provincial university and is a freelance writer who specialises in modern military affairs. He has contributed to numerous journals and is currently engaged on research to do with the American involvement in Vietnam. (Chapter 7)

INTRODUCTION

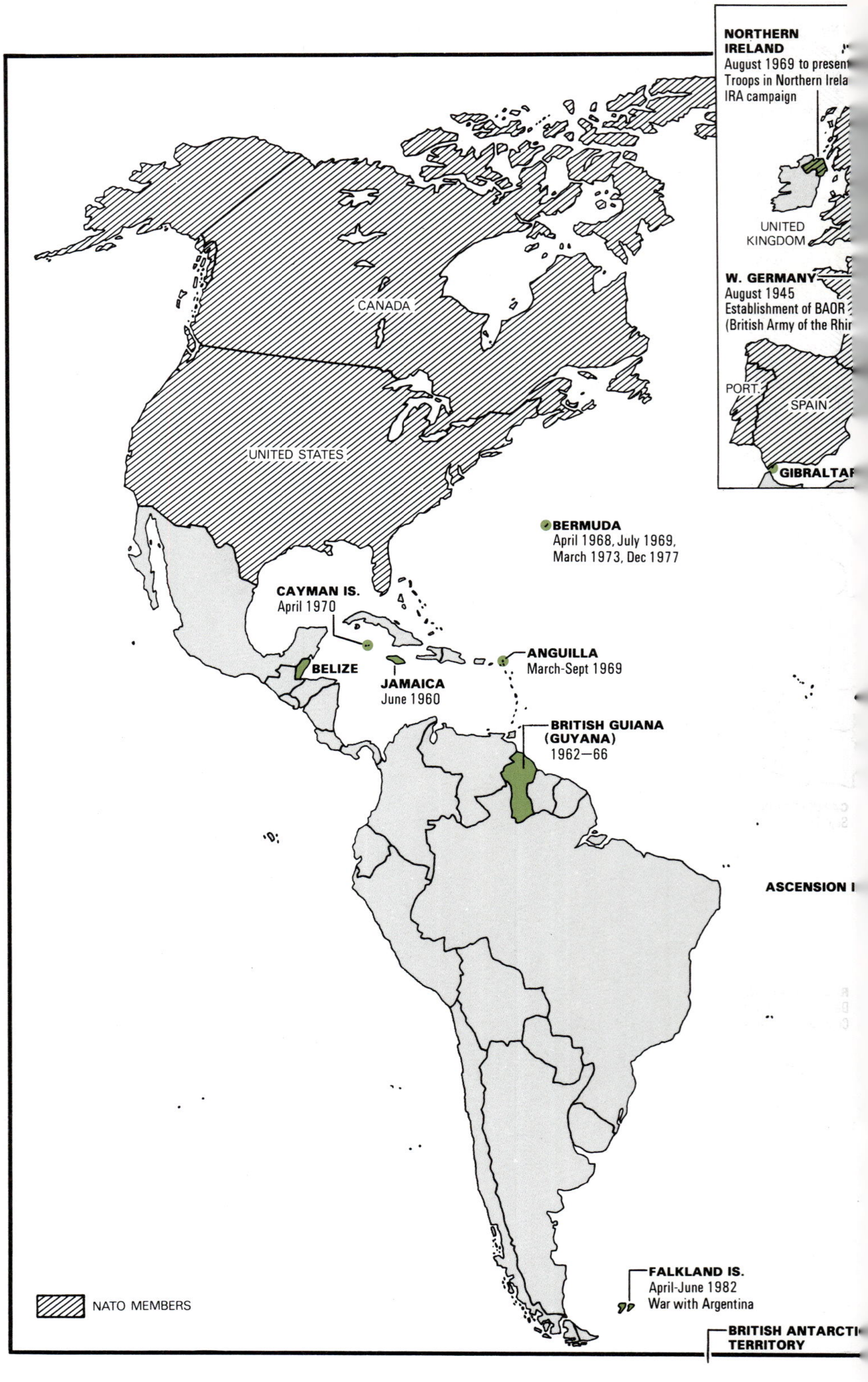

Britain is justifiably proud of her armed services. Although they may be small in number (about 320,000 personnel in 1983-84), they are undeniably efficient and highly professional in their approach to a wide range of difficult tasks. Since 1945 they have gained an enviable reputation for success in the delicate art of counter-insurgency, helping to contain guerrilla movements as far afield as Malaya, Cyprus and Northern Ireland, while at the same time retaining conventional war-fighting capability of the type displayed so recently in the Falklands. They have served with equal efficiency in the jungles of the Far East, the deserts of Arabia and the arctic wastes of northern Norway, and although their permanent presence overseas has been reduced dramatically over the last 40 years, they continue to play a part in global affairs, whether in defence of the last remnants of Britain's imperial past or as contributors to international peacekeeping efforts in Cyprus, Sinai or Lebanon. At home, they have proved adept at countering terrorism and valuable in 'aiding the civil power' at lower levels, maintaining essential services in time of crisis or clearing up after natural disasters. Most impressively, they are armed with sophisticated equipment, including strategic nuclear weapons, yet have at no time abused society's trust in them by interfering in the political processes of the state. Some of their roles and duties may not receive universal backing in a country of divergent political views, but with constant media coverage of events in Northern Ireland, Beirut or the Falklands, there can be no doubt that the armed services are firmly in the public eye and that most people accept the need to maintain them.

But this is a very modern development, for traditionally Britain has shown a marked reluctance to support her armed forces in circumstances short of grave national danger. The reasons were many and varied. Low pay, appalling living conditions, savage discipline and a short life expectancy made the prospect of enlisting in either the Navy or Army unattractive, while the unwillingness of politicians to pay for improvements merely exacerbated neglect. But these were only the natural results of Britain's security needs. As an island, she was remarkably secure from direct attack and her main concern was to protect her trading routes and colonial resource areas, the vital components of wealth and power. The main emphasis of defence efforts was therefore maritime, with the army distributed far and wide in protection of colonial possessions, and as a result the majority of campaigns were fought in a vacuum of public ignorance and a long way from home. Commitment of military forces to Europe was rare – Britain preferred to take the opportunity of European war to expand her overseas empire, subsidising allies to tie the enemy down in his own home areas – and even when it did occur, success was difficult to achieve against continental armies geared to such campaigns. Both Marlborough in the early-eighteenth century and Wellington a hundred years later found the going hard and neither would have been able to gain the victories he did without substantial help from allied forces. In such circumstances, with the exception of occasional invasion scares, the British people were content to dismiss the armed forces for the simple reason that they were rarely seen.

This began to change in the late-nineteenth century as the politics and structure of Europe developed. Before the rise of a unified Germany,

Above: British Military Operations 1945-84 and continuing military alliances and commitments.

Right: HMS *Illustrious* leaves her home port heading for the Falkland Islands immediately after the end of the fighting in 1982. *Illustrious* relieved *Invincible* on the station. Note the Phalanx multiple-barrel anti-aircraft cannon system fitted at the after end of the flight deck. This installation was rapidly provided because of the experience in the Falklands.

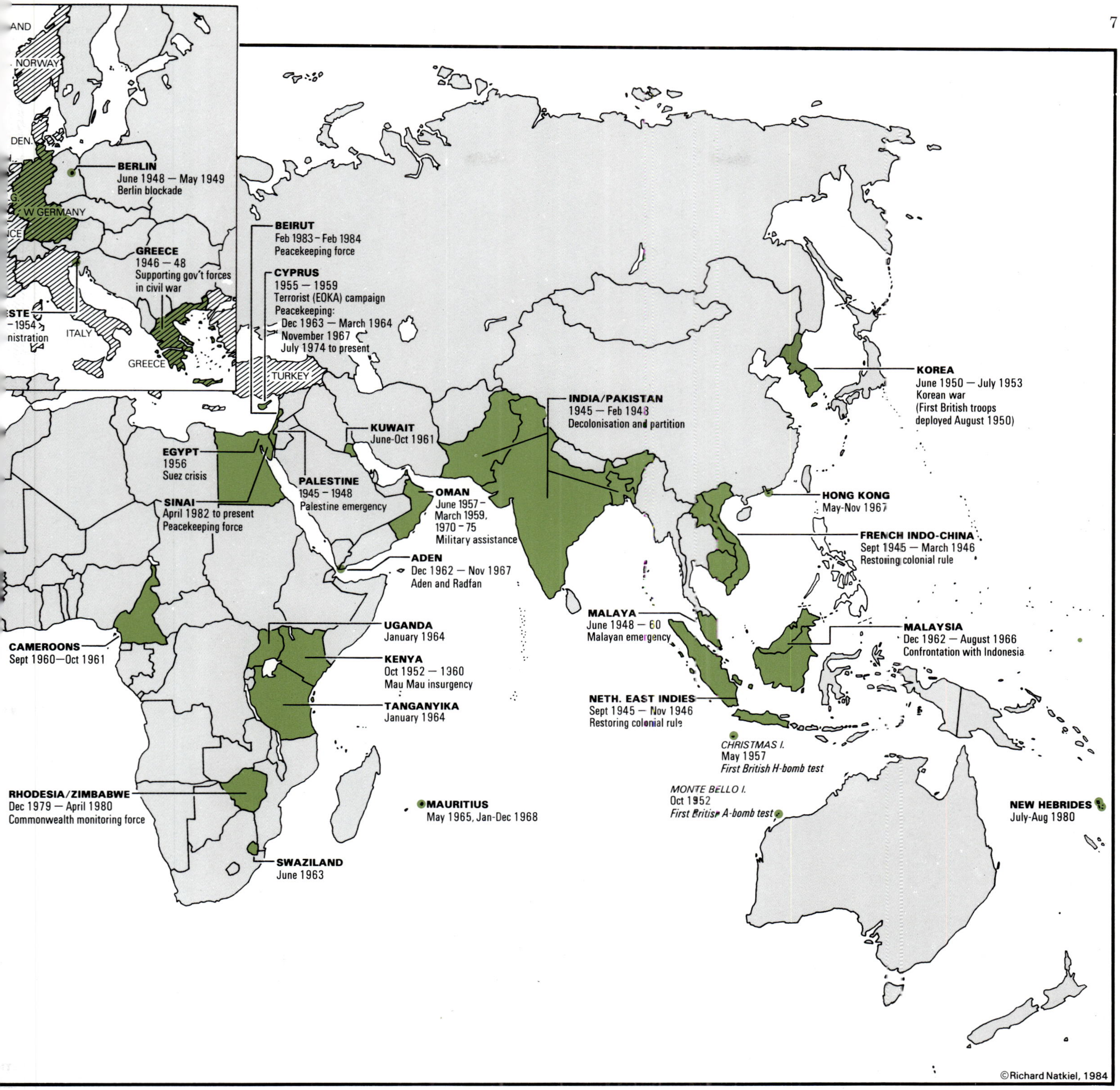
NORWAY
DEN.
W GERMANY
ITALY
GREECE
TURKEY
BERLIN
June 1948 — May 1949
Berlin blockade
GREECE
1946 — 48
Supporting gov't forces
in civil war
BEIRUT
Feb 1983 – Feb 1984
Peacekeeping force
CYPRUS
1955 — 1959
Terrorist (EOKA) campaign
Peacekeeping:
Dec 1963 — March 1964
November 1967
July 1974 to present
KOREA
June 1950 — July 1953
Korean war
(First British troops
deployed August 1950)
INDIA/PAKISTAN
1945 — Feb 1948
Decolonisation and partition
KUWAIT
June-Oct 1961
EGYPT
1956
Suez crisis
PALESTINE
1945 – 1948
Palestine emergency
SINAI
April 1982 to present
Peacekeeping force
OMAN
June 1957 –
March 1959,
1970 – 75
Military assistance
HONG KONG
May-Nov 1967
FRENCH INDO-CHINA
Sept 1945 — March 1946
Restoring colonial rule
ADEN
Dec 1962 — Nov 1967
Aden and Radfan
UGANDA
January 1964
KENYA
Oct 1952 — 1360
Mau Mau insurgency
TANGANYIKA
January 1964
CAMEROONS
Sept 1960—Oct 1961
MALAYA
June 1948 — 60
Malayan emergency
MALAYSIA
Dec 1962 — August 1966
Confrontation with Indonesia
NETH. EAST INDIES
Sept 1945 — Nov 1946
Restoring colonial rule
CHRISTMAS I.
May 1957
First British H-bomb test
MONTE BELLO I.
Oct 1952
First British A-bomb test
RHODESIA/ZIMBABWE
Dec 1979 — April 1980
Commonwealth monitoring force
MAURITIUS
May 1965, Jan-Dec 1968
NEW HEBRIDES
July-Aug 1980
SWAZILAND
June 1963
©Richard Natkiel, 1984

R06

A

Above: Practicing stalking in the Malayan jungle in the early 1950s. The soldier is armed with an air rifle and wears a fencing mask to protect his face and eyes from pellets.

Above left: British troops patrolling a bleak winter road near Maghera, County Tyrone in Northern Ireland in 1979.

Left: A Whirlwind helicopter sets down in a clearing in the Malayan jungle.

for example, Britain could always play one German state off against another to create a continental balance of power favourable to British interests, but once those states came together to form a solid territorial block, capable of projecting its own considerable influence, such expedients were less likely to succeed. Moreover, certain of the European powers, notably France and Germany, began to play Britain at her own game, creating large navies to challenge Britain's control of the sea-lanes and carving out empires which threatened the very bases of Britain's wealth. This had a number of adverse effects. Firstly, it undermined Britain's position as the manufacturing centre of Europe, for as soon as rival powers gained access to their own overseas resources they found that they could undercut British prices and take over key markets, weakening Britain's economic strength and forcing her to take more than a passing interest in European affairs. Secondly, in order to maintain a balance of power in Europe, more structured alliances had to be negotiated. Gone were the days of manipulating minor states; now if Britain wanted the security of continental allies, she had to promise something in return – usually military aid in the event of a future war. The creation of a British Expeditionary Force in 1908, designed specifically for European commitment if the need arose, marked a crucial step in this direction. Admittedly the force was small, but its existence implied an acceptance of a major shift in British security needs. From this time onwards, Britain would have to face the necessity of maintaining forces not just for colonial or trade-route protection but also for the vastly different campaigns of continental war.

Full acceptance of this new reality was painfully slow to emerge. Although British forces became involved in all aspects of the First World War (1914-18) – from Flanders and the Atlantic sea-lanes to the Middle East and Gallipoli – the conflict tended to be seen as a hideously expensive aberration which would never be repeated. In 1918, despite the inherent instability of post-war Europe and Britain's role in creating the peace settlement, her armed forces were withdrawn from continental commitment and devoted almost entirely to the protection of imperial possessions and trading routes – roles which Britain could afford to carry out now that both France and Germany had been weakened by the war. But such insularity could never last, contributing as it did to the vacuum of European politics which the fascist parties were swift to fill. Once they had emerged in Italy and Germany, Britain faced a direct threat to her homeland which could not be ignored and her involvement in renewed European commitment became inevitable. When this degenerated into the Second World War (1939-45), the long-term results were dramatic. By 1945, even if she had wanted to, Britain could not withdraw from a continent shattered by five and a half years of total war. European commitment during the ensuing peacetime period was unavoidable, particularly as the threat from the Soviet Union emerged, yet the economic importance of the imperial trading system remained. The scene was set for a period of strategic uncertainty and deep division over defence priorities as it became obvious that the country could not afford such a wide range of responsibilities.

The resolution of this dilemma constitutes the main theme of the present book, tracing as it does the pressures of global commitment in the 1940s and 1950s, the gradual decline of the imperial system through decolonisation in the 1960s and the trend towards European defence as top priority in the 1970s. The process of change has been undeniably slow and the ramifications of continued overstretch damaging to Britain's financial well-being, but it has occurred. In the process the armed forces have gained an enormous wealth of experience and faced a host of complex challenges, their response to which has invariably produced public approbation and contributed to their reputation, richly deserved, for professionalism and efficiency. Financial problems remain and may yet prove crippling, even to a purely European defence role, but nothing can alter the achievements of the last 40 years.

J L Pimlott

INDIA
AND ADJACENT COUNTRIES

THE RESPONSIBILITIES OF WORLD POWER

Britain emerged from the Second World War with high prestige, large armed forces and an unavoidable commitment to world affairs. Whereas before 1939 she had been interested primarily in policing and protecting her empire, after 1945 she was faced with vastly increased responsibilities and a need to concentrate resources in certain key areas. Not only was the original empire to be maintained as an essential source of potential wealth, needed if the country was to stand any chance at all of recovering from the financially crippling effects of total war, but the new commitment to Europe, unavoidable as a consequence of the total defeat of Germany, could not be cut down. Furthermore, many areas of the empire were demanding the same sort of political independence that the recent war had been fought to provide for the European powers and, in the Middle East especially, new nationalisms were emerging to challenge the British position. It was a complex package of commitments and problems, made worse by the fact that Britain, having devoted an estimated quarter of her pre-war national wealth to the defeat of the Axis, was close to economic collapse.

The central dilemma of Britain's post-war position in the world – that she is a country with global interests and influence but only limited economic strength – thus became apparent as early as 1945. So far as the armed forces were concerned, this was manifested in a potentially crippling degree of overstretch. At the end of the Second World War there were nearly five million members of the British armed forces, many of whom had been conscripted for the duration of hostilities only, and once their demands for demobilisation had been satisfied, it was apparent that there would not be enough service personnel remaining to carry out the new range of defence commitments. In 1947, therefore, National Service had to be introduced for the first time during a period of settled peace and for the next 15 years Britain was to face the political, social and economic problems of maintaining large conscript forces. The National Servicemen were to fight as well as their regular comrades in a host of difficult campaigns, but their existence served to symbolise the pressures of Britain's unprecedented world responsibilities.

These became apparent initially in the Far East, where the sudden surrender of Japan in August 1945 left a large number of occupied European colonies bereft of government. So far as the British were concerned, contingency plans for the liberation of their possessions had already been laid down and these were put into effect immediately, with unopposed landings in Malaya and Singapore. However, as neither the French nor the Dutch had adequate forces in the Far East, their colonies posed problems. To prevent a slide into disorder, it was decided by the Anglo-American Joint Chiefs of Staff that whatever troops were available should be used in these areas to disarm and repatriate the Japanese and restore civil administration; a policy that was to result in British-Indian forces becoming involved in the Netherlands East Indies (NEI) and the southern part of French Indochina. Unfortunately both territories contained strong nationalist movements which were determined to resist a return to colonial status, and the British found themselves caught in the midst of bitter confrontations as the Dutch and French governments sought to impose their erstwhile rule.

At first, however, it was assumed that the reoccupation would be a routine affair, especially in the NEI where it was believed that the

Above: HMS *Vanguard*, the last British battleship.

Previous page: Indian independence is confirmed, July 1947: (L to R) Nehru; Lord Ismay, British adviser; Mountbatten and Jinnah.

Right: Military policemen disperse a Black Market crowd in West Berlin, 1948.

Below: HMS *Volage*, blasted by mines off the coast of Albania, 1946.

local Indonesian people would be likely to accept a Dutch return without too great a protest. This proved to be a mistake, for during the period of Japanese rule Indonesian nationalism had developed and had been nurtured by the occupying authorities. When British forces arrived in 1945, therefore, they were quickly associated with the Dutch by local people to whom independence was a real ambition.

The first British landing took place on 29 September 1945 at Batavia (now Jakarta), the capital of Java, and it was already known from reports by a small advance group and from a naval force in NEI waters that the Indonesians were far from happy about the arrival of foreign troops. The Indonesian nationalists, led by Ahmed Sukarno, had already formed a government and achieved a semblance of political control over most of Java, so that when the British landed, accompanied by Dutch administrators intent upon reassuming colonial rule, there existed a recipe for disorders which the newly arrived troops would have to control.

It had originally been intended to reoccupy the NEI with only three brigades – two in Java and one on the neighbouring island of Sumatra.

Right: British servicemen are demobilised, December 1945, as part of a process designed to reduce the size of the armed forces for their peacetime roles. The boxes contain civilian clothes.

Main picture: The frigate HMS *Amethyst* arrives in Hong Kong, August 1949. Damaged by gunfire on the Yangtse River, between the Nationalist and Communist forces in China, on 20 April, *Amethyst* had endured three months of 'captivity' before breaking out (30/31 July) in an epic dash for the open sea.

However, the early arrival of Dutch military units and the fact that the Indonesians had already organised bodies of troops (armed and trained by the Japanese) meant that there were inevitable military clashes between the British, Dutch and Indonesians in Java and political clashes between the British and Dutch governments. In the end the decision was taken to augment the original allocation of forces and by early October 1945 the HQ of XV Corps and the 23rd Indian Division, together with HQ RAF NEI, had arrived in Batavia. By the end of the month the RAF had two fighter squadrons and a transport squadron on the island. These forces were further built up until they comprised a corps of three divisions and an armoured brigade, supported by a significant air force and the use of Royal Navy warships when they were needed.

Lieutenant General Sir Philip Christison, appointed to command Allied Forces NEI, de-

ployed his troops principally in the area of Batavia, with detachments at Semarang on the north coast and Sourabaya at the north-eastern end of Java. On arrival the first units to land found little semblance of law and order, but after they had deployed they gradually restored some degree of normality, curbing the looting, arson and murder that had been rife. In many cases local commanders used Japanese units to help them in this task, ordering them to do so in accordance with the terms of surrender which had been negotiated.

There remained, however, the problem posed by what were termed 'extremists' among the Indonesian people – those who were armed and organised into military groups, intent upon resisting a return of the Dutch. In Sourabaya Brigadier Mallaby, commander of 49th Brigade, tried to negotiate with the local Indonesian leaders as soon as he arrived on 25 October. Despite an agreement, fighting broke out between British and Indonesian forces and Mallaby was murdered when he personally attempted to organise a ceasefire. Further efforts to restore peace were unsuccessful and with the aid of reinforcements and supported by both the Royal Navy and the RAF, the town had to be taken by force. The operation was completed by 22 December 1945, by which time an advance party of Dutch forces had arrived to take over from the British. In the event, this did not happen until the autumn of 1946. Similar problems occurred with the landing at Semarang, although the fighting was not on the same scale. Even so, reinforcements had to be moved in and the area was not secured until January 1946.

In Batavia it was a different story. To ensure control there, it proved necessary to deploy forces well inland from the coastal region and this provided an opportunity for well-armed bands of Indonesians to ambush the roads between garrisons. These attacks went on for a year with little respite for the British troops, who lived in fortified positions and expended much effort in picketing roads to protect their lines of communication. In March 1946 Dutch forces began to build up effective strength, but it was not until the following November that the last British troops could be withdrawn. Men of the 26th Indian Division, deployed to Sumatra to restore order at the end of 1945, were among the last to leave. It had been a difficult operation and one which the British forces had not expected to carry out. The fact that they did so in an unfamiliar country against active opposition says much for their inherent flexibility and military skill.

Such attributes were also needed in southern Indochina at the same time, for when British-Indian forces arrived in Saigon in September 1945 as part of an allied move to clear the former French possessions of Vietnam, Laos and Cambodia, they entered an area in which indigenous nationalist groups, centred upon the communist-controlled Viet Minh, had already seized effective power from the surrendering Japanese and set up a revolutionary government in Hanoi. Viet Minh strength was concentrated in the northern region known as Tonkin, but their organisation had also been built up in the south where the British were involved, and when the Nationalist Chinese, who moved into the north to repatriate Japan-

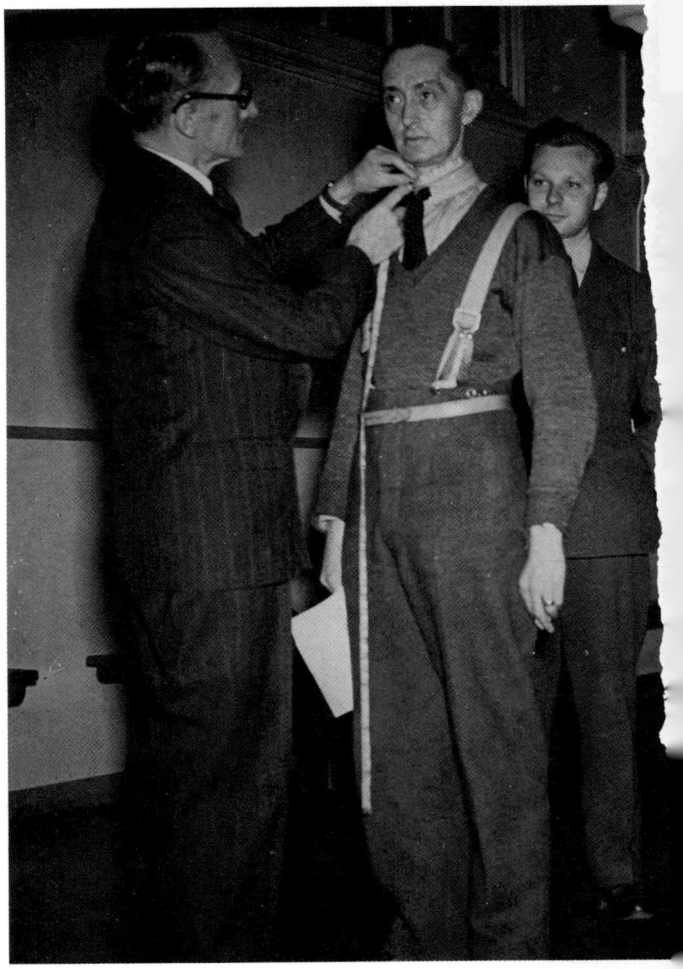

Right: RAF personnel, waiting to be demobilised, are measured for the civilian clothes which every serviceman received on his return to civilian life, 1945.

Below: The last British rulers of India: Field Marshal Lord Wavell (left) greets his replacement as Viceroy, Lord Mountbatten, at New Delhi, March 1947. Mountbatten's task was to prepare the way for independence.

ese troops, did nothing to destroy the new government, many Vietnamese presumed that the French were not going to return. The British, therefore, faced a situation very similar to that which pertained in the NEI, and despite initial orders that they were merely to supervise the Japanese surrender and restore law and order up to the 16th parallel, it soon became apparent that the French were intent upon reasserting their authority, using the British presence as a preliminary move.

The first British troops landed by air near Saigon on 8 September 1945 and thereafter the build up continued until by the middle of October all three brigades of Major General D D Gracey's 20th Indian Division were present. They faced a very tense situation in which it was clear that a return to colonial status was unwelcome. In many areas a state of lawlessness prevailed and active resistance broke out in numerous places as British and then French troops made their appearance. This took the form of attacks on individuals and on convoys of vehicles, and it soon became obvious to Gracey that he would not be able to deploy his forces throughout the whole of southern Indochina in sufficient strength to secure universal law and order. As a consequence he sought and obtained authority to concentrate his men in the general area of Saigon, with the intention of holding this as a base until sufficient French forces had arrived from elsewhere in the Far East and from France itself for the French to assume

Below: Indonesian policemen (second from left and far right) are marched away under British guard after having been disarmed, Batavia (Jakarta), September 1945.

Above: British troops on the streets of Calcutta, August 1946, in an attempt to separate Hindu and Moslem rioters. They could do little to prevent the bloodshed of intercommunal fighting which preceded Indian independence.

responsibility and allow the British to depart.

Despite an initial shortage of troops, Gracey acted with considerable firmness to restore order in Saigon. He issued directives prohibiting demonstrations, meetings and the carrying of weapons, and imposed a rigorous curfew, proclaiming that anyone disobeying his orders would be summarily shot. Nevertheless, throughout September the situation continued to deteriorate, with persistent attacks on radio stations, power plants and water supplies. Roads were also blocked, impeding the necessary movement of troops and, with only one brigade as yet deployed, Gracey, like his counterparts in the NEI, was forced to turn to the Japanese for help, rearming units to assist British troops to bring an end to violence.

The remaining two brigades of 20th Division arrived during the first half of October and with them came the first major French military units under General Leclerc. The three British brigades were all deployed in and around Saigon and once they were in position they soon established a reasonably effective control of the city and the roads leading into it. This enabled the French to assume a larger measure of control in November, relieving the British 32nd and 80th Brigades before the end of the month. By 19 December 100th Brigade to the north of Saigon had also been relieved and by early February 1946 virtually all British forces had been withdrawn. A few remained behind until March to supervise the last of the Japanese repatriations, but by then the French had as-

sumed full responsibility in the region. The brief period of British occupation had witnessed none of the large-scale operations which characterised the commitment to the NEI, but the problems of unfamiliar terrain and maintaining law and order were the same. The experience was to prove valuable as the British in turn faced the first of the demands for political independence from their own colonial possessions.

These demands were heard most forcibly from India, where the clamour for independence had developed during the Second World War and had been nurtured by promises that it would be granted in the long term. But the mood of the Indian people was that it should happen quickly and tension rose in the winter of 1945-46 as the country fell into the grip of heady emotions. Mutinies occurred in units of the Indian Army, necessitating the commitment of British battalions to put them down. In March 1946 the British government attempted to persuade Indian political leaders to work together to decide on the type of government they wished for themselves, but in the discussions that followed it soon became obvious that the Congress Party (largely composed of Hindus) and the Moslem League could not co-operate. The Moslems, in the minority, feared domination by the Hindus and their fears were fuelled by a wave of brutal inter-communal battles.

The worst fighting, looting and destruction occurred in Calcutta in August 1946 and the police quickly proved unable to cope. Six British battalions were called into the city to restore order. For five days and nights the troops were deployed against the violent mobs and when at last the city fell silent, these same troops were left with the task of cleaning up and removing the hundreds of corpses which lay in every street and yard. One company disposed of no fewer than 517 bodies found in its area of operations. But the violence did not subside, inter-communal fighting broke out in Bombay, Delhi and the Punjab, and as Indian Army units joined the British troops in quelling the disturbances, India seemed close to anarchy.

In February 1947 the British government announced that it intended to grant India independence by June 1948 at the latest. This merely led to more outbreaks of violence as the Indian people gave vent to their fears for the future. In June 1947 it was agreed that India should become two states – Hindu India and Moslem Pakistan – and on 18 July independence was confirmed for 15 August in a desperate attempt to restore stability. In the last stages before independence British troops were withdrawn from operations in support of the civil power and prepared for departure. Units of the Indian Army were formed into the Punjab Frontier Force to sustain law and order along the frontier between the two new countries, although this did little to stop the fighting. The last British troops withdrew from the sub-continent in February 1948, bringing to an end some two centuries of service in the region.

There was more to the 'loss' of India than mere emotion, for the withdrawal undermined much of the *raison d'être* of the empire. The host of far-flung possessions which came under British rule in the nineteenth and early twentieth centuries were designed principally to protect the trading routes to and from the apparently limitless wealth of India, and once that was no longer available, the strategic necessity of the empire ceased to exist. In addition, with the imperial trading system now disrupted, one of the main sources of Britain's wealth declined dramatically, at a time when post-war economic problems were already chronic. Finally, the loss of the Indian Army, usually deployed to protect British interests in the Far East and even Arabia as well as to defend India itself, effectively halved the

Right: A British soldier with a Bren light machine gun at a street corner in Bombay, September 1946. Inter-communal rioting was as bad here as in Calcutta, resulting in hundreds of deaths.

number of troops available for colonial policing. The British Army and RAF may no longer have had to provide large numbers of men for commitment to India after 1947, but they were left to defend the rest of a still-substantial empire on their own. The problem of overstretch was hardly solved by Indian independence and it began to seem as if Britain would have to make a major reassessment of her defence policy, based upon a gradual withdrawal from the remains of the declining empire. Events in the mandate of Palestine, a region of importance to the protection of the Suez Canal (a central core of the imperial trading system), appeared to suggest that such a reassessment was taking place in the late 1940s.

Opposition to continued British rule in Palestine came principally from the Jews, angry at official policies which restricted the flow of refugees from war-torn Europe and intent upon the creation of an independent state of Israel. At first Jewish groups attempted to whip up large-scale riots in both Jerusalem and Tel Aviv, but when British forces effectively countered these, more violent tactics were used by the Jewish secret army, the *Haganah*, and its ferocious breakaway elements, the *Irgun Zvai Leumi* and Stern Gang. British problems were not eased by the fact that the Arabs, quick to recognise what was in store for them, also exerted pressure, especially after the decision to withdraw from the mandate was announced in 1947.

Throughout the period 1945-48 the British Army in Palestine faced resourceful and relentless enemies who not only attacked the British but also fought each other to secure advantage for their own cause. As a result the army became ever more stretched and reinforcements had to be deployed. At the end of the Second World War the 1st Infantry Division was the only formation in Palestine, but was also responsible for stabilising a difficult situation in neighbouring Syria and Lebanon. It was reinforced in autumn 1945 by the 6th Airborne Division from Germany although, as an indication of the beginnings of overstretch, this formation should have been held back as part of the Middle Eastern strategic reserve. In March 1947 the 3rd Infantry Division was deployed to southern Palestine, completing a commitment which Britain was hard-pressed to afford.

The tasks faced by these units were many and varied; quite frequently dangerous, often routine and boring. Acting as they were in aid of the civil power, the troops were nearly always employed in support of the police or, as increasingly became the case, instead of the police when the latter found themselves overwhelmed and unable to sustain law and order. Intelligence, particularly about the Jewish groups, was invariably poor and soldiers found it extremely frustrating to be constantly reacting to situations about which they had no prior knowledge. Operations, therefore, tended to be confined to controlling riots – as in autumn 1945 when men of the 6th Airborne Division were deployed to Tel Aviv – or preserving at least an element of law and order, invigilating curfews and guarding important points such as power stations, telephone exchanges or military installations. Occasionally a more positive move would be authorised, such as after the Jewish bombing of the King David Hotel in July 1946, when a major cordon-and-search operation was mounted into Jewish areas. It lasted four days and resulted in the detention of some 700 suspects. But against guerrilla groups with strong support among the local population of their own faith, long-term results were rarely achieved.

Thus by September 1947 the British government, acknowledging the intractable nature of the Palestinian problem and aware that such a large commitment of resources was impossible to maintain indefinitely, announced that it would be relinquishing the mandate in the following year, handing the question over to the United Nations. From then onwards, the emphasis of the fighting shifted from attacks on

Above: Sabotage in Palestine: a train carrying supplies has been derailed, probably by Jewish guerrillas, near Hadera, January 1946.

Left: An ELAS stronghold in Athens is attacked by British paras.

Right: A British para NCO, accompanied by a member of the Palestine Police, displays part of a Jewish arms cache, Palestine, 2 September 1946.

Far right: British officer Orde Wingate, famous as the leader of the Chindits in Burma (1943-44), helped to train the first Jewish fighters ('Special Night Squads' of the *Haganah*) in the late 1930s, inadvertently sowing the seeds for anti-British actions ten years later.

6

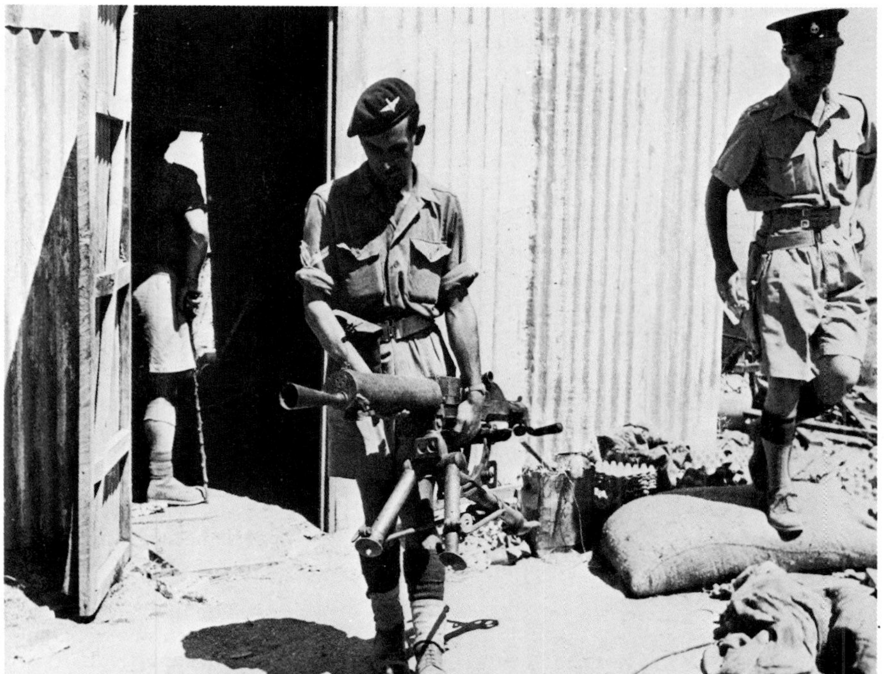

Above: Jewish dissidents received some of their training in the British Army: here Brigadier E S Benjamin (standing) addresses officers of the Jewish Brigade Group, March 1945. Formed in September 1944, this Group fought in Italy under the British Eighth Army, but many of its members later joined the *Haganah* and other anti-British formations.

the British Army to conflict between Jews and Arabs intent upon securing their respective positions. British units still had to be deployed to hold the two sides apart whenever possible, particularly as the date for withdrawal came nearer, but when the mandate expired on 15 May 1948 the situation was one in which the British were no longer involved. The campaign as a whole had cost 338 British lives (soldiers, police and civilians): a small price in terms of the nature of the fighting but one which contributed yet more to the pressures of overstretch.

Nevertheless, the end of the mandate did release badly needed troops for duty elsewhere and implied a recognition of the problems of post-war over-commitment. This was apparently reinforced, also in 1948, when Britain withdrew from her involvement in Greece, where a civil war between monarchists and communists had been raging since 1946. British interest in the outcome had been manifested in the deployment of substantial forces to northern Greece in support of the existing anti-communist government. These forces were never heavily committed to fighting the communists, but their existence acted as a powerful symbol of Western concern and it was only after the United States had agreed to take Britain's place in supporting the Greek government that withdrawal could occur. As in the NEI, Indochina, India and Palestine, the fighting was to continue in Greece after the British had left, but their decision to go did begin to rationalise an impossible crisis of global overstretch.

Right: British paras guard Jewish suspects, rounded up in Haifa during one of the periodic cordon-and-sweep operations designed to root out the guerrillas, 1946.

The main reason for this crisis lay in Europe, where in May 1945 the British found themselves unavoidably committed to the occupation of a specific area of Germany, together with similar responsibilities in Austria and northern Italy. Because of the terms of unconditonal surrender imposed on the defeated Axis powers, there was no civilian government left in authority and British troops, in common with their American, Russian and French allies, found themselves deployed to administer a defeated population. In the British zone of occupation in northern Germany, this amounted to some 20 million native Germans plus approximately a million refugees and 'displaced persons' and over two million members of the German armed forces who had surrendered.

Well before the war in Europe had ended, the Allies had agreed on the division of Germany into zones and the creation of an Allied Control Council, comprising the four Commanders-in-

Above: A tramp steamer, packed with Jewish refugees, approaches the coast of Palestine, July 1946. The interception of such vessels and the refusal to allow their occupants to enter Palestine, did little to help Britain in the eyes of the world.

Left: People run for cover as the King David Hotel, Jerusalem, blows up, 22 July 1946. Housing the British secretariat, the Hotel was hit by Irgun terrorists in one of the most spectacular acts of the Palestinian campaign.

Right: British Security Force personnel view the damage inflicted on the Palestine Police CID Headquarters, Jerusalem, by a Jewish bomb, January 1946.

Below: British paras display the contents of a Jewish arms cache, September 1946. The soldier in the centre is holding a German MG34 light machine gun. Sten guns, pistols, rifles and even a heavy machine gun (of German World War I vintage) complete the haul.

Chief of the victorious armies, which was effectively the government of the defeated state. The system was mirrored within each zone, where special Control Commissions were set up by elements of the armed forces, and similar organisations were established to administer occupied Austria. In such circumstances, where the alternative would have been to leave millions of people to starve in an anarchistic vacuum which the Soviets would probably have been pleased to fill, the Western Allies had no choice but to maintain substantial armed forces in Europe despite the onset of peace. To the British, this was just one more responsibility and one more contribution to overstretch.

At the grass-roots level of the British zone of occupation in Germany, the necessary administrative work was carried out by men of the 12 divisions of the 21st Army Group which, led by Field Marshal Viscount Montgomery, had fought its way from Normandy, across the Rhine and onto the north German plain in 1944-45. In August 1945, however, 21st Army Group ceased to exist and the army in Germany was renamed the British Army of the Rhine (BAOR). This formation supported the British Military Government, but was also organised into a military hierarchy capable of taking the field if the need arose. Unfortunately, its strength was gradually whittled away over the next 12 months as demobilisation went ahead. By early 1948 it comprised only the 2nd Infantry and 7th Armoured Divisions, together with 16th Parachute Brigade and a separate brigade in Berlin. By then, the situation in Europe had begun to change and the forces were needed for more than mere occupation duties.

Even before the cessation of hostilities in May 1945 there had been signs that the wartime alliance between the Western powers and the Soviet Union was beginning to crumble. While the German armies had continued to fight, the Allies had been equally bent on their destruction, but when thoughts turned to what should happen in Europe after the war, there was much room for argument and misunderstanding. It soon became apparent that the Soviet Union was determined to secure its borders by controlling the east European countries that lay adjacent to it. After the war, the Soviets gave clear indications that their zone of Germany fell into this category and that they had no intention of allowing a reunited Germany to enter the family of European nations. The Western allies saw these moves as aggressive and expansionist rather than defensive and in consequence the role of their armies in western Europe changed from that of administering a defeated nation to one of defence against a possible move on the part of the Soviets. In Britain's case, any hopes of a return to traditional military aloofness from the affairs of Europe rapidly disappeared, and BAOR gradually developed into a more effective fighting organisation geared to resist any threat from the Soviet forces.

By 1948, the Soviets had clearly demonstrated their determination not to co-operate further with the West and in that year they increased the build-up of pressure in Germany and began actively to threaten the Western garrisons in the enclave of Berlin. To get to the city, the Western allies had to cross some 160km (100 miles) of Soviet-occupied Germany and, although no written agreement had been signed between them and the Russians regarding communications, they had used road, rail, canal and air routes to support their isolated garrisons in Berlin since 1945. These proved to be extremely vulnerable as consensus between the powers over the future of the city and of Germany as a whole deteriorated, and from January 1948 onwards the Soviets began to impose small, almost unnoticed, restrictions on Western movement in and out of Berlin. Passenger traffic was curbed in a variety of ways and by one means or another the movement of supplies was slowed down. In early June, under a somewhat bogus pretext, the Soviets insisted on inspecting all freight routed to the city and then, on 15 June, the autobahn was closed, ostensibly for repairs to the bridge over the River Elbe. By the 24th all routes overland to the city had been closed and only aircraft remained to move men and supplies, including all the food and necessities of life for the Berliners within the Western sectors.

Above: Casualties are carried from the wreckage of the King David Hotel, 22 July 1946. They are among the lucky ones: 91 of their colleagues died in the blast.

Left: David Ben-Gurion, Jewish political leader who declared the formation of the State of Israel on 14 May 1948, 24 hours before the British withdrew from the troubled mandate of Palestine.

The problem which now confronted the West was one of enormous magnitude. A daily average of 12,000 tons of supplies had normally been channelled into the city to provide for the garrison and the civilian population. Faced with a choice of either abandoning their position in Berlin or attempting to break the blockade, the West instigated an airlift. Within two days of the closure of the land routes, the RAF flew 48 Dakotas into Gatow, the only airfield in the British sector, and the French and Americans followed suit in their areas of responsibility. An intricate flight programme soon developed, and was to increase in scope as the weeks went by.

The RAF flew not only Dakotas but also Yorks and Lancasters, as well as its latest transport aircraft, the Hastings. Small British civil aviation companies came into being and earned respect as well as profit from flying in cargoes which were often of a dangerous nature, such as petrol, paraffin and oil. At its peak the combined allied airlift was delivering a daily average of 7000 tons of essential supplies to Berlin; on one memorable day (16 April 1949) no less than 12,941 tons were shifted. Nor was it just the RAF involved on the British side, for the army too was heavily committed. The British zone of occupation in Germany lay closest to Berlin, so to shorten flights as far as possible, all the allied air fleets required airfields within it. The Royal Engineers worked day and night to develop existing facilities and to refurbish old wartime grass strips long neglected; the Royal Army Service Corps developed procedures for receiving, loading, unloading and distributing a vast array of supplies both in the zone of occupation and in Berlin itself. It was an elaborate organisation, but one that worked remarkably well during the difficult and often dangerous conditions of the winter of 1948-49.

Despite continual harassment of the airlift, the Russians stopped short of mounting a full-scale attack on the supply aircraft that lumbered ceaselessly over their zone of Germany towards the beleaguered city and in the end were forced to admit defeat. In May 1949, after 11 gruelling months, the blockade was lifted, communication routes were gradually reopened and life in Berlin returned to a more normal footing. The crisis had demonstrated once and for all that relations between the Soviet Union and the West were now hostile, and the latter took firm steps to build up its defences against any further threats that might develop. Already, in March 1948, Britain, France and the Benelux countries had put their signatures to the Brussels Treaty, pledging mutual support, and although there may have been doubts about their ability to defend themselves against the might of the Soviet forces, they had at least recognised the existence of a threat from the East. As the Berlin Blockade developed, the Americans moved to join their European allies and, in an unprecedented step, on 4 April 1949 committed themselves to the protection of Western Europe by signing an agreement with 11 other

Left: Map showing the three main air corridors from the allied occupation zones of western Germany into West Berlin, 1948-49. Road and rail links were closed by the Russians in June 1948, causing the crisis and necessitating the airlift.

Right: A Sunderland V flying-boat of No 201 Squadron RAF, helps to evacuate children from the Havel See, two miles south of Gatow in the British sector of West Berlin, November 1948. The idea, having brought in supplies, was to move out unnecessary civilians, so reducing the numbers who had to be sustained.

Below right: Men of the Royal Welch Fusiliers travel to Berlin by Dakota to relieve the Royal Norfolk Regiment as part of the British garrison, 1948.

Below: Jewish civilians, rounded up in a cordon-and-search operation in Tel Aviv, are interrogated by members of the Palestine Police in the aftermath of the King David Hotel blast, July 1946. Little hard information was discovered.

countries (Britain, France, Canada, the Netherlands, Belgium, Luxembourg, Italy, Portugal, Denmark, Norway and Iceland) to form the North Atlantic Treaty Organisation (NATO). Once this had happened the British, like the Americans, were pledged to contribute to the long-term collective defence of the European continent.

It was a turning-point in modern British defence policy, the ramifications of which were to be enormous. Gone were the days of aloofness from European affairs and isolation within the protective strength of an imperial system. As events since 1945 had already served to indicate, that imperial system was declining and, with the loss of India in 1947, no longer economically viable, while the importance of Europe to the defence of Britain itself was obviously growing. It was to take another 20 years for the shift in priorities to be fully recognised, but by 1949 the writing was on the wall. Even so, the conflicts continued and the armed forces, drawing on the wealth of experience already gained since 1945, faced a variety of new challenges. One of the most difficult of these began in 1950, a long way from Europe and outside the empire, as Britain, in concert with United Nations allies, fought against a communist attack in Korea. It was to be a bitter war.

THE KOREAN WAR

On 25 June 1950 the North Korean Army, trained and armed by the communists, stormed across the 38th parallel and invaded the South. Even while the hopelessly outmatched and outgunned South Korean Army fell back in disarray through the capital city of Seoul, its patron, the United States, took prompt action. On 27 June the US ambassador tabled an emergency resolution before the Security Council which called upon member states of the United Nations to lend military support to the embattled Republic. The absence of the Soviet delegation (a protest at the continued presence of the Nationalist Chinese on the Security Council) allowed the resolution to be passed. On the following day Royal Navy units from the Pacific Fleet based in Japanese waters were placed under the command of General MacArthur, America's supremo in Tokyo.

Above: A British sniper, camouflaged in his hide and forward of the battle line, observes the enemy positions and awaits a target of opportunity.

Previous page: A 25-pounder of 14th Field Regt RA firing in support of the Commonwealth Division. By the summer of 1952 the war had become a largely static affair where artillery played a major part in countering the numerical superiority of the communist forces.

It was another six weeks before the first British military contingents set foot on Korean soil. By that time Seoul had long since fallen, American troops, hastily rushed from occupation duties in Japan, had been humbled in battle, and the confused survivors were holding on grimly to a last line of defence in the far south, the Pusan Perimeter. It was there, on 28 August 1950, that the 1st Battalions of the Middlesex Regiment and the Argyll and Sutherland Highlanders came ashore. At first it was intended that the troops would spend a while adjusting to local conditions before moving into the line under overall American command. However, within a matter of days the North Koreans unleashed an offensive across the Naktong River which then formed part of the front held by the 2nd (US) Infantry Division. The Americans, unable to contain the attack, fell back and the British troops were rushed forward to fill the breach in the line. The two battalions found themselves responsible for an immense front of 16,500m (18,000 yards) of mountainous and rugged terrain. Fortunately, by the time the deployment was complete, the communist forces had exhausted their resources and the offensive had lost its momentum.

Relief to the Pusan Perimeter came on 15 September with MacArthur's brilliant landings at Inchon. The newly formed Eighth Army now planned to break out of Pusan, advance north and link up with the US Marines at Inchon. The two British battalions, under the command of the 24th (US) Infantry Division, were ordered to protect the left flank of the advance. At first the North Koreans resisted furiously. Isolated pockets of the enemy clung tenaciously to

Right: Men of the 1st Battalion, the Middlesex Regiment, travelling in US transport, move towards the front near Chilgok during the bitter fighting in the Pusan Perimeter, 3 September 1950.

Left: Men of 41 Commando, Royal Marines, wearing American-issued combat clothing against the bitter Siberian winter, await an air supply drop near Koto-Ri, December 1950.

U.S.A.
4867921

mountain tops and ridgelines from which they could only be prised with the utmost difficulty. British troops were involved in one such operation when in a freak accident an air strike by American Mustangs hit the wrong hill. Two companies of Argylls were on a feature known as Point 282, and although the recognition panels were clearly displayed, napalm bombs very soon turned the whole position into a blazing inferno which left less than 40 men able to fight. In the ensuing confusion the North Koreans attacked and drove the dazed Scots from the hill. Major Muir, the battalion's second-in-command, led the survivors in an immediate counterattack and retook the hill. But there were by now only 20 men left, their position was quite untenable and they were ordered to withdraw. Muir was mortally wounded in the engagement and subsequently awarded a posthumous Victoria Cross. Six officers and 80 men from the Argylls were casualties in that first bloody battle.

By the end of September the Eighth Army had broken the back of enemy resistance and, as their survivors streamed north in confusion, linked up with the US Marines who were by then fighting in Seoul. The British battalions regrouped and were joined by the 3rd Battalion, Royal Australian Regiment, to complete the 27th Commonwealth Infantry Brigade.

The Brigade, now part of the 1st (US) Cavalry Division, joined in the headlong pursuit of an elusive enemy across the 38th parallel, deep into North Korea towards the Yalu River. The victorious UN forces were confident of a quick and easy victory. Commonwealth battalions took it in turn to spearhead an advance which, in the fog of war, found itself on occasion inextricably mixed with fleeing columns of the enemy. The Middlesex played a prominent part in the capture of Pyongyang, capital of the North, which fell on 20 October. There was minimum resistance and the war seemed to be as good as won.

In the absence of any clear directives it now seemed to be the UN intention to bring the remaining communist forces to battle, capture their government and possibly unite the

Left: Soldiers of Princess Patricia's Canadian Light Infantry assemble in a rear area and prepare their equipment before moving forward into the front line, February 1951.

Bottom left: From the outset, UN air strikes against communist lines of communication proved a decisive factor. This bridge in North Korea has been destroyed by Royal Navy Fireflys from the carrier HMS *Theseus*, December 1950.

Below: In the early days, the UN Forces had to rely on armoured support provided by tanks of Second World War vintage. This is a Comet, probably from C Sqdn, 7th Royal Tank Regiment moving forward to the front line, 1950.

country under Seoul. The US Marines were, therefore, deployed by sea to the east coast for an advance northwards towards the mountainous Chosin Reservoir to cut off the enemy before he could reach the Manchurian border. Attached to the American force was the 41st Royal Marine Independent Commando which had earlier been formed in Hong Kong.

In the meanwhile British battalions continued to lead the main advance north from Pyongyang against an enemy which chose to flee rather than stand and fight a major battle. Nevertheless rearguard action and engagements against isolated pockets of resistance still caused casualties. The Commonwealth Brigade completed its final action in this phase of the war when on 30 October it captured the important port at Chongchen. As the foremost UN forces they were now within 19km (12 miles) of the Yalu River and only 64km (40 miles) south of the Manchurian border. After eight weeks of continuous action the Brigade was withdrawn into Army Reserve at Taechon.

MacArthur discounted any significant Chinese intervention in Korea despite repeated and increasingly persistent warnings to the contrary from both the international diplomatic community and intelligence sources. In any case the Chinese were regarded by MacArthur as 'militarily uncouth' whose only saving grace lay in their numerical strength.

But even as the UN forces began to experience the discomforts of their first Korean winter, the Chinese attacked. Two hundred thousand hardy peasants, well used to the extremes of the Asian winter, fell upon the UN troops and within a short while forced them to retreat. MacArthur was right to assume that the Chinese could not match the Western armies in the sophistication of their weapons division for division, but they were led by officers who themselves were veterans. They were indeed a formidable opponent.

On 3 November the three battalions of the 27th Commonwealth Brigade held a bridgehead north of the Chongchen River while the frightened, cold and scattered units of the Eighth Army moved through to re-form along a new defence line to the south. The British and Australians in turn came under increasing Chinese pressure but they held their ground until the enemy suddenly withdrew, having completed his 'reconnaissance in force'.

There now occurred one of the most controversial actions of the war. Instead of consolidating their defences, MacArthur ordered the UN forces to resume the advance northwards to the Yalu. Over 160km (100 miles) of high mountains separated the Eighth Army from the Marines of X Corps and it was through this seemingly impassable terrain that the Chinese infiltrated a new and even bigger army. The Chinese fell upon the UN forces for a second time and the surprise was just as great. The 1st South Korean Division took the full brunt of the enemy attack and within hours had simply ceased to exist as a coherent fighting unit. Panic is contagious and the UN retreat at times assumed all the worst characteristics of an undignified rout.

It was 193km (120 miles) to the original defence lines in the hills above Seoul and it was there that the Eighth Army turned to face the enemy in the weeks before Christmas. At the same time the Marines in X Corps fought their way eastwards to the sea. In this epic retreat the 250 men of the Royal Marine Independent Commando formed the rearguard as part of a battle group which had been hastily thrown together from the 1st (US) Marine Division. The Chinese attacked them in overwhelming numbers and the rearguard had to fight its way out to reach the sea and evacuation at Hungnam. In a month of bitter conflict the Royal Marines suffered 80 battle casualties.

The Chinese, with their logistics and lines of communication hampered by foul weather and UN air strikes, were forced to regroup in mid-December. The British troops enjoyed an uneasy and cold Christmas in the hills above Seoul.

The Chinese and North Korean forces unleashed their new offensive on New Year's Eve. Once again the enemy concentrated the full weight of attack on the South Koreans. The latter fell back in disarray and the Chinese

Above: A trooper from the 8th Kings Royal Irish Hussars shepherds a group of refugees.

Right: The venerable Vickers heavy machine gun more than proved its worth in the sustained fire role.

Below: After the first winter campaign, Royal Marine Commandos, supported by the US Navy, carried out a number of raids behind communist lines. This photograph shows one such raid on 14 June 1951 at Chinnapo.

Above: In a scene reminiscent of the trenches of the Great War, two young riflemen relax before their dugout in the front line in Korea.

Above right: In the static phase of the war in 1952, and with the communists occupying the high ground, dust and movement was a constant problem. One method of defeating enemy observed artillery fire is illustrated here. The road leading across the exposed valley to the forward position is hung with camouflage netting.

poured through the gap in the line, rolling up the UN forces from the flanks. Yet again the Commonwealth Brigade found itself as rear-guard. The Middlesex, Australians and Argylls leapfrogged southwards with practiced ease and mutual confidence. In a classic operation of its kind their performance was in sad contrast to the panic, chaos and carnage around them.

The newly arrived 29th Infantry Brigade – comprising the 1st Battalions of the Royal Northumberland Fusiliers, the Gloucestershire Regiment and the Royal Ulster Rifles, with tanks of the 8th King's Royal Irish Hussars and 25-pounder field guns of the 45th Field Regiment, Royal Artillery, in support – had a more difficult time. The Northumberland Fusiliers were able to break off contact while in defensive positions some 16km (10 miles) north of Seoul. 'C' Squadron, 7th Royal Tanks (attached to the 8th Hussars) kept the enemy at bay, but snow and icebound tracks caused a near fatal delay for the Ulster Rifles. Their transport became bogged down and this gave the Chinese, past masters at infiltration, time to place a number of ambushes and road-blocks along the line of retreat. It was only with the greatest difficulty, and often at the point of the bayonet, that such obstacles could be cleared, and the Ulster Rifles suffered over 200 casualties before the battalion was able to rejoin the main force.

In early January 1951 the Argylls and the Middlesex held the bridges over the Han River while the Eighth Army continued its retreat. The bridges were then blown and the door slammed in the face of the Chinese, though luckless Seoul was abandoned to the communists for a second time. The UN retreat finally came to rest along a line that ran from east to west across the peninsula and some 64km (40 miles) south of Seoul. The Chinese by this time had outrun their long and tenuous line of communication, which was in any case hammered from the air by day and night. The enemy did not have the strength to sustain the momentum of his advance and so it fell to the UN forces to regain the initiative.

After a short pause to regroup, the Eighth Army began to advance northwards again. At first the Chinese resisted stubbornly but the sheer volume of firepower delivered by UN artillery and air strikes proved too much and they were forced to give ground.

In the early phases the Commonwealth Brigade was held in reserve, but the Glosters and the Ulster Rifles, supported by the tanks of the 8th Hussars, were in the thick of the action. It proved to be a thankless and bloody task to attack, always uphill, in an effort to clear the ridgelines and mountain tops. Each position, once captured, had to be secured against the threat of infiltration before the battalion could move on to the next objective. It was a slow and methodical advance and quite unlike the rapid war of movement in the campaign of the previous autumn.

Eventually the Argylls, the Middlesex and the Australians were called into battle against the stubborn Chinese. The 27th Infantry Brigade was now a truly Commonwealth force since on its return to the conflict it had in support a battery of New Zealand artillery and an Indian Army Field Ambulance.

On 8 March the UN forces broke the back of Chinese resistance and the enemy withdrew. Within the week American troops had liberated Seoul, for a second time, and the Eighth Army was in headlong pursuit of a retreating enemy. However, this time there was to be no frantic advance into the North; instead the Eighth Army was ordered to dig in astride the 38th parallel. The mobile phase of the Korean War was over.

The onset of spring and more clement weather naturally brought with it an increase in military activity along the front line. The UN High Command feared that the Chinese were massing their forces in readiness for a new offensive, and aerial reconnaissance confirmed this judgement. The problem was that the Eighth Army was not well placed to meet such an attack, the front line lacking the depth which had proved so vital to defeat the human-

wave tactics of the Chinese. In addition, the defence lines lay just 48km (30 miles) from Seoul. Should the Chinese achieve a break-through and the capital fall for a third time, it would be a political calamity which might possibly endanger the war effort.

General Ridgway, commanding Eighth Army, decided upon a bold course of action: he ordered the army to advance northwards a few miles and onto higher ground. On the right flank this took the UN force beyond the 38th parallel. The new positions were easier to defend and allowed space for a fallback line before Seoul. There was also the hope that such an advance might pre-empt and disrupt the Chinese in their own preparations.

The battalions of the 29th Infantry Brigade now found themselves holding the ground from Choksong on the left to the junction of the Imjin and Hanton Rivers on the right. In this sector the terrain was less severe and quite different from the more mountainous regions to the east. The Imjin River flowed through a broad valley, but now that the spring thaw had receded it was easily fordable and no real obstacle. To the south of the river the main battalion positions were dug in along barren hillsides where only the occasional scrub offered cover and concealment. On the afternoon of 22 April combat patrols reported significant enemy movement: it was clear that an attack was imminent.

The Glosters occupied the most crucial part of the brigade front since they guarded the main highway which ran south towards Seoul. The commanding officer, Colonel Carne (who was to receive a Victoria Cross for his subsequent actions), deployed his troops to receive the brunt of the enemy attack. The battalion was very thin on the ground and herein lay its main problem, for there was so much ground to cover that Carne could only afford to have two rifle companies forward, close to the river. 'A' Company occupied a dominant feature which was called Castle Hill, overlooking the south bank of the Imjin River. Protection of the right flank was the task of 'D' Company.

The two remaining companies ('B' and 'C') were placed, together with the mortars, some 1830m (2000 yards) from the river with their backs against Kamak San, the highest feature in the region. The Assault Pioneers occupied Hill 235 while Vickers heavy machine guns were sited throughout the battalion wherever they could command a good field of fire. The British expected that the Chinese would make their attack in two phases. The first would be a

Above: Two North Korean soldiers surrendering to the Glosters.

Below: Lt Col J P Carne VC DSO of the Glorious Glosters, together with another member of the Regiment at Buckingham Palace in October 1953.

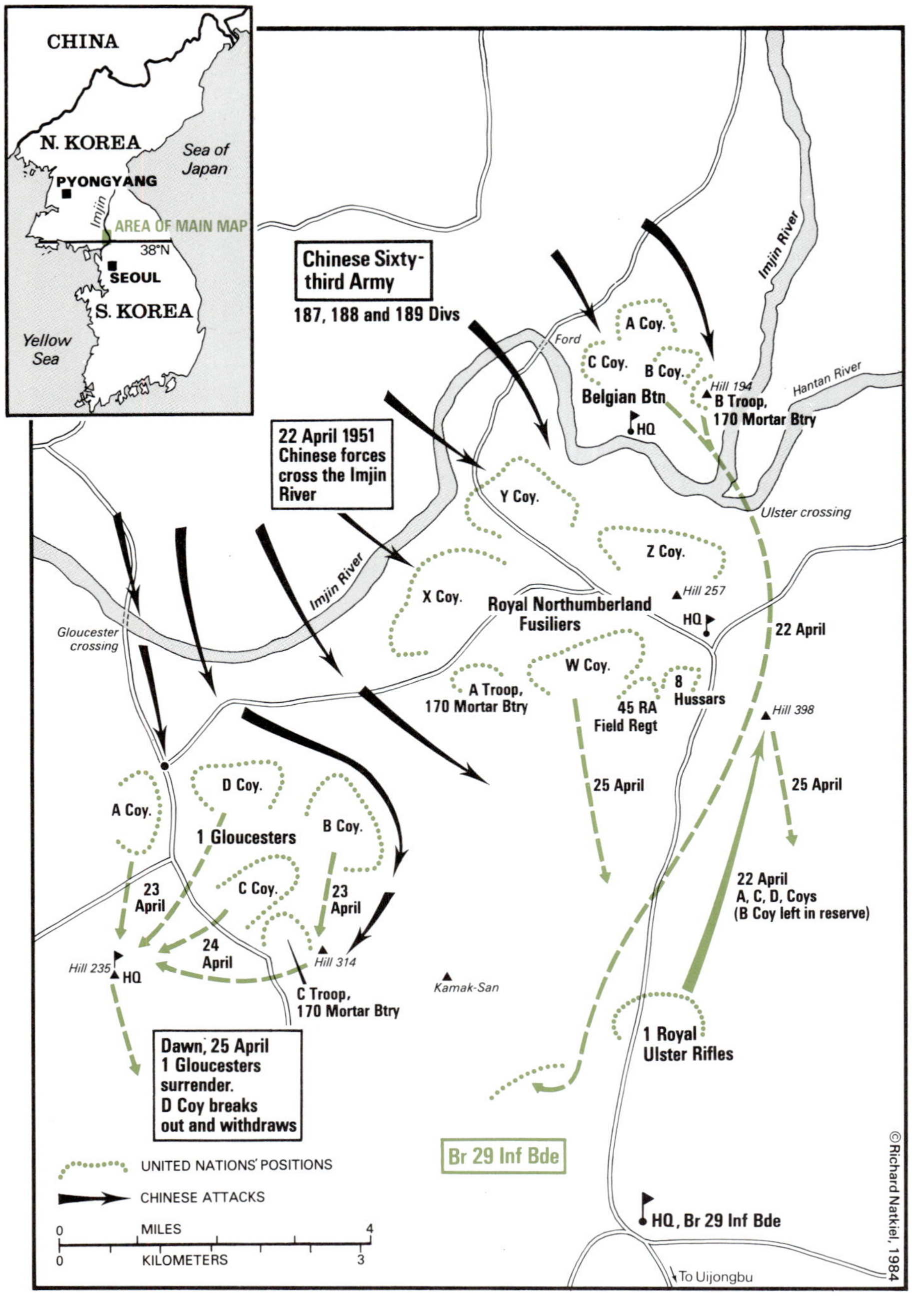

Map: The Battle of the Imjin River, 22-25 April 1951.

night assault to secure a bridgehead, followed at first light with the main thrust for the highway to Seoul.

In the initial stages the battle went exceedingly well for the Glosters. A fighting patrol under Lieutenant Guy Temple covered the main ford across the river. The Chinese made four attempts to force a crossing and on each occasion were repulsed with heavy casualties. It was only when his ammunition was exhausted that Temple withdrew his platoon intact to the main company position. But it soon became clear that the Chinese had little intention of fighting a two-phased operation. Instead, with the crossing-point secured, they poured their forces across in ever-increasing numbers and unleashed a rolling offensive against the British positions. By midnight the battle had spilled over to embrace the Northumberland Fusiliers and a battalion of Belgians who were attached to the brigade at this time.

When dawn came, the Chinese increased the pressure and 'A' Company, which had lost half its number during the night, was forced to relinquish Castle Hill. The company consolidated along the lower slopes and then launched a series of counterattacks which were led by Lieutenant Curtis, an ex-ranker and reserve officer from the Duke of Cornwall's Light Infantry. The Chinese poured down a hail of fire which forced the attackers to go to ground; all, that is, except Curtis, who charged on alone hurling grenades into machine-gun nests and enemy strongpoints. He was cut down by enemy gunfire and killed, earning a posthumous Victoria Cross.

As the day progressed, the fighting became even more bitter and intense. To a cacophony of blaring bugles, wave upon wave of Chinese troops were hurled against the brigade. The Northumberland Fusiliers were forced to give

ground and shorten their perimeter, while the Belgians were redeployed to cover the rather ominous gap that now appeared in the line.

It was the Glosters who bore the brunt of the battle. Artillery and air strikes pounded away at the enemy's rear areas but there was little that could be done to support the main battle directly since by this time the engagement was invariably at close quarters and frequently hand to hand.

On the evening of 23 April and after some 24 hours of continuous battle, Carne concentrated his battalion into a single perimeter. Survivors moved onto Hill 235 and held a perimeter which was little more than 550m (600 yards). Casualties had been so heavy that the remnants of 'B' and 'C' Companies did not amount to a single platoon. There were perhaps 300 men who were still able to fight in the battalion.

On 24 April the remainder of the brigade, which had itself been under intense pressure, was forced to pull back as the rest of the army withdrew the 8km (5 miles) to their original positions along the 38th parallel. The Glosters were now surrounded, but still they defied the enemy and in so doing denied him the highway south to Seoul.

Colonel Carne, in the face of mounting casualties, reduced the perimeter and prepared to make a last stand on Hill 235, forever immortalised as Gloster Hill. The 25-pounders of 45th Field Regiment and US Air Force fighter-bombers continued to bombard the Chinese positions; relief columns tried desperately to break through to the beleaguered troops and effect a rescue. A detachment of Filipino tanks got to within 3km (2 miles), a second attempt saw the 8th Hussars spearhead a battlegroup of Belgian, Puerto Rican and American infantry, but all to no avail.

By the morning of 25 April the brigade had completed its deployment into new positions and the guns in support of the Glosters fell silent. Colonel Carne ordered his companies to break out and try to rejoin the UN lines. In the end nearly all were either killed or captured. The survivors, 39 officers and men of 'D' Company, were the only members of the 1st Battalion, Gloucestershire Regiment to reach the sanctuary of the UN lines. Though the battalion had been to all intents and purposes wiped out, its sacrifice had not been in vain. The Glosters had destroyed the momentum of the Chinese offensive and so delayed their timetable that the enemy retired, enabling Eighth Army to move back to its original positions astride the 38th parallel.

By the summer of 1951 there were sufficient troops in Korea to form the Commonwealth Division. Major General A J H Cassels was its first commander. The division was allowed a little while out of the line and away from the battle to settle down, resolve its inevitable teething troubles, and allow men from different nationalities to become used to one another. Operational control of the division was exercised by the Americans while it was administered by C-in-C Commonwealth Forces in Japan, so there were bound to be some difficulties in the early period.

On 10 July 1951 the truce talks began in Kaesong and hopes ran high that the war would soon be over. However, as the summer gave way to the second autumn of the war it became apparent that the communists saw these negotiations as a political extension of the military conflict. Consequently the ground taken, held or lost on the battlefield acquired a new and more sinister significance at the conference table.

Above: Hill 235, where the Glosters made their epic last stand in April 1951. With the ground recaptured, a surviving officer from the battalion indicates the salient features of the battle to a military observer.

Right: The Centurion tank first saw action in Korea. The picture shows a troop crossing the Imjin River by way of an American pontoon bridge.

A Mark IV Firefly of the Royal Navy flies a reconnaissance mission along the eastern seaboard of Korea, September 1952. The Royal Navy Carrier Task Force was responsible for securing this coastline against communist infiltration by sea.

Right: A mortar team watches for targets across the valley in the summer of 1952.

Opposite: The light fleet carrier HMS *Ocean* en route from Japan to assume patrol duties off Korea's east coast with the Carrier Task Force, July 1952.

Below: General Eisenhower, US President-elect, visited Korea in 1952. The photograph shows him meeting with the Commanding General of the Commonwealth Division, General West.

By this time the Commonwealth Division had been deployed into the front and along the line of the Imjin River. In September it launched a series of limited attacks which took the division onto higher ground beyond the river line. Later in October the division launched Operation 'Commando' which was a set-piece battle against a defended position. The success of these operations 'blooded the division', ironed out the flaws and built confidence between the troops.

The onset of winter found the division in difficult and hilly country holding a front of some 1830m (2000 yards). The mass of hills and valleys seemed to swallow up troops to such a degree that seven out of the nine battalions were deployed forward and there was little defence in depth – a risky business with the Chinese as enemy.

In November 1951 the Chinese returned to the offensive, preceded by their heaviest artillery bombardment of the war. A series of probing attacks was launched against positions held by the King's Shropshire Light Infantry and the Australians. Then the Chinese turned the full weight of the assault against the King's Own Scottish Borderers; the enemy force was estimated to be a division of some 6000 men. Once they had been contained in bitter fighting, the Borderers counterattacked. Private William Speakman, attached from the Black Watch, led attack after attack against the Chinese. Though he was severely wounded, Speakman, in acts of great bravery, hurled grenades at the enemy until he was overcome by his injuries. He was awarded the Victoria Cross.

The Chinese switched their attack and concentrated against the Shropshire Light In-

Below: Carrier operations were never without incident. Though the ceasefire had come into effect, maritime air patrols were still maintained throughout the summer months of 1953. This Sea Fury crash-landed on the deck of HMS *Ocean*, 22 August 1953.

fantry. This battalion suffered more than 100 casualties and was forced at first to yield ground. Their mortars gave tremendous support, firing four and a half tons of shells during the engagement. Even the Chinese could not take the appalling casualties which had by this time been inflicted upon them and with nightfall they retired, leaving behind more than 1000 dead on the battlefield. Thereafter the battle became one of mortar and artillery fire, fought at longer range while the US Air Force bombed the Chinese rear areas and lines of communication. Low cloud hampered air strikes and the rain turned the ground into a quagmire.

The onset of winter marked the end of the Chinese offensive. For the Commonwealth Division it had been a harrowing ordeal; though its battalions had fought the enemy to a standstill, the absence of a strong defence in depth had been a telling factor. With the lull in the fighting the division was able to shorten its front. The brigade which had taken the main brunt of the offensive moved into reserve.

The winter sleet gave way to blizzards and for the soldiers it became a battle against the elements. It was not unusual to record 16 degrees of frost at night. But even under these conditions the war continued and battle became the province of the platoon commander. It was the young lieutenants who commanded on lonely hill tops or led the fighting patrols into no-man's-land in search of the prisoners demanded by the intelligence staff at headquarters. Such operations hardly ever made the headlines at home but they produced a steady attrition in casualties.

On 27 November 1951 the armistice negotiations, which were then being held at Panmunjon, reached an agreement over the 'demarcation line'. The protagonists agreed a demilitarised zone from which the forces were to withdraw in accordance with a schedule which had still to be negotiated. Hopes ran high that the war would soon be over. In the event nothing could have been further from the truth and the war was destined to drag on for another 20 months, with the slightest piece of ground

Left: The notorious 'Hook', scene of some of the most bitter fighting of the war, 1952-53.

Main picture: Men of the Black Watch in the front line in the summer of 1952. They are armed with an American Browning .30in calibre machine gun.

won or lost having significance in terms of negotiating strength at the conference table. Both sides were now so evenly matched that neither had the military capability or the political will to inflict a telling defeat on the other.

So long as the Chinese were unwilling to negotiate and come to terms the war was stalemated. This in turn meant that British troops fought and died to uphold the prestige of the UN and to maintain the principle of international relations which stated that aggression cannot be allowed to pay. Domestic support fell away and the troops felt increasingly isolated and bitter, particularly as the battles could still be hard-fought affairs.

This was especially the case at the 'Hook', so named because it formed a hinge in the UN positions where the front line turned sharply southwestwards away from the Samichon and Ko Dong Valleys. The actual 'hook' was a sinister, towering, horseshoe-shaped ridge, overlooking the two bridges which engineers had constructed across the Imjin River and guarding the vital highway south to Seoul. It was to this already notorious stretch of the front that the Commonwealth Division returned in the summer of 1952 after a period of rest and rehabilitation.

In November 1952 the Chinese unleashed a particularly heavy bombardment against the British positions, followed closely by an infantry advance. The defenders were forced to use the most desperate of stratagems, to call down defensive fire while cowering deep in the trenches. On this occasion it succeeded.

In the remaining weeks of the year the British battalions were heavily involved in aggressive patrolling. On occasion set-piece attacks were launched against enemy strongpoints or features. The objective was to dominate no-man's-land and take the initiative away from the enemy. Though such tactics did result in casualties, it seemed to be better than simply waiting for the Chinese to attack first. Indeed all the available evidence seemed to point to its success, for when the division was relieved in January 1953 this once-tempestuous sector of the front was secure.

The onset of spring and the early summer allowed both sides to construct stronger and deeper defensive works. The new strongpoints were protected by the inevitable barbed wire and thickly sown minefields. Such military architecture in turn severely constrained the activities of the fighting patrols, which became an increasingly hazardous undertaking.

In April 1953 the Commonwealth Division returned once more to the 'Hook' where it relieved the 2nd (US) Infantry Division in that sector. Air reconnaissance confirmed intelligence assessments that the Chinese were massing men and material in readiness for another offensive against the 'Hook'. On the night of 7/8 May a series of probing attacks was sent in to test the mettle of the defenders and seek for weak spots in the line. The 1st Battalion, Black Watch, who were in the line, were reinforced by the 1st Battalions, King's and Duke of Wellington's Regiments.

The Chinese kept up a continuous artillery and mortar bombardment which increased in volume and intensity. On the night of 28 May the positions were hit by what seasoned veterans believed was the heaviest bombardment of the war. Trenches and dug-outs, deluged in fire, collapsed under the weight of shell and soldiers were entombed in the debris.

Suddenly the bombardment ceased and the night echoed to the sound of bugles which heralded the Chinese attack. Even as the dazed defenders rushed to man their shattered trenches, assault engineers blasted a path

British Army units in Korea August 1950/July 1953

Formation and units	Month of Arrival	Departure
Armour		
8th King's Royal Irish Hussars	Nov 1950	Dec 1951
'C' Sqn 7th Royal Tank Regt	Nov 1950	Oct 1951
5th Royal Inniskilling Dragoon Guards	Dec 1951	Dec 1952
1st Royal Tank Regt	Dec 1952	Dec 1953
Artillery		
45th Field Regiment RA	Nov 1950	Nov 1951
11th Independent Light AA Bty RA (converted to 4.2in. mortars June 51)	Nov 1950	Nov 1951
170th Independent Mortar Bty RA	Nov 1950	Oct 1951
14th Field Regt RA	Nov 1951	Dec 1952
120th Lt AA Bty RA	Oct 1951	—
42nd Lt Bty RA	Nov 1951	—
61st Lt Regt RA	Jan 1952	—
20th Field Regt RA	Dec 1952	Dec 1953
Infantry		
1st Bn Middlesex Regt	Aug 1950	May 1951
1st Bn Argyll & Sutherland Highlanders	Aug 1950	Apr 1951
1st Bn Royal Northumberland Fusiliers	Nov 1950	Nov 1951
1st Bn The Gloucestershire Regt	Nov 1950	Nov 1951
1st Bn Royal Ulster Rifles	Nov 1950	Oct 1951
1st Bn King's Own Scottish Borderers	Apr 1951	Aug 1952
1st Bn The King's Shropshire Light Infantry	May 1951	Sept 1952
1st Bn The Royal Norfolk Regt	Oct 1951	Sept 1952
1st Bn The Royal Leicestershire Regt	Oct 1951	June 1952
1st Bn The Welch Regt	Nov 1951	Nov 1952
1st Bn The Black Watch	June 1952	July 1953
1st Bn The Royal Fusiliers	Aug 1952	Aug 1953
1st Bn Durham Light Infantry	Sept 1952	Sept 1953
1st Bn The King's Regt	Sept 1952	Oct 1953
1st Bn The Duke of Wellington's Regt	Oct 1952	Nov 1953
1st Bn The Royal Scots	July 1953	

Casualties

	Officers	Other ranks
Killed	71	615
Wounded	187	2311
Missing	52	1050
TOTALS	310	3976

Above: An Australian machine-gunner from B Coy, 2 Btn The Australian Regiment takes a break for a quick wash during the battle for the 'Hook', 1953.

Above: Roll Call for the Black Watch after the Battle for the 'Hook', May 1953.

through mines and barbed wire. Chinese infantry, firing their burp-guns and hurling concussion grenades, attacked the forward companies of the King's. Divisional artillery responded immediately and a barrage caught the follow-up waves of the enemy before they could reach the front line.

Throughout the rest of that terrible night the outcome remained in doubt. British guns effectively sealed off the sector so that very few enemy troops were able to make it through such a lethal bombardment. Reinforcements (platoons from the Dukes) drove through the Chinese barrage to lend support to the hard-pressed King's, who by this time were involved in a hand-to-hand battle where quarter was neither asked nor given.

The Chinese tried desperately to sustain the momentum of the battle and paid dearly every time a fresh regiment attempted to negotiate the barrage of no-man's-land. The King's, with the Dukes in support, returned to the offensive and by dawn had eliminated the last few pockets of enemy resistance.

Daylight revealed the awful destruction of the battlefield. The two British battalions between them had 150 casualties, but they counted more than 1000 enemy dead. Once the wounded had been removed, the main task was to rebuild the shattered defences. Royal Engineers came forward with their heavy equipment and expertise to reconstruct a line which in places had been obliterated.

In the event this proved to be the last major engagement fought by British troops in Korea. As the armistice drew nearer, the Chinese still launched attacks aimed at securing some piece of ground, a hill or ridgeline which had suddenly assumed a new importance, but they left the 'Hook' well alone and chose instead to hit those parts of the line which were manned by South Korean divisions.

The armistice came into effect on 25 July 1953 and the battlefield fell silent. It was two years and 11 months since the first British troops from the Middlesex and the Argyll and Sutherland Highlanders had stepped onto Korean soil. In the intervening period 16 battalions of British infantry had seen action with the United Nations Forces and throughout it all they had received full support from armour and artillery units. But they were not the only British forces committed to Korea. Ships of the Royal Navy helped to maintain naval supremacy and, through such command of the sea, guarantee the safe passage of the transports carrying UN forces and supplies to the battle. The coastline was patrolled to prevent infiltration and any attempt to outflank the UN line from the sea. A Royal Navy carrier task force provided air cover, supporting amphibious operations and the land battle ashore.

Air support for the British troops came from the US Fifth Air Force which included South African and Australian squadrons. Contrary to popular belief no Royal Air Force squadrons or aircraft served in Korea, though pilots flew on attachment with Commonwealth and American units. However, three squadrons in turn from the RAF Flying Boat Wing helped to maintain an offensive blockade of the Korean coast and provided long-range maritime air reconnaissance alongside American Martin Mariners. The RAF flew Mark V Sunderlands from squadron bases at Iwakuni in Japan.

Elements of all three armed services, therefore, contributed to the conflict in Korea, symbolising Britain's commitment to the UN and international law. It was a costly campaign – the Army lost 71 officers and 615 soldiers – and one which stretched the country's resources virtually to breaking-point. But the experience in conventional warfare was invaluable, enhancing the deterrent strength and prestige of the forces at a time when they were also beginning to gain a reputation for success in a totally different kind of combat – counter-insurgency.

The Commonwealth Division July 1951 Korea

HQ The Commonwealth Division

- **25th Canadian Inf BDE**
  - 2 Bn R CDN Regt
  - 2 Bn R 22ᵉ Regt*
  - 2 Bn PPCLI*
- **28th BR Commonwealth BDE**
  - 1 KOSB
  - 1 RAR*
  - 1 KSLI
- **29th BR Inf BDE**
  - 1RNF
  - 1RUR
  - 1 Glosters
- **Divisional Troops**
  - 8th Royal Irish Hussars
  - 'C' Sqn Lord Strathcona's Horse (CDN)
  - 2 Regt Royal CDN Horse Arty
  - 16th Field Regt R NZ Arty
  - 45th Field Regt RA
  - 170th Lt Bty RA
  - 11th Lt AA Bty RA
  - 28th Field Eng Regt RE
  - 57th Indep Field Sqd R CDN Engineers
  - 64th Field Park RE
  - 25th (CDN) Field Ambulance RCAMC
  - 26th Field Ambulance RAMC
  - 60th Indian (Para) Field Ambulance IMC
  - Service Troops
  - [attached
  - 1 Belgian Inf Bn
  - 1 Norwegian MASH]

* PPCLI – Princess Patricia's Canadian Light Infantry
R 22ᵉ Regt – Royal 22 Regiment
RAR – Royal Australian Regiment

POLICING THE EMPIRE

From 1948-60 British forces were involved in three major campaigns of counter-insurgency – Malaya (1948-60), Kenya (1952-60) and Cyprus (1955-59). Each of these campaigns was a considerable political, economic and military commitment and, as for the greater part of the 1950s they were being fought concurrently , they were a major strain on British resources. The British did not lack experience in counter-insurgency operations, as they had been involved in Palestine and India before and after the Second World War, albeit under different circumstances. Certain common experiences and lessons emerged from the campaigns in Malaya, Kenya and Cyprus and these were to form the basis for future British counter-insurgency operations.

After 1945 all the European colonial powers were to face the demands of their colonial subjects for national independence and this was sometimes combined with communist ideology and revolutionary guerrilla warfare. The British faced their first major challenge in the Far East. When the High Commissioner for Malaya declared a state of emergency in June 1948 it was the culmination of several months of political unrest and acts of terror by elements of the Malayan Communist Party (MCP). During the Second World War resistance to the Japanese had been mainly led by the communist Malayan People's Anti-Japanese Army (MPAJA), who had gained considerable support from the local Chinese. Although the MCP would have liked to seize power following the collapse of the Japanese in August 1945, it was unable to prevent the re-establishment of British authority. The British disbanded the MPAJA and recognised the MCP as a legal political party. However, many weapons were concealed in secret jungle hides.

A combination of political and industrial unrest in Malaya and the decision by the MCP to launch an armed struggle, created the ingredients for an insurgency campaign that began in 1948. In an effort to create a semblance of unity between the Malayan and Chinese peoples, the MPAJA and the MCP formed the Malayan Races' Liberation Army (MRLA) under Chin Peng and moved into the jungle. From this secure base and relying upon support from Chinese squatters and the Chinese urban population, terrorist groups could strike at the police, local officials, mines and plantations.

Initially, the terrorists had considerable success as they were frequently able to achieve surprise against the security forces. The geography and terrain of Malaya was advantageous to the insurgents as four-fifths of the country was primaeval jungle and the west and east coasts were divided by a 1830 m (6000 ft) mountain range. The security forces were at a low ebb at the beginning of the emergency with the 10,000 police suffering from poor morale, little experience and lack of resources, whilst the army largely consisted of Gurkha units that were in the process of being reorganised. The civil administration under the High Commissioner was attempting to rebuild its authority following the Japanese occupation. There was little co-ordination of policy and resources between the civil, the police and the military authorities.

The High Commissioner was concerned that the rule of law through the normal courts be maintained. However, a series of emergency laws was introduced to meet the increasing threat from terrorism, including the right of the government to detain suspects for up to two years without trial, to search without a warrant, to control movement and to impose curfews. Severe penalties were introduced for aiding insurgents, and the death penalty was imposed for carrying weapons and ammunition. Finally, there was a compulsory registration of the civil population with all citizens over the age of 12 required to possess an identity card bearing their fingerprints and photograph. Although these measures laid the government open to accusations of totalitarian behaviour, they were considered vital in the campaign of

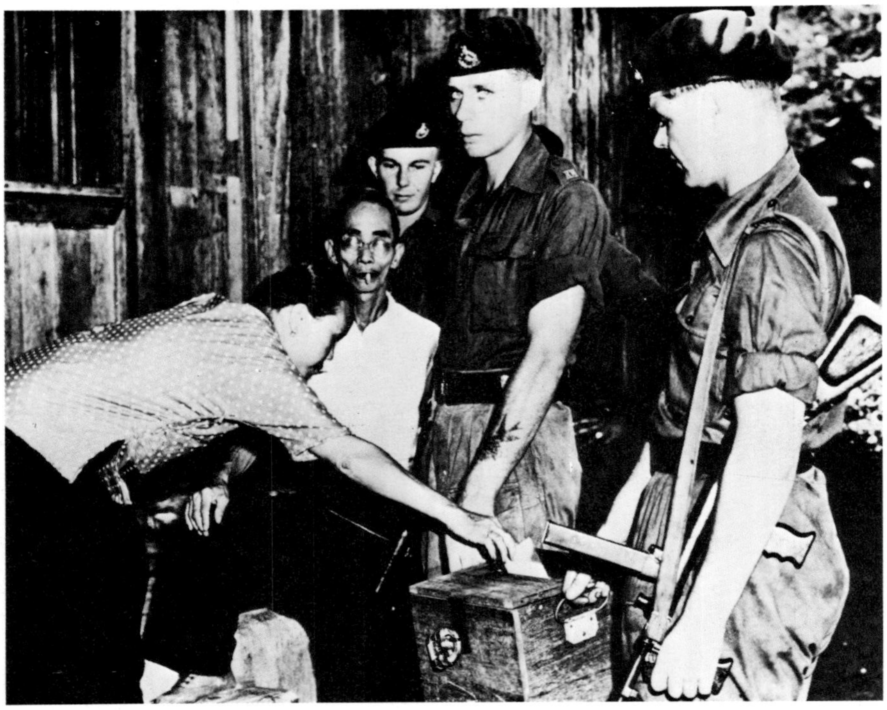

Right: Training 'Ferrets'. Such 'Ferret' units were made up of Malay, Gurkha and British troops who operated in the jungle, ambushing the CTs.

Left: Background information. Local Chinese women hand in questionnaires to British Marines. General Templer used such methods to gain information about the CTs.

Previous page: 'Jungle Bashing': a British Army patrol in Malaya in 1952. Thousands of such manhours were needed for every CT contact.

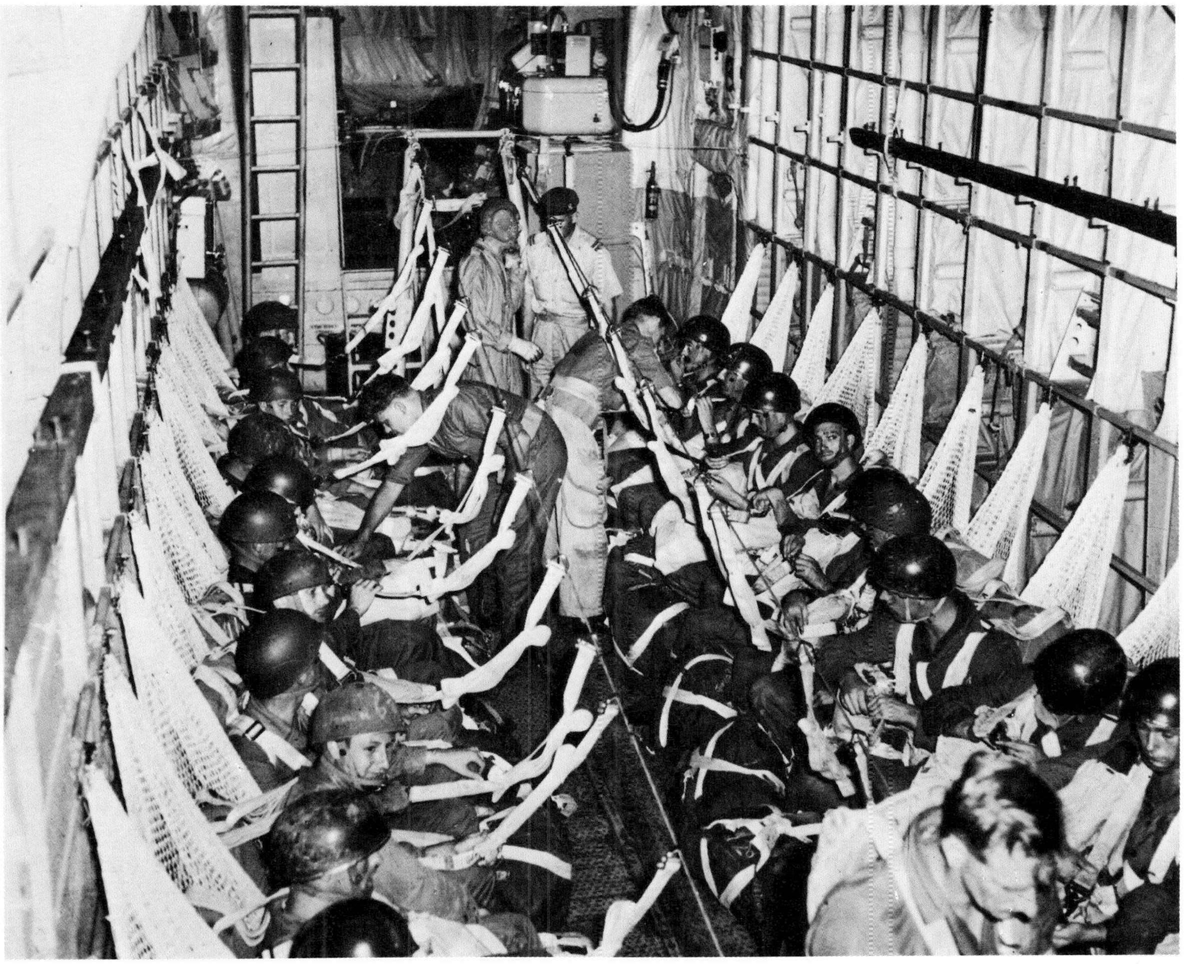

Above: An Abban tracker advises a British NCO commanding a patrol in Malaya, 1950. Local guides were essential in helping locate the enemy.

Right: Soldiers of 22nd SAS on board an RAF Beverley prior to being dropped into the Malayan jungle. The SAS was used for long-range penetration operations.

counter-insurgency and were subject to continuous review.

The success of the insurgents and the absence of any one person responsible for co-ordinating the efforts of the civil, police and military authorities prompted the High Commissioner, Sir Henry Gurney, to request the services of an experienced soldier as Director of Operations. In 1950 Lieutenant General (retired) Sir Harold Briggs was appointed to the job 'to plan, coordinate and to direct the anti-bandit operations of the police and fighting forces'.

Within a fortnight of his arrival in Malaya and after a hasty tour of inspection, Briggs issued his plan of operations. The 'Briggs' Plan' set out four main aims – to dominate the populated areas and to build up a feeling of complete security, which would in time result in a steady and increasing flow of information coming from all sources; to break up the communist organisations within the populated areas; to isolate the insurgents from their food and supply organisations in the populated areas; and to destroy the insurgents by forcing them to attack the security forces on the latter's own ground. To achieve these aims Briggs persuaded Gurney to establish an integrated civil, police and military organisation to emphasise the joint approach to the emergency. At federal, state and district levels joint integrated committees were established, joint police-military operations rooms were set up and intelligence resources were pooled under one Chief of Intelligence. The principle of joint control of the emergency was firmly established and an organisation was created through which joint decisions were taken and then implemented.

The Police and Special Branch were reorganised to gather intelligence and to seek out and destroy the communist infrastructure in the populated areas. Police and troops moved in to secure bases in the villages and forced the insurgents to move deeper into the jungle. A 'food

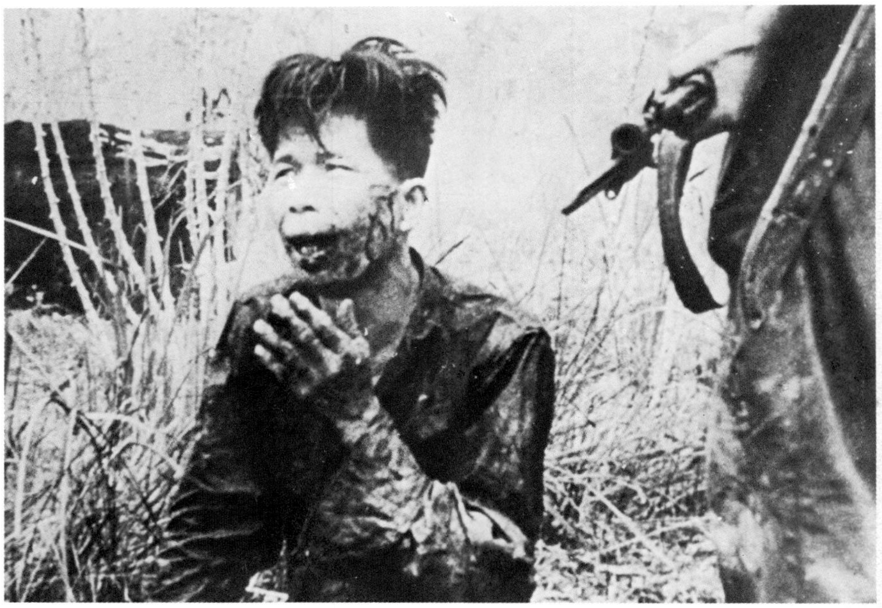

Left: A 'New Village' in Malaya, 1952. Under the Briggs Plan some 500,000 Chinese squatters were resettled in 500 such villages, away from CT influence and intimidation.

Below left: A wounded CT captured and under guard.

Below: A soldier, armed with an Owen sub-machine gun, checks a Chinese woman worker's identity card. Such checks inhibited the movement of CTs and their sympathisers.

Bottom: A train in Malaya derailed by CT ambush, 1951. During the early years of the emergency, communications were particularly vunerable.

Bottom right: The value of airpower: a British soldier on patrol in the Malayan jungle recovers supplies dropped by parachute.

denial' policy was adopted which in the long run proved devastatingly successful. The main problem for the security forces was how to deny the insurgents the support they received from some 500,000 Chinese squatters who lived on the edges of the jungle. The government decided to resettle the squatters in some 500 new villages where they could be controlled and protected from intimidation. In many cases the squatters had to be forcibly resettled and the operation called for both firmness and tact by the Police and the Army. By the end of 1951 some 400,000 of the squatters had been resettled, forcing the insurgents to split up into smaller groups or move further afield to seek food supplies.

Despite all these measures and the gradual reinforcement of the Police and the military, insurgent attacks continued, culminating in the death of Gurney in an ambush on 6 October 1951. The British government decided to take the opportunity to combine the posts of High Commissioner and Director of Operations in one person. In January 1952 General Sir Gerald Templer, a serving soldier, took up the controversial appointment. A forceful, dynamic man with a flair for publicity, Templer gave the security forces the necessary fillip required to take the offensive and build on the achievements of Gurney and Briggs. He laid down four main principles – the conduct of the emergency and normal civil government were completely inter-related and would be handled as one problem; the whole population had to play its part in fighting the communists; the insurgents had to be defeated before Malaya could expect self-government; and, above all, 'the answer lies not in pouring in more troops into the jungle, but rests in the hearts and minds of the Malayan people'.

Templer seized the political intiative from the insurgents by promising early elections to the legislature with independence to follow, something which was to happen in 1957. Both the Police and the Army had been reinforced and improved intelligence and a locally recruited Home Guard freed the security forces for offensive action. The contact rate with insurgents increased and more and more of them began to surrender. By the time Templer left Malaya in 1954 the insurgents were on the defensive. In 1955 the Alliance Party under Tunku Abdul Rahman won a resounding

Right: Unloading a casualty from an RAF Sycamore helicopter at Kuala Lumpur. Helicopters were invaluable for quick evacuation of wounded from deep in the jungle.

victory at the polls and an amnesty was offered to the MRLA. This was refused, and between 1955 and 1960 the security forces steadily pushed the insurgents back to the Thai border and reduced their effectiveness to comparative insignificance.

The victory in Malaya against communist insurgency occurred after a protracted struggle and was due to many factors. The fact that the majority of the insurgents were drawn from the Chinese population helped to isolate them from the rest of the community and in turn they were physically isolated from any external support. The dedication and expertise of the colonial civil servants at all levels of the administration, coupled with the bravery and loyalty of the majority of the owners and managers of the mines and plantations, was a very important factor. Once a political and military aim had been established and a joint command and control structure set up, the necessary framework existed for success. At the beginning of the emergency the Police had been overstretched and on the defensive, and it took time to expand the force from 10,000 to 40,000 men at the height of the struggle. The Army had supported the Police and had been expanded from some 10,000 to 35,000 men. An important element was provided by Commonwealth contingents and locally recruited Malays.

The security forces had gradually to build up an intelligence organisation before they could take effective offensive action against the insurgents. Operating without accurate intelligence meant hours of fruitless 'jungle bashing' and the dispersal of forces. Both the Special Branch and the Special Air Service (SAS) conducted deep penetration operations into the jungle to ambush, capture or kill insurgents. Air power was important for resupply, limited fire-support missions, and the use of helicopters for the movement of small numbers of men and the quick evacuation of the wounded. The Navy was able to provide transport and close fire support along the coast and up some rivers. But the basic job on the ground had to be done by the infantry who had to learn to live and fight in the jungle.

Over 6000 insurgents were killed, 1200 captured and 2700 surrendered during the emergency. Some 1300 police were killed and over 500 soldiers. Civilian casualties were over 3000. But for the British and many foreign observers the emergency in Malaya was regarded as an example of a successful counter-insurgency campaign.

Many of the methods were used to equal effect at much the same time in Kenya, a British

Below: Lieutenant General Sir George Erskine (centre), GOC Kenya, observing operations against Mau Mau, 1953. Erskine was criticised by local white settlers for being 'too soft' on Mau Mau.

Above: The new proconsul of Empire, General Sir Gerald Templer. As High Commissioner of Malaya, Templer combined civil and military authority.

Left: Alan Lennox-Boyd, Colonial Secretary (in trilby, centre), inspects members of a Kikuyu village Home Guard.

Below: Members of a British Army patrol surprise a Mau Mau suspect.

Above: British Army patrol in Kenya keeping a watchful eye out for Mau Mau suspects.

Below: Captured home-made Mau Mau weapons. The Mau Mau had few proper guns and were forced to rely on such weapons, which were more dangerous to the user than to the enemy.

colony ruled by a Governor appointed by the Colonial Office. Although there were British settlers, the Africans outnumbered them by one hundred to one. The colony was administered by district commissioners and officers, there was a small police force and some three battalions of the King's African Rifles.

In October 1952 the Governor declared a state of emergency following a period of disorder around Nairobi and the murder of a leading Kikuyu chieftain loyal to Britain. It was from the Kikuyu tribe, who lived north of Nairobi, that the insurgent Mau Mau movement was formed. Although nearly all Mau Mau were Kikuyu not all Kikuyu were Mau Mau. The insurgency was tribal-based, and few other Kenyan tribes supported Mau Mau. The Kikuyu were particularly susceptible to dissatisfaction over the economic and agricultural policies of the colonial administration. Kikuyu grievances had been simmering for several years before 1952 and yet the administration had largely discounted them.

Mau Mau had very little organisation outside Nairobi and no real command structure or doctrine that could be comparable to the MCP. Mau Mau groups gained cohesion through binding oaths, acts of terror and ritualistic murder. They had a few handguns, axes and pangas; their main tactics were surprise attack and terror. Although their targets were to include white settlers and the security forces, the majority of their victims were members of the Kikuyu tribe who refused to support them. At the beginning of the emergency there were some 12,500 Mau Mau insurgents.

Unlike Malaya, the British government decided not to appoint one official to combine both civil and military authority. It was considered that as the emergency only affected one part of Kenya this was unnecessary, and there was pressure from colonial civil servants and white settlers against appointing some military supremo on the Templer model. However, it was

Right: British soldiers on patrol in Kenya take a short rest.

Below: Jomo Kenyatta – the Kenyan leader whom the British suspected of being the real head of Mau Mau. He was detained.

necessary to reorganise the military command structure and recognise that an independent HQ was required in Kenya quite separate from GHQ Cairo. The main problem for civil-military relations came from the white settlers who at times made virulent criticisms of the GOC, Lieutenant General Sir George Erskine, alleging that the effects of his policies were 'too soft' on Mau Mau.

The colonial administration had two immediate tasks: to build up a joint police-military intelligence organisation to piece together what little was known about Mau Mau, and to expand the security forces. It took some considerable time to set up a decent intelligence system and unity of command and control was never properly achieved in Kenya. Expansion of the Police meant recruiting more black Africans and using the white Kenya Police Reserve. The Army was gradually reinforced so that by 1955 there were some five British battalions and six battalions of King's African Rifles in Kenya. As in Malaya a local Home Guard was recruited. Even so, it took nearly a year before the administration was able to take the offensive. Before that Mau Mau terrorists were able to achieve some spectacular successes such as the massacre of the Kikuyu village of Lari and the attack on the Naivasha police post, both on 26 March 1953.

In 1954 sufficient army reinforcements had arrived to enable the security forces to start major operations. It was decided to destroy the Mau Mau organisation in Nairobi by a systematic cordon-and-search of the capital. Operation 'Anvil', launched in April 1954, lasted over a month and resulted in the detention of over 16,000 Mau Mau suspects. It destroyed the Mau Mau organisation in Nairobi and cut links with Mau Mau groups on Mount Kenya and in the Aberdares. The security forces then moved out of Nairobi into neighbouring areas, clearing out Mau Mau suspects and attempting to resettle Kikuyu villages. As in Malaya, the administration used emergency powers to back up its policy and the detention of suspects was a major factor, with some 32,000 detainees held in

Above: Kikuyu tribesmen, working as members of a counter-gang which tracked down Mau Mau groups.

Below: Kikuyu witch doctor (right), suspected of being a member of Mau Mau. Blood oaths and sacrifices were important elements in Mau Mau proceedures.

prison camps by the end of 1956. Resettlement of Kikuyu villages outside areas where Mau Mau operated was also attempted, but was not as successful as the resettlement of Chinese squatters in Malaya.

The administration divided Kenya into two types of area. Those designated Special Areas meant that the security forces operated within existing law, whilst those designated Prohibited Areas (the Aberdares and Mount Kenya), were treated almost like war zones. The virtual absence of any population centres meant that the security forces were under no real constraint. To clear the Prohibited Areas of Mau Mau gangs the security forces organised massive cordon-and-search operations, mobilising thousands of African 'beaters' armed with machetes to clear a path towards the stop lines held by the security forces. Patrols were put into these areas to lay ambushes and the RAF bombed designated zones.

One of the most effective measures used against Mau Mau for gathering intelligence, setting ambushes and persuading members of the gangs to desert, was the use of 'counter-gangs'. The British had used this technique during the Boer War, in Palestine and in Malaya. In Kenya these had originally consisted of small groups of loyal black Africans led by suitably disguised British police or army officers, who went into the forests masquarading as Mau Mau gangs. Soon, many of these 'counter-gangs' consisted of former Mau Mau activists who had been successfully turned against and willingly operated against their former associates.

By 1960 the last remnants of the Mau Mau gangs had been killed or had surrendered. The tribal nature of Mau Mau had limited their appeal in Kenya, and their lack of organisation and weapons meant that after the initial impact of their acts of terror they were on the defensive.

Apart from the operations of the security forces, a very important element behind the success of the administration was in the area of political and economic reform which cut away what black African support there had been for Mau Mau. Agrarian reform programmes, the establishment of minimum rates of pay for urban blacks, and the breakdown of racial barriers within the civil service were all important.

Over 600 members of the security forces and about 2000 (mostly black African) civilians lost their lives during the emergency. Nearly 12,000 insurgents were killed and some 2500 were captured, whilst 73,000 black Africans were detained or imprisoned. Once again, the violence had been contained and law and order upheld, but such success was not universal. Elsewhere in the empire, more intractable problems were being experienced.

Cyprus was a British colony ruled by a Governor and administered by colonial civil servants. It had been of strategic importance as a British base in the eastern Mediterranean since 1878, and with the deteriorating situation in the Middle East after 1945, this importance had increased. About 80 per cent of the population of 520,000 were Greek, and although Cyprus had never been part of modern Greece, successive Greek governments had claimed the island and the mainland Greeks and the Greek Cypriots wanted *Enosis* or union. Some 18 per cent of the remaining population were Turkish, and the Turks had been the legal owners of the

Left: George Grivas, EOKA leader in Cyprus, poses for the camera in the Troodos mountains. Although he succeeded in forcing the British to deploy many troops in Cyprus, he failed to achieve *Enosis*.

Below: Royal Marine Commandos with RAVC tracker dogs hunt for EOKA groups in the Troodos mountains, 1956.

island until 1923. The Turkish Cypriots looked to Turkey as their national homeland, and the Turkish government wanted Cyprus returned to their rule or to be partitioned. In July 1954 the British government announced that because of its strategic importance, Cyprus could not expect independence.

The leader of the Greek Cypriots, Archbishop Makarios, was the driving force behind the *Enosis* movement and he helped create an organisation needed to sustain a campaign to persuade the British to grant it. He recruited a right-wing, Cypriot-born Greek Army Colonel, George Grivas, to organise the military arm of the movement, which was called EOKA, the National Organisation of Cypriot Fighters.

In the autumn of 1954 British forces began arriving in Cyprus after being withdrawn from Egypt. The Greek Cypriots regarded this as a provocation which was combined with a refusal by the United Nations to consider the question of Cyprus. EOKA decided to begin a campaign to force the British to accede to *Enosis*. The campaign was aimed at controlling the Greek Cypriot community, wearing the British down, and mobilising world opinion behind *Enosis*.

Although EOKA started their campaign with about 100 men, and even at the end only had some 300 in the Troodos mountains, they were

Above: EOKA ambush of a British car. Such shooting incidents were common practice in Cyprus.

Above left: Cordon-and-search by troops of the Royal Warwickshire Regiment, looking for EOKA suspects in Nicosia. The majority of Greek Cypriots supported EOKA.

Left: After the Greek-Turkish agreement to establish an independent Cyprus in 1959, EOKA members appear in public in Nicosia.

able to rely upon considerable support from the Greek community. The methods used by EOKA were a combination of guerrilla warfare, terrorism and propaganda. They organised riots, boycotts, strikes and civil disobedience amongst the Greek Cypriots, and fought a bitter rural and urban guerrilla war against the British security forces. EOKA realised that the British could not be defeated in a conventional war, but sought to gain propaganda victories and to attack the police and intelligence agencies and thus blind the authorities.

Recognising the potential danger of the situation, the British government appointed an experienced soldier, Field Marshal Sir John Harding, as Governor in September 1955. Harding immediately began to prepare a campaign based upon the ideas and methods that were proving successful in Malaya. He took up the appointment of Director of Operations and set up a joint command and control structure for the civil, police and army authorities and a joint intelligence organisation. Harding intensified operations against EOKA and at the same time opened direct negotiations with Makarios All this occurred before the proclamation of a state of emergency in November 1955.

Initially, Harding and the security forces were very much on the defensive. The 1700 Cypriot Police were not very effective and had divided loyalties, so it was necessary to bring in outside help. The armed forces were available to support the Police, but many of them were administrative and support units, mainly concerned with meeting their own security needs. Intelligence was poor and it was months before there was proper co-ordination between the Police and the Army and information could be fully collated and disseminated.

Grivas based his command headquarters in the Troodos mountains and organised mountain groups of EOKA who emerged from the caves to carry out swift ambushes and raids. In conjunction with the mountain groups, town groups controlled the urban terrorism. At first the main target of the mountain groups was the Police, but when they in turn became vulnerable to attack by the Army, Grivas switched his emphasis to civil disobedience and terror in the urban areas.

In June 1956 Harding was able to go over to the offensive using reinforcements which included a parachute brigade. Operation 'Pepperpot' was a major cordon-and-search of the Troodos mountains. Although Grivas escaped from the Army he lost two mountain groups and decided that the mountains were no longer a safe base. Despite a short truce, the situation in

Cyprus deteriorated when British troops were withdrawn temporarily for the Suez operation in late 1956. However, at the beginning of 1957 with the return of these troops, Harding was able to form an independent striking force. He also received the significant reinforcement of helicopters, which enabled the security forces to carry out offensive actions.

In November 1957 Harding retired as Governor and was replaced by Sir Hugh Foot. The new Governor was concerned to begin a period of diplomacy and conciliation in which military action was to be used only as a last resort. The political dimensions of the Cyprus crisis had assumed international proportions with the situation being debated at the UN; Turkish concern had been aroused following inter-communal riots; the British government had been stimulated to seek a compromise solution. So the role of the security forces was to contain the situation while political negotiations proceeded. A Greek-Turkish plan to make Cyprus an independent state was finally endorsed by Makarios in 1959 and Grivas returned to Greece a hero, but one who had failed to achieve his objective. For the British, the outcome was less than satisfactory, although they were able to maintain their sovereign bases.

Over 100 British soldiers and 50 policemen were killed during the emergency. Some 240 civilians, of whom 26 were British, also lost their lives, plus at least 90 insurgents.

The campaigns fought by the British in Malaya, Kenya and Cyprus established a number of essential requirements for successful counter-insurgency. It was important that the political and military aims were agreed by all concerned from the very beginning and clearly stated in a directive. As the military aim was dependent on political considerations it was necessary that the political directive should state three things – the purpose and scope of military operations; the short-term political and military aims governing the campaign; and finally the long-term political aim which it was hoped to achieve when the military operations were concluded. In Malaya and Kenya it took some time before the aim became clear and a directive was issued. In Cyprus, the aim was never very clear and this undoubtedly hampered operations as policy oscillated between negotiation and military action.

Given the importance of the political factors involved in counter-insurgency operations, it was essential to establish good civil-military relations. The greatest potential area for conflict was between the civil and military administrations in the field. The civil authorities were primarily concerned with a long-term settlement based upon the goodwill of the people and were sometimes suspicious that the military were only interested in short-term successes. For their part, the military sometimes believed that their freedom of action was being unduly restricted by political considerations. But good civil-military relations were usually maintained because of a common purpose and a compatibility of educational and social background between the civil and military leaders.

Effective civil-military co-operation was based upon a unified command, with preferably

Below: Field Marshal Sir John Harding (right), Governor of Cyprus, with Archbishop Makarios, leader of the Greek Cypriots, January 1956. A number of such meetings were arranged by the British in the hope of stopping the EOKA campaign.

Above: Soldiers of the Suffolk Regiment guard the barrier between the Greek and Turkish areas of Nicosia following inter-communal violence, 1958.

the direction and control of policy and operations in the hands of one individual. In Malaya, for a significant period of time, this was achieved by appointing Templer as High Commissioner, and in Cyprus Harding as Governor. But the political circumstances did not always permit this to happen and it was not always possible to find the right man for the job.

To implement successful counter-insurgency operations meant establishing a joint command and control structure embracing the civil, police, military, intelligence and information services. Experience in Malaya, Kenya and Cyprus proved that the four essentials were a director of operations, a joint committee structure, a secretariat and joint operations rooms.

Left: EOKA terrorists operating in the Paphos area, 1958. The photograph was found in an arms cache by British troops.

Left: Following Cypriot independence, Archbishop Makarios talks with British paras on exercise.

The blueprint for joint command and control had been established in Malaya and was adapted, although less successfully, in Kenya and Cyprus. The fundamental point was that it was necessary to co-ordinate the separate policies and services involved in counter--insurgency to prevent muddle and a waste of resources. Such a joint command and control structure had to exist at every level.

In both politics and war the importance of accurate intelligence cannot be over-emphasised. In counter-insurgency the very fact that insurgency has begun either means the failure of intelligence or a refusal by the responsible authorities to believe it. In Malaya, Kenya and Cyprus the civil authorities relied mainly upon the Police and the Special Branch for such intelligence, and their knowledge or lack of it could be crucial. Once insurgency had begun, the Army became more directly involved, and here there were fundamental differences between police and military approaches to the acquisition and dissemination of intelligence which could not be fully resolved until some form of joint intelligence was established.

The organisation of intelligence during counter-insurgency operations usually followed three phases. The first phase was that leading up to the outbreak of insurgency when effective action against the insurgents did not occur either because of a lack of accurate intelligence or a failure to take action by the civil authorities. In Cyprus in 1955 there were only three Special Branch officers, and two of them were quickly murdered. In Malaya in 1948 there were some 30 Special Branch officers, who had completed a fairly accurate assessment of the activities of the MCP, but they were not confident about predicting communist intentions.

The second phase was when the insurgents went underground and the armed forces were called in to support the Police. This was a crucial period because there was usually a paucity of accurate intelligence, the security forces were very much on the defensive, and there was an understandable tendency to over-react against insurgent attacks, thus risking alienating the local population.

The third phase began when the security forces had built up sufficient background information about the whole population, thus discovering the identities of the insurgents and their supporters and converting this into contact information. This involved isolating the insurgents from the civil population and collecting and analysing information from a variety of sources. Penetration of the insurgent organisation by agents and using 'converted' insurgents enabled the security forces to take the offensive. In Malaya and Kenya it was found that intelligence began with the ordinary soldier at section level watching and reporting on everything he saw.

The quality and quantity of the security forces available for counter-insurgency was also crucial. In all the colonial territories the Police stood in the front line and were usually local recruits at the NCO and other-rank level with British officers. In Malaya the Police were initially weak, suffering from poor morale and inadequate resources. The Police in Cyprus were largely drawn from the Greek-Cypriot community and their effectiveness was suspect. In Kenya, the Police were effective and reliable but had insufficient manpower to deal with Mau Mau. Following the outbreak of the emergencies the Police were usually reorganised, given more weapons and equipment and greatly expanded. Additional manpower came in the first instance from former British members of the Palestine Police and then from the British police forces on attachment. But the most substantial reinforcements came from the local population in both Malaya and Kenya, and without their loyal and efficient service it would have proved very difficult to have defeated the

MRLA and Mau Mau. Even so, the commitment of regular British forces was essential.

Relevant training for counter-insurgency was very important for such forces. Initially, there were some problems as many senior officers had only just experienced large-scale conventional war and found it difficult to adapt to a conflict which had a very high political content. There were many practical problems of acclimatisation, acquiring the correct clothing, weapons and equipment and learning to operate in frequently hostile terrain and climate. Before accurate intelligence began to pinpoint insurgent groups, the majority of time had to be spent in hours of patrolling, guard duties and cordon-and-sweeps. Mobility did give the security forces an important edge over the enemy, although the use of roads could attract ambushes.

The political content of insurgency required the counter-insurgents to develop propaganda and psychological warfare, later to be called information policy. This worked at several levels. Firstly, it was aimed at the local population to convince them that the insurgents were wrong and would lose, the counter-insurgents were right and would win, and it was in their own interests to support the latter. A powerful argument in Malaya was the announcement of future independence, while in Kenya the tribal divisions and atrocities of Mau Mau helped the security forces. Secondly, information policy was aimed at maintaining the morale of the security forces. Thirdly, it was vital to persuade the insurgents that they were losing and that if they surrendered they would be well treated. Finally, it was necessary to win the support of international opinion, which in the case of Cyprus was the main aim of EOKA and had to be strongly countered by the British.

Right: EOKA prisoner, captured by men of the Duke of Wellington's Regiment in the Troodos after a fierce gun battle.

Below: British troops and Cypriot police stop and search the passengers of a local bus following the burning of a post office.

'Winning the hearts and minds' of the local population could become rather a glib phrase, but in general terms the British succeeded in doing this in Malaya and Kenya, although not in Cyprus. By its very nature counter-insurgency can mean the restriction of civil liberties and possible excesses by the security forces desperate to contain insurgency and provoked by acts of terrorism. Undoubtedly, there were acts of brutality committed by the security forces, such as against Mau Mau suspects by the Kenya Police Reservists, but generally these were isolated and were investigated. The forced resettlement of the Chinese squatters was strongly resisted, but in general the British attempted to act within the law and refused to respond to acts of provocative terror. It was only with the support of the majority of the local population that counter-insurgency was successful in Malaya and Kenya.

Finally, the British emerged from Malaya, Kenya and Cyprus with a general sense of achievement, and in the case of Malaya, the admiration of other nations who had conducted similar but less successful operations. The experience gained in the difficult art of counter-insurgency was to prove useful as the withdrawal from the empire gathered pace in the 1960s and the problems of Northern Ireland developed into violence at the end of the decade. Refinements to the art would be constantly needed, but the campaigns of the 1950s provided a solid base of practical knowledge and skill which could never be destroyed, even when overlaid by more conventional operations such as those in the Middle East.

59
O22R71

SUEZ–THE WATERSHED

British influence in the Middle East, built up since the 1870s to protect the vital trade and communications route through the Suez Canal, began to decline in the years immediately after the Second World War. The granting of independence to India in 1947 destroyed the core of the imperial trading system and undermined the validity of maintaining a presence in countries such as Egypt, Sudan, Libya, Transjordan, Aden and Somaliland. At the same time, the decision to withdraw from the mandate of Palestine suggested a weakness of resolve and the rise of Arab nationalism created a political force which Britain could never hope to match. As the pressures developed, Britain faced the choice of either losing prestige or fighting for continued influence. Neither was attractive and for some time official policy veered erratically between the two.

The dilemma was particularly acute in Egypt, ostensibly an independent state in which British troops were present as 'guests' under the terms of a treaty signed in 1936. Ten years later, demands for military withdrawal produced riots in the streets of Alexandria and attacks upon British property which were sufficient to persuade the London government to compromise. By March 1947 troops had been withdrawn from barracks in Cairo and Alexandria and concentrated in the Canal Zone, a collection of camps and base workshops set up during the Desert War of 1940-43, centred upon Ismailia. It was an unfortunate precedent, implying that Britain was weak and susceptible to pressure.

The result was renewed demands for withdrawal and when these failed to have any effect the Egyptian prime minister, Nahas Pasha, formally abrogated the 1936 Treaty, destroying at a stroke the legal right of British troops to remain even in the Canal Zone. When this was announced on 15 October 1951, anti-British riots swept the Canal towns and service families were openly attacked. Britain, determined to retain prestige, refused to be intimidated and this time committed troops to protect her interests. By 14 November a total of 6000 soldiers had been sent to reinforce the Canal Zone and they, together with the original garrison, soon contained the trouble.

The Egyptians responded by withdrawing all civilian labour from the British base and by using para-military police auxiliaries, the *Bulak Nizam*, to conduct a campaign of escalating violence. In Ismailia, Port Said and Suez Town, elements of the *Bulak Nizam*, armed by the Egyptian authorities but rarely under their full control, attacked service families, base facilities and even army patrols. To begin with, the GOC Middle East Land Forces, Lieutenant General Sir George Erskine (later to achieve wider fame in Kenya during the Mau Mau emergency) favoured a low-profile response, but as British deaths mounted he ordered overt retaliation. On 25 January 1952 he initiated a full-scale offensive against police and *Bulak Nizam* strongpoints in Ismailia. Unfortunately this proved to be more difficult than envisaged and at least 40 policemen were killed. In response, British property in Cairo was burned down and it began to look as if the only solution would be a British reoccupation of the Egyptian capital. Such a prospect forced the head of state, King Farouk, hitherto content to let events take their course, to dismiss Nahas and call in his army to disarm the police. The violence, which had cost the lives of 40 British servicemen, gradually died down.

In purely military terms this was a victory for Britain, but politically the results were more complex. In London the government felt obliged to reassess the strategic necessity of a base which cost so much to maintain, while in Egypt

Previous page: A Centurion tank of 6 RTR emerges from the bowels of an LST, Port Said, 1956. Despite problems of finding and transporting armour to Egypt, the tanks of 6 RTR played a crucial role in the capture of Port Said on 6 November 1956.

Below: As British troops stand guard, captured members of the Egyptian *Bulak Nizam* (police auxiliaries) are marched away from their barracks, Ismailia, January 1952.

Below right: Soldiers of the Lancashire Fusiliers advance against *Bulak Nizam* positions in Ismailia, January 1952.

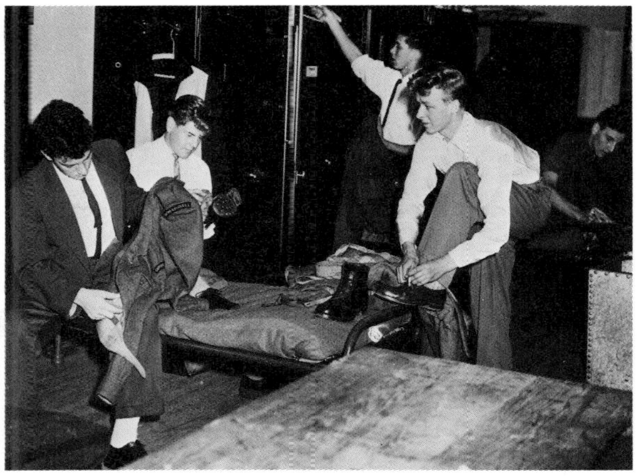

Above: Anthony Nutting (left), Minister of State for the Middle East, signs the agreement with President Gamal Abdul Nasser (right) whereby the British are to withdraw from Egypt, 19 October 1954.

Above right: Reservists of the Oxfordshire and Buckinghamshire Light Infantry change into their uniforms, August 1956. Over 20,000 Army reservists were recalled during the Suez Crisis, although very few saw action.

Right: Men of the Duke of Wellington's Regiment load supplies on board a transport plane at Blackbushe airport, August 1956. The supplies are bound for the invasion force gathering in the Mediterranean.

Farouk's intervention, apparently in support of the British, helped to concentrate opposition to him among army officers. Thus when Farouk was deposed in July 1952 and replaced by a military council headed by Major General Mohammed Neguib, the atmosphere had changed. Neguib, aware of the need for international sympathy, adopted a more moderate line and agreed to enter negotiations about the Canal Zone. The ensuing talks were by no means easy, punctuated by yet more riots and, in April 1954, by the overthrow of Neguib in favour of the more chauvinistic Colonel Gamal Abdul Nasser, but an agreement was eventually hammered out. Signed on 19 October 1954, it gave the British 20 months in which to withdraw their troops, after which the Canal Zone base would be maintained by civilian technicians with a British right to move forces back in should the freedom of the Canal be threatened by outside powers. On 24 March 1956 the last of the fighting troops – 2nd Battalion, Grenadier Guards – withdrew. It seemed as if the British had at last resolved their dilemma.

By that time, however, relations between Nasser and the Western powers had deteriorated. His strident calls for pan-Arab consolidation threatened Britain's remaining influence in Jordan, Libya and Aden, his support of Algerian rebels alienated France, and his re-

Right: Political leaders discuss the crisis, August 1956: (L to R) Christian Pineau, French Foreign Minister, Anthony Eden, British Prime Minister, and John Foster Dulles, US Secretary of State. The meeting was unlikely to have been as amicable as the smiles imply.

Below: Marines of 3rd Commando Brigade come ashore during an amphibious exercise, Malta, September 1956.

fusal to join the Baghdad Pact in 1955 displeased the Americans. Finally, his vehement opposition to Israel threatened renewed conflict in the Middle East and, as a result, his requests for military equipment from the West were refused. When in July 1955 he turned instead to the Eastern bloc, concluding an agreement with Czechoslovakia which provided 530 Soviet-built armoured vehicles, 500 artillery pieces and over 200 modern aircraft, many in the West began to regard the Egyptian leader as a Soviet puppet, intent upon aggression. Opposition to his policies was manifested in a withdrawal of promised finances for his dream project, the Aswan High Dam, in mid-July 1956. Nasser

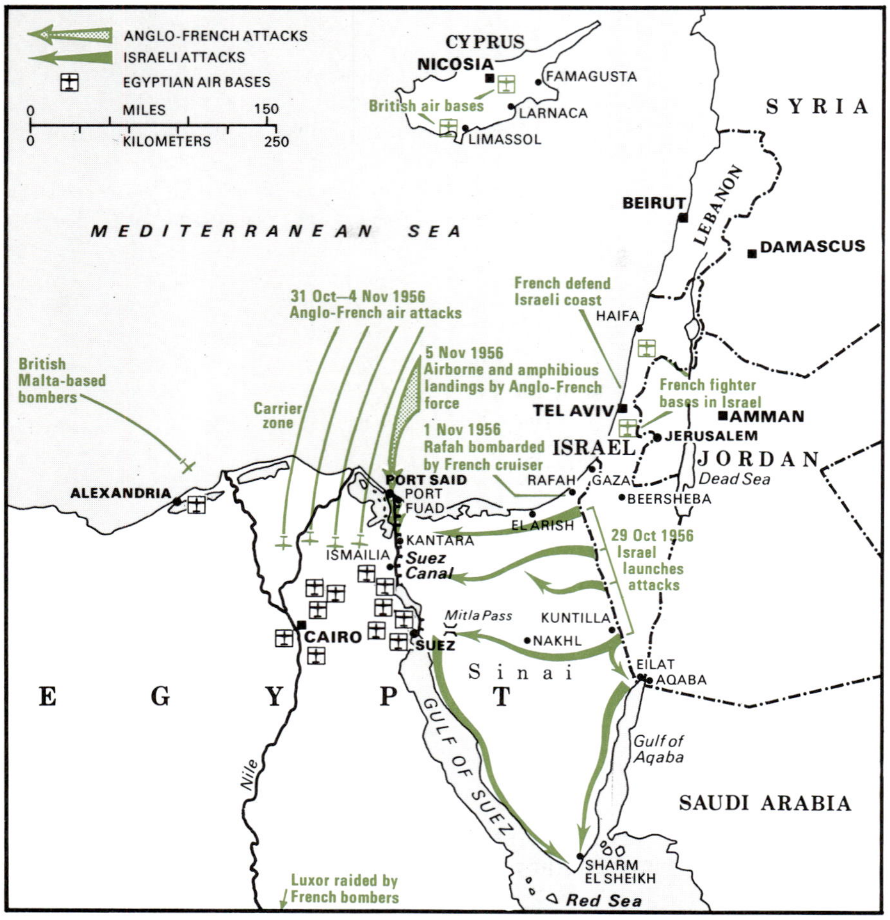

Above: Map showing the military events of October-November 1956. The problems facing Nasser, attacked from the east by the Israelis and from the north by the Anglo-French forces, may be easily appreciated.

was left with the problem of finding an alternative source of income. His solution was announced on 26 July when he nationalised the Suez Canal Company, forcing all users of the waterway to pay tolls to the Egyptian government instead of to an Anglo-French consortium based in Paris.

In itself this was hardly a cause for war, but to both Britain and France it symbolised a greater threat. Afraid for their right of access to the Canal, angry at the arbitrary dispossession of Company shareholders and aware of their declining influence in the Middle East, they were ready to blame Nasser for all their problems, regarding him as a new Hitler who had to be stopped. On 27 July Britain began to prepare a military force for operations in Egypt and three days later the French announced that they would contribute two divisions – the 10th Colonial Parachute and 7th Light Mechanised, both currently in Algeria – supported by air and naval units.

At first the preparations appeared to go well. On 2 August a Royal Proclamation recalled over 20,000 British Army reservists to the colours and five days later Anglo-French staff talks in London set up a co-ordinated command structure. As Britain was to provide the bulk of the projected expeditionary force (50,000 of the intended 80,000 troops, plus 100 warships and 300 aircraft), she was given the top command posts, with French officers acting as deputies. General Sir Charles Keightley, GOC Middle East Land Forces, was appointed overall commander, with Vice-Admiral d'Escadre Barjot, commander of the French Mediterranean Fleet, as his deputy. Land forces were to be under Lieutenant General Sir Hugh Stockwell and General André Beaufre; air elements under Air Marshal Denis Barnett and General Raymond Brohon; and naval units under Vice-Admiral M Richmond (later replaced by Vice-Admiral D F Durnford-Slater) and Contre-Amiral Lancelot. By that time the first of the naval forces were already being prepared. The French fleet, organised around the aircraft carriers *Lafayette* and *Arromanches*, was concentrating in Toulon and three British carriers – HMS *Bulwark, Theseus* and *Ocean* – were being made ready to join HMS *Eagle* in the Mediterranean. RAF Transport Command had been alerted for a possible airlift and Cyprus had been chosen as the operational base.

But much of this was a facade, hiding a host of practical problems which seriously weakened the military option. Despite declared intentions and initial deployments, neither Britain nor France had armed forces available to mount an immediate operation. For the French the problem lay in Algeria, where large numbers of troops were tied down fighting nationalist guerrillas, but for the British the difficulties were more general. Since the end of the Second World War, British defence commitments had been enormous, with forces deployed in Europe as well as throughout the empire, and had been satisfied only by a policy of conscription which was both expensive and unpopular. Money was scarce, preventing the introduction of new

Left: The Anglo-French commanders, Operation Musketeer: (L to R) General André Beaufre, deputy land force commander, General Sir Charles Keightley, overall commander, Vice-Admiral d'Escadre Barjot, deputy overall commander, and Lieutenant General Sir Hugh Stockwell, land force commander.

equipment (to the extent that the Egyptians, with their Soviet-built weapons, enjoyed superiority in certain key areas, notably small-arms and jet aircraft) and, by the mid-1950s, the armed services were stretched to their limits, fighting counter-insurgency campaigns simultaneously in Malaya, Kenya and Cyprus. Indeed, the high incidence of such operations had led to a marked decline in conventional warfare capabilities, with specialist troops such as marines and parachutists – essential elements in any expeditionary force – deployed to combat guerrillas. In July 1956 the bulk of the strategic reserve – 3rd Commando and 16th

Below: Men of 3rd Battalion, Parachute Regiment check their equipment before boarding their planes, Cyprus, early morning, 5 November 1956. Next stop – Gamil Airfield.

Right: Members of 6 RTR wait to board LSTs, Malta, October 1956. This was a time of boredom and inaction.

Independent Parachute Brigades – which should have been instantly available, had been committed to fighting EOKA gangs in Cyprus and had not trained together for nearly a year. Even if they had, a shortage of amphibious assault ships, landing craft and transport aircraft would have seriously limited their effectiveness.

Nor did the problems end there. Although Britain and France, as powerful states in their own right, should have been sufficient to deter or defeat Nasser, they were operating in a world now dominated by the superpowers and without the backing of America their policies were unlikely to succeed. But America was approaching a presidential election and neither the incumbent, Dwight D Eisenhower, nor his Secretary of State, John Foster Dulles, was prepared to support the use of force over the Canal. Dulles travelled to London as soon as the crisis

Below: The Paras go in: the scene on 5 November 1956 as men of 3 Para capture Gamil Airfield.

developed, and although he failed to stop Anglo-French military prepartions, his constant calls for peaceful negotiations and international conferences forced the Europeans to proceed with caution. Letters from the Soviet premier to his British and French counterparts (the first of which were received in early September), warning of the 'grave consequences' of military action in the Middle East, increased the sense of international isolation, especially as they seemed to reflect the general feelings of the United Nations.

The result was a lack of clear political objectives for the expeditionary force, leading to constant changes of plan which did little to improve efficiency. The basic aim was to occupy the Canal Zone, but an early suggestion by the French that this should be achieved immediately using parachute forces was vetoed by the more cautious British and thereafter the issue was complicated by political demands for the overthrow of Nasser. As this would clearly entail the occupation of Cairo and the defeat of the Egyptian armed forces, something more elaborate was needed. After further staff talks, it was decided that the initial objective would have to be Alexandria, the nearest port to Cairo, and that it should be taken by seaborne assault. An operational plan, originally code-named 'Hamilcar' but soon to be altered to 'Musketeer', was put forward on 15 August. Preceded by air and naval bombardments and the establishment of air superiority, an airborne assault would be mounted to the south west of Alexandria to block Egyptian reinforcement routes, after which seaborne forces would take the town. Once in control and joined by follow-up units, they would break out towards both Cairo and the Canal. D-Day for the operation was set for 15 September.

Above: Against a backdrop of a burning building, men of C Coy, 3 Para consolidate their positions around the control tower, Gamil Airfield, 5 November 1956.

It was an over-ambitious scheme which produced more problems than it solved. The timetable was wildly optimistic and as early as 25 August the date for the attack had to be put back by 10 days, chiefly because the new plan necessitated the provision of a large invasion force which could not be gathered together quickly. Warships had to be taken out of mothballs, merchant ships and tankers requisitioned and adequate base facilities established. This last consideration posed its own problems, for the original base of Cyprus lacked deep-water ports and suitable airfields. The fleet had, therefore, to be gathered at Malta, but as this island lay some six days' sailing time away from Egypt, any hopes of achieving surprise were dashed.

Delays were also experienced in preparing the military units involved. Commandos and paratroops had to be withdrawn from Cyprus

Below: Men of A Coy, 3 Para land at the northwestern end of the runway, Gamil Airfield, 5 November 1956. The airport buildings and control tower are in the background.

and retrained in their specialised roles, something which was both time-consuming and, in the event, unsatisfactory. The men of 16th Parachute Brigade, for example, found that they were expected to jump from obsolete side-loading Hastings and Valetta transports (by comparison, the more experienced French had rear-loading Nordatlas machines) and that there were only enough of these to lift one battalion, with no heavy-weapons support. Similarly, because of a shortage of landing craft, 45 Commando, one of the constitutents of 3rd Commando Brigade, was suddenly told to prepare for a helicopter-borne assault, something that had not been attempted before. Sycamore and Whirlwind helicopters of 845 Squadron, Royal Navy, and the Joint (Army-RAF) Experimental Helicopter Unit (JEHU) were hurriedly shipped out aboard the carriers *Ocean* and *Theseus* in late September, leaving the commandos very little time to acquire new skills. Finally, despite the lessons of the Second World War, none of the formations involved in the invasion force – the two strategic reserve brigades and, as follow-up, 3rd Infantry Division – had an armoured element. A new armoured brigade, comprising the 1st and 6th Royal Tank Regiment (1 and 6 RTR), was created in August, but was put together too fast to be effective. Both units were strung out on training duties in England when the crisis broke and it was only through the use of civilian transporters, provided by Pickfords, the haulage company, that 6 RTR managed to reach Southampton at all. Once there, a shortage of tank landing ships (only 18 were available) restricted their strength to 47 Centurions. 1 RTR, with a further 46 Centurions, embarked too late to take part in the invasion.

Meanwhile, the operational plan had been changed yet again, this time at the instigation of the French. On 25 August they had suggested that the landing site be shifted to Port Said, from where an advance down the Canal would split Egyptian forces facing Israel in Sinai from those in the Delta and considerably ease a subsequent advance on Cairo. This was formally adopted by the Joint Chiefs of Staff on 10 September, although without alteration to the existing timetable. D-Day was still set for 25 September, but as the fleet would have to leave home waters by the 12th to meet the deadline, it was quickly recognised that this was impossible. The assault date had to be put back yet again – this time to 1 October – under the new code-name 'Musketeer Revised'.

But the French, exasperated by the constant delays, had begun to look elsewhere for support, initiating secret talks with Israel about a co-ordinated assault on Egypt. Despite subsequent denials, there can be no doubt that Britain was aware of these and probably welcomed them because they postponed the need for military action for at least another month. After preliminary negotiations, a new plan – the fourth in three months – was finalised during a meeting of British, French and Israeli representatives at Sèvres, just outside Paris, between 22 and 24 October. The Israelis proposed to attack Egyptian forces in Sinai at the end of the month, on the understanding that Britain and France would immediately intervene, delivering an ultimatum to both sides which would demand the creation of a 16km (10 mile) demilitarised zone on either side of the Canal. This the Israelis would accept – a simple task as none of their forces would be within such a zone – leaving Nasser to suffer the consequences of refusal

Left: RAF armourers prepare to load six 454kg (1000lb) bombs on board a Canberra bomber, Cyprus, November 1956. The aircraft is painted with black and white 'invasion' recognition stripes on fuselage and wings.

Below left: Through the smoke of air and naval bombardment, the invasion fleet approaches Port Said, 6 November 1956.

Below: Men of 40 Commando, Royal Marines, raise the White Ensign over Navy House, Port Said, 6 November 1956, at the end of a difficult advance along the eastern waterfront.

or the ignominy of abandoning a sizeable area of his state. The former was the more likely response and this would trigger a sustained Anglo-French air attack, designed to destroy the Egyptian Air Force and clear the way for a more general Israeli advance.

The air assault would last for about six days – the time needed to move invasion convoys from Malta – at the end of which an allied air and seaborne landing would take place at Port Said. The details took some time to be finalised, but in the end it was decided that on D-1 a single British battalion – 3rd Battalion, Parachute Regiment (3 Para) – would be dropped onto Gamil airfield to the west of the town and a French unit – the 2nd Colonial Parachute Regiment (2 RCP) – would assault Port Fuad to the east, clearing the vital Raswa bridges which linked the two assault areas. On D-Day itself, the two airborne units would advance into Port Said while British commandos (40, 42 and 45 Commando, Royal Marines), the remainder of 16th Parachute Brigade (1 and 2 Para) and the Centurions of 6 RTR stormed ashore. At the same time, the French 10th Parachute Division would complete its deployment into Port Fuad by sea and air. Once Port Said had been cleared, the invaders would advance down the Canal towards Ismailia and Suez Town while reinforcements – the British 3rd Infantry and

French 7th Light Mechanised Divisions – disembarked. With his forces split to face enemy threats in Sinai and along the Canal, Nasser would be defeated, it was hoped, in about six days.

The Israeli attack (Operation 'Kadesh') began just before 1700 hours on 29 October with a paradrop to the east of the Mitla Pass, and soon developed into a three-pronged armoured advance across the Sinai desert. By then the Anglo-French invasion force had at last been brought together. It was a formidable armada, with the British providing a total of 45,000 men, 12,000 vehicles, 300 aircraft and 100 warships, centred upon five aircraft carriers – *Eagle, Ocean, Theseus, Bulwark* and *Albion* – while the French contributed 34,000 men, 9000 vehicles, 200 aircraft and 30 warships, including the carriers *Lafayette* and *Arromanches*. Most of the naval units were already at sea and forces earmarked for the initial assault were concentrated in the Mediterranean area. The RAF had 17 bomber squadrons, equipped with Canberras and Valiants, in Malta and Cyprus, supported by Venom, Hunter and Meteor land-based fighters and Sea Venom, Wyvern and Sea Hawk strike aircraft on board the carriers; the French had F4U Corsairs and TBM-3 Avengers with the fleet and Mystère IVAs and F-84F Thunderstreaks in Cyprus and Israel. 16th Parachute Brigade and 10th Parachute Division were in Cyprus and follow-up units were on their way from Britain and Algeria. As the convoys all came together, they were shadowed by elements of the US Sixth Fleet but no interference took place. The first shots of the naval war were fired on 1 November, when the British cruiser *Newfoundland* engaged and sank the Egyptian frigate *Domiat* in the Gulf of Suez.

By then the air attacks had already begun. As

Right: French AMX-13 light tanks deploy in the streets of Port Said, November 1956.

Below right: Lieutenant General Sir Hugh Stockwell (left), land force commander for Musketeer, visits a 25-pounder gunpit at El Cap, December 1956. El Cap marked the southern limit of the Anglo-French advance.

Below: British troops examine Egyptian weapons, captured in Port Said, 6 November 1956.

soon as the Israelis advanced into Sinai the proposed ultimatum was issued and, as expected, Nasser promptly rejected it. Consequently, late on 31 October a Canberra of No 10 Squadron RAF initiated the Anglo-French response by dropping 225kg (500lb) bombs onto an Egyptian airfield at Almaza, north of Cairo. Throughout that night Canberras and Valiants hit a wide range of other airfields – three more in the Nile Delta and eight in the Canal Zone – although the damage inflicted was not decisive. Most of the Egyptian MiG-15 fighters and Ilyushin Il-28 bombers had been moved to safety during the period of the ultimatum and it was not until 1 November, when the carrier strike aircraft were committed, that more accurate and destructive raids took place. By the end of the first day an estimated 50 Egyptian aircraft had been located and destroyed and about 40 others damaged, with no British or French losses. For the next 72 hours this pattern of high-altitude night and low-altitude day attacks was repeated, virtually wiping out the Egyptian Air Force and disrupting ground defences. On 4 November the process of 'softening up' Port Said began, prepartory to the allied invasion. Coastal artillery positions, barracks, supply dumps and anti-aircraft defences were all hit, and although by then a total of seven aircraft (two Wyverns, a Venom, two Sea Hawks, a Thunderstreak and a Corsair) had been shot down, enough damage had been inflicted to enable the bulk of the carrier air strength to be diverted to close-support tasks when the invasion began. It went ahead in the knowledge that the Israelis had already defeated Egyptian forces in Sinai.

Early on 5 November, men of 3 Para and 2 RCP began to emplane at airfields in Cyprus. The British battalion was to be dropped first and at 0415 hours GMT three companies and their supplies were lifted from Nicosia aboard a fleet of 26 Hastings and Valettas. Their intended drop-zone (DZ) – Gamil airfield – was a narrow strip of land 2400m long and 800m wide (one and a half miles by half a mile), bounded to north and south by sea. Protected by fighters and ground-attack aircraft, the heavily laden transports approached the DZ at 0515, flying

from the north-west directly into the sun. Despite the delays associated with side-loading, 85 per cent of the force was on the ground within 10 minutes, having suffered only one fatality and few major injuries. 'A' Company rushed to secure the north-western end of the airfield, encountering only spasmodic resistance from Egyptian defenders; 'B' Company moved towards the Port Said end to block Egyptian reinforcement routes, fighting a short but bloody hand-to-hand engagement on the way; 'C' Company cleared the airfield itself, setting up a command post and mortar positions among oil drums strewn across the runway by the Egyptians in an effort to prevent its use. Within 30 minutes the objective was firmly in British hands and, while a second lift brought in the rest of 3 Para and helicopters evacuated the wounded to the fleet offshore, 'B' Company began to push towards Port Said.

2 RCP parachuted onto an even smaller DZ – 460m by 185m (500 by 200 yards), bounded by buildings, roads and water – to the south of the Raswa bridges at 0530. They landed in the incredibly short time of four minutes but had to fight to establish their hold, having dropped literally onto the heads of Egyptian defenders. Nevertheless, supported by a 'cab rank' of strike aircraft, they advanced to capture the western Raswa bridge (the eastern bridge had been destroyed) by 0900. They dug in around their prize, sending out probing patrols into Port

Said, and at about 1530 were joined by a second battalion which dropped onto salt pans to the east and cleared Port Fuad. Meanwhile a small detachment of British paras (from 9th Independent Squadron Royal Engineers and Guards Parachute Company) which had landed with the first French wave, conducted a reconnaissance down the Canal road towards Ismailia. They returned with the news that it appeared to be undefended.

By then the main British para force had pushed through stiffening opposition from Gamil, clearing defenders from positions in a sewage farm, a cemetery, a coastguard barracks and blocks of flats on the outskirts of Port Said. By 1300 hours they were running short of ammunition and the order was given to dig in. They remained in their positions, under sniper fire, and awaited the seaborne landing.

This began at 0400 on 6 November with air strikes against Egyptian positions on the chosen beaches, closely followed by a short intense naval bombardment. As soon as this was lifted, at 0430, the first of the tracked landing vehicles, each with 30 commandos on board, came ashore. 40 Commando landed on the allied left (Sierra Red Beach) with the task of clearing the harbour and 42 Commando assaulted on the right (Sierra Green Beach) with orders to advance through Port Said to make contact with the French at Raswa. As they came ashore they encountered little opposition from defenders demoralised by the air and naval bombardment, but as they pushed into built-up areas beyond the beaches they came under sustained sniper fire. Fortunately they were soon joined by 14 Centurions of 'C' Squadron 6 RTR, which had landed to the left of 40 Commando as soon as the beach was clear and thereafter, in a remarkable display of inter-arm co-operation, commandos could call up heavy armour whenever they encountered pockets of enemy resistance. The process was time-consuming and destructive, but as the morning wore on the superior numbers and firepower of the Anglo-French forces began to take effect. At 0540 the first elements of 45 Commando arrived, landing near the Casino Palace from 22 helicopters of 845 Squadron and JEHU, and as they were gradually reinforced they began to clear a path through the centre of Port Said, aiming to link up with 3 Para to the west. As they did so, 40 Commando to the east slowly advanced along the waterfront, using armour and air strikes to clear the police station, the Canal Company offices and, eventually, Navy House; while to the south 42 Commando moved steadily towards the French positions at Raswa. Meanwhile 3 Para resumed their attacks from the direction of Gamil and 2 RCP, reinforced from the sea by the 1st Foreign Legion Parachute Regiment and a unit of AMX-13 light tanks, consolidated their hold on the important Raswa bridge and Port Fuad. House-clearing operations were to continue throughout the day but by 1200, when Centurions of the newly landed 'A' Squadron 6 RTR finally linked up with 2 RCP, Egyptian positions in Port Said were no longer tenable.

The emphasis now shifted to the next objective – the Canal road running south towards Ismailia. All the evidence seemed to suggest that this was clear and 'A' Squadron 6 RTR, with French para support, began to advance down the narrow causeway towards more open ground at El Cap without delay. However, the main unit earmarked for the task – 2 Para – could not be deployed quickly. It arrived in the harbour aboard the troopship *Empire Parkeston* sometime in the afternoon, but congestion both afloat and ashore delayed disembarkation and it was not until 1900 that the battalion assembled at Raswa to spearhead the advance. By then the allied commanders were inclined to wait until morning before proceeding further and it was only after receiving the startling news that a ceasefire was to be imposed from midnight that they resumed the drive south. The aim was to establish positions beyond the causeway by the time of the ceasefire so as to gain room for manoeuvre should the fighting flare up again, but as 2 Para could not set out until 2300, this was a tall order. In the event, accompanied by the tanks of 'A' Squadron 6 RTR, the British troops did manage to reach El Cap, about 40km (25 miles) south of Port Said, by the appointed hour. There they dug in, convinced that another few hours would have seen them in Ismailia.

The ceasefire had been forced on the British and French by international pressure. Since 20 October the United Nations had been calling for an end to hostilities in the Middle East and had even initiated the formation of a special Emergency Force to relieve Anglo-French troops in Egypt. At the same time the Soviets threatened to intervene in support of Nasser. This latter development seriously alarmed the Americans and, as it turned out, it was they who held the whip-hand, particularly over an economically weak Britain. The war had led to a run on sterling and a sudden decline in Britain's gold reserves. Although loans from the International Monetary Fund promised to ease the pressure, American backing for these was essential, leaving Britain with no choice but to

Above: Egyptian prisoners are marched away, guarded by French paras, November 1956. In the background is the western Raswa bridge, French airborne objective on 5 November.

Left: British paras face an unruly mob as they distribute food to the inhabitants of Port Said, November 1956. It was this sort of task which would be handed over thankfully to the UN.

Right: Soldiers of 3rd Infantry Division, souvenirs in hand, pose for a street camera, Port Said, November 1956.

bow to demands from Washington for a ceasefire. The French, lacking independence of command in Port Said, had to comply. It was a sobering lesson in the realities of world politics: neither Britain nor France was powerful enough to pursue policies which acted against superpower interests.

UN forces began to arrive in Egypt on 14 November, taking over Anglo-French positions which were now being held by 3rd Infantry Division. Riots and sniper fire continued to cause problems but as more UN contingents were deployed the violence died down, enabling the last of the allied troops to withdraw on 23 December. They had done a difficult job well, for despite the problems experienced during the lengthy preparation phase of 'Musketeer', the assault troops had fought with skill and daring once committed. Casualties had been kept to a minimum (the entire operation cost the British 22 dead and 97 wounded and the French 10 dead and 33 wounded, with 10 aircraft – eight British and two French – destroyed) and valuable lessons, particularly in helicopter operations, had been learnt for the future.

However, politically the Suez affair was a disaster. The sudden ceasefire and subsequent withdrawal constituted a stunning humiliation for both Britain and France, marking the end of the era of European domination in the Middle East. In Britain's case, this should have led to serious policy reassessments. So far as defence commitments were concerned, it was now obvious that Britain was hopelessly overstretched, trying to do too much with too little, and that even if a global role was to be retained it would have to be subordinate to superpower interests. In this sense, the Suez crisis was a watershed in the post-1945 period: before it Britain had all the trappings of world power and a reputation for greatness; after 1956 the reputation lay discredited and the maintenance of a global empire, already undermined by the loss of India, was no longer viable. The long and difficult process of decolonisation was about to begin, presenting the armed forces with new challenges and campaigns.

Unfortunately they were not well prepared to meet these, for despite the 'lessons' of Suez, the British government refused to face reality. Instead of cutting commitments abroad, a subsequent Defence White Paper, presented in April 1957 by Minister of Defence Duncan Sandys, tried to disguise the problems of overstretch by substituting technology for manpower. In Europe greater emphasis was to be placed upon nuclear weapons and in the empire smaller garrisons were to be maintained, particularly east of Suez, on the presumption that they could be reinforced quickly by air should a crisis develop. It was a poor policy, little different to that which had caused the problems of 1956, but it was made worse by the simultaneous decision to phase out conscription after 1960. This was undoubtedly a popular move and it certainly opened the way towards high service professionalism, but by effectively halving the size of the armed forces (from 690,000 to 375,000) it served to exacerbate already chronic defence difficulties.

Right: The scene at the entrance to the Suez Canal, November 1956, showing the blockships sunk by the Egyptians.

Main picture: Men of 42 Field Squadron, Royal Engineers, leave Port Said on board the LST *Evan Gibb*, December 1956.

31
01CC86

WITHDRAWAL FROM EMPIRE

Britain's post-war imperial withdrawal was a slow and rather difficult process. Despite the loss of India in 1947, the habit of an empire died hard. There were allies to defend, treaties to fulfil, trade routes to secure and colonies to prepare for independence. During the late-1940s and early-1950s, therefore, Britain remained unable or unwilling to disengage from the empire. The Suez debacle of 1956 produced no immediate changes to this attitude; in its aftermath, Britain seemed to be in no hurry to cut her imperial commitments. Two colonies – the Gold Coast (subsequently Ghana) and Malaya – were freed in 1957, but both had long been earmarked for early release and, in the case of Malaya, British forces stayed on even after independence. Thus, as late as 1957, Britain still regarded herself as a great imperial power.

Before very long, however, the British government began to reassess its policies. Recognising that the political, economic and military costs of an empire had become prohibitive, Harold Macmillan's Conservative government (January 1957-October 1963) decided upon a policy of imperial disengagement. The new policy, heralded by Macmillan's 'wind of change' speech of 3 February 1960, was soon put into effect. During the next four years. Conservative governments under Macmillan and Sir Alec Douglas-Home granted independence to most of Britain's colonies in Africa as well as to many in the Caribbean, Mediterranean, Near and Middle East, Far East and Pacific. The succeeding Labour government (October 1964 to June 1970) under Harold Wilson accelerated the imperial withdrawal. With its traditional aversion to imperial adventure and its dislike of high defence spending, Labour sought to wind up Britain's imperial commitments as quickly as possible. By November 1967, Britain's last major possession east of Suez – Aden – had been evacuated and only the remnants of the empire remained.

This withdrawal from the empire had profound repercussions for Britain's armed forces. As one imperial outpost after another was abandoned, the need for an imperial *gendarmerie* declined and Britain was able to concentrate more and more upon her NATO role. This did not mean, however, that the armed forces had no active duties to perform during the period of imperial withdrawal. On the contrary, the transition from globalism to regionalism was a gradual and troublesome process, and Britain was compelled to mount a whole series of military operations, during the early and mid-1960s, in order to cover her retreat from the empire. These multifarious operations ranged from peace-keeping duties to counter-insurgency campaigns and were carried out in areas as diverse as the Caribbean, Africa, the Middle East and the Far East.

The operations undertaken in the Caribbean were relatively minor affairs. One of the first took place on the central island of Jamaica, the home of the British Headquarters Caribbean Area. In June 1960 one company of the resident British battalion was called upon to help the Police and West Indies Regiment to quell Rastafarian unrest. This was achieved quickly and with little loss of life. Two years later, Jamaica became independent (August 1962), and British forces left the island.

This departure did not end Britain's involvement in the region, however. Britain was still responsible for numerous Caribbean territories and in one of these – British Guiana (subse-

Previous page: Britain's withdrawal from empire during the 1960s was accompanied by numerous military operations, including major campaigns in Brunei/Borneo and South Arabia. Shown here is a Saladin armoured car of the Queen's Royal Irish Hussars taking up position in Brunei Town, September 1963.

Below left: Even after the Suez debacle, Britain continued to perform an active military role in the Middle East. In this photo British paratroopers drill with a bazooka at Amman airport, Jordan, July 1958. The paratroopers had arrived in response to a request for assistance from King Hussein.

Below: A British military policeman in conversation with a local policeman and member of the Arab Legion, Amman, July 1958. British forces were able to rely upon the full co-operation of the Jordanian security forces.

quently Guyana) – British troops were given the task of maintaining the peace between people of Indian descent and those of Afro-Caribbean stock; a task that required a military presence from 1962 until independence in May 1966. Few casualties were incurred, but the assignment was a difficult one, and from May 1964 two battalions of infantry were required. One of these was withdrawn just before independence while the other stayed on until October 1966 in order to train the new Guyana Defence Force.

Britain's withdrawal from Africa was also accompanied by a number of minor military operations. Five were mounted between September 1960 and January 1964, each being fulfilled efficiently, successfully and with no loss of life on the British side.

The first of these operations took place in the British-administered Trust Territory of the Cameroons and began in September 1960. The purpose of the operation was to maintain the peace until the constitutional status of the territory had been settled by plebiscite. In the event the plebiscite was conducted without incident and the territory was partitioned by Nigeria and the Cameroon Republic. By October 1961, Britain had withdrawn.

A second operation, carried out in June 1963, involved the despatch of British troops to the southern African territory of Swaziland. The troops in question were sent to deal with

Above: Destination Jordan: British paratroopers board a Royal Air Force Beverley in Cyprus, July 1958.

internal unrest. Strikes and disorders had occurred in May 1963 and when the situation deteriorated in early June, Britain airlifted a battalion of infantry into Swaziland from their base in Kenya. The arrival of these troops stabilised the situation. The Police were then able to restore order swiftly and within a week the country had returned to normal.

Seven months later, British troops were back in action in another part of the continent – East Africa – carrying out more or less simultaneous operations in Tanganyika (subsequently Tanzania), Uganda and Kenya. These operations differed in two important respects from the Cameroon and Swaziland operations. Whereas the latter were carried out in territories still under British administration, the East African operations were executed in countries recently freed from British rule. Moreover, the East African operations had a different purpose. British forces were not called in to maintain the peace or restore order, but to put down mutinies by units of the fledgling armies of Tanganyika, Uganda and Kenya. These operations – or rather interventions – were potentially hazardous, because in all three countries the mutineers were sizeable in number and well armed.

The basic cause of the mutinies appears to have been the same in all three states: the African soldiers involved in the revolts wanted improvements to their pay and conditions and resented the fact that senior positions in their armies were still held by seconded British officers. Whether the mutinies were linked or not is unclear, but certainly there was a common pattern. In all three cases army units went out of control and the governments concerned were forced to call upon the former colonial power – Britain – to quell the rebellions.

The first of the three states to be affected was Tanganyika. On 20 January 1964 soldiers of the 1st Tanganyika Rifles, based at Colito near the capital, Dar-es-Salaam, revolted against their officers and detained some 30 British officers and NCOs. The mutineers went on to seize the airport and enter the capital. Four days later the country's president, Julius Nyerere, asked the British government to intervene. Britain responded positively, the action taken being short and sharp. As a precautionary measure, the British government had already ordered the aircraft carrier HMS *Centaur* to make its way from Aden to Dar-es-Salaam. By 24 January

Right: Soldiers of the 1st Battalion, Royal Ulster Rifles on a routine river patrol in Borneo, August 1964.

Main picture: HMS *Victorious* and HMS *Bulwark* off the coast of Kuwait, 1961. British forces deterred a projected Iraqi invasion.

Below: British forces in Kuwait, July 1961. In the background, a Centurion tank; in the foreground, a Bren-gun post amidst the sand and stone.

1964 *Centaur*, carrying 45 Commando, Royal Marines plus a complement of 21 aircraft, lay off the Tanganyikan coastline. In the early hours of the next day a company of Marines was ferried ashore by helicopter and put down near the mutineers' barracks. The Marines proceeded to attack the barracks and after a brief fight the mutineers surrendered. Other companies of the Commando were given the job of rounding up those mutineers who were still roaming the streets of the capital.

The mutinies in Uganda and Kenya were suppressed swiftly and decisively. In Uganda the trouble-spot was Jinja, where the 1st Uganda Rifles and elements of a newly formed second battalion were based. On 23 January 1964 several hundred of these soldiers rebelled and took control of the camp's armoury; British officers and NCOs were forced to take refuge in an orderly room. When the Ugandan prime minister, Milton Obote, appealed for assistance, the British government responded promptly. Over 400 men were flown into Uganda's Entebbe airport and while some of these troops were detailed to secure the airfield itself, others drove on to Jinja, about 112km (70 miles) away. Having been met *en route* by two British soldiers who had escaped from the camp, the advancing column decided to act boldly: they would drive straight into the camp and take the mutineers by surprise. This plan was effected. In the early hours of 25 January British forces rushed into the camp; as dawn broke, the rebels found themselves surrounded by bayonets and gave up without a fight.

In Kenya the trouble began at Lanet, where some 250 men of the 11th Kenya Rifles were based. Disturbances at this camp, on 23 January 1964, led the government of Kenya to request military assistance. The British authorities in Kenya responded by ordering a battery of the 3rd Royal Horse Artillery, based at Gilgil some 32km (20 miles) from Lanet, to the trouble-spot. On the following day, British forces reconnoitered the camp, established radio contact with British personnel still inside and proceeded to mount an attack. Most of the camp was recaptured, though the rebels refused to parley. The next day, however, the mutineers agreed to negotiate and after making an unsuccessful break-out attempt, they surrendered. Thus the Kenyan government, like its Tanganyikan and Ugandan counterparts, was saved from possible collapse by bold, resolute operations.

One of the operations associated with Britain's withdrawal from east of Suez can also be classified as a rearguard action designed to assist an erstwhile colonial regime. The operation in question was carried out in Kuwait, a small but oil-rich Arab state formerly 'guided' by the British government. On 19 June 1961 a new treaty was introduced whereby Kuwait assumed full responsibility for its foreign

Left: Gunners of the 3rd Royal Horse Artillery prepare to move against mutineers at Lanet, Kenya, January 1964.

Right: An Iban tribesman in Borneo. With their almost superhuman tracking abilities, the Iban proved a valuable asset to the British.

Below, far left: During the Brunei revolt of December 1962 a considerable number of civilians were taken hostage by the rebels, but most survived the ordeal. This photograph shows a group of Europeans at Seria, soon after they had been liberated by soldiers of the Queen's Own Highlanders.

Main picture: All three services contributed to the Borneo campaign. The photo shows Royal Navy Wessex helicopters aboard HMS *Albion*, with the coastline of Borneo in the background.

affairs whilst continuing to rely on Britain for military protection. This new treaty was soon put to the test. On 25 June 1961 neighbouring Iraq threatened to annex Kuwait and the latter duly appealed to Britain for help. As luck would have it, the British government was in a strong position to offer assistance, because the aircraft carrier HMS *Bulwark* with 42 Commando, Royal Marines aboard, was already in the vicinity. Other forces were despatched from Aden, Cyprus and Kenya. Whether these forces could have repulsed an Iraqi attack remains

purely conjectural, however, since no fighting actually took place. Faced by this British show of strength, the Iraqis decided not to invade. British forces were subsequently withdrawn, a process which was completed by 19 October 1961.

Just over a year later, British forces were back on active service in a completely different setting east of Suez: the jungles of Borneo. Conflict had arisen over the disposition of Britain's remaining colonies in South East Asia, these being Singapore and the three territories that constituted British Borneo – Sarawak, Brunei and North Borneo or Sabah. The prime minister of Malaya, Tunku Abdul Rahman, wanted to bring these territories into closer association with Malaya to form a Malaysian Federation, a proposal that was also looked upon with favour by Britain and by the majority of the peoples of the territories in question. On the other hand, Indonesia's president, Ahmed Sukarno, was strongly opposed to the proposal, regarding it as a threat to his plan for

a greater Indonesia. Most of the island of Borneo formed part of Indonesia, and Sukarno wanted to incorporate the northern, that is British, part of the island (Kalimantan Utara) into his own country. Sukarno, therefore, sought to crush the Malaysian idea while it was still in embryo.

The first opportunity for him to do so arose in December 1962, when the Sultanate of Brunei flared into revolt. The rebellion was masterminded by A M Azahari, an absentee politician with pro-Sukarno leanings, and was led in the field by Yassin Affendi, whose forces numbered some 4000. Affendi's plan was to obtain firearms from police stations (apparently only about 1000 of his men were armed with guns), seize the oilfields at Seria, capture the sultan and, by achieving all these objectives, win converts to the rebel cause. The revolt began on 8 December 1962.

Initially the rebels met with some success. They managed to take control of several outlying towns, notably Seria, Tutong, Limbang

Right: Infantry operations in Borneo were often given artillery support. This photo shows British gunners pounding border crossing points with 105mm howitzers, October 1964.

Far left: The largest of the helicopters used in Borneo was the Belvedere, a general-purpose, rescue and transport aircraft. Seen here is a Belvedere of No 66 Squadron, Royal Air Force.

Below: A Royal Air Force Whirlwind helicopter in Borneo. By using helicopters for the rapid deployment and collection of troops, as well as for casualty evacuation and supply, British forces were able to overcome many of the problems posed by the jungle terrain.

and Bangar, and they also captured the power station and other buildings within the town of Brunei. However, the rebels were nowhere near as successful as they had hoped. The Police had received advanced warning that trouble was coming and resistance was stronger than expected. The rebels failed to capture the sultan's palace, failed to hold the airport in Brunei Town and lost control of the power station. Moreover, British forces soon began to arrive from their base at Singapore, 1200km (750 miles) away; by the evening of 8 December two companies of Gurkhas had been airlifted into Brunei. Over the next few days other units arrived by air and sea and Brigadier Glennie, the British commander, was ordered to restore the territory of Brunei to the rule of the sultan.

This he did. Within six days, the rebels had been routed. The swift arrival and bold deployment of British forces threw the rebels into confusion. Brunei Town was secured by 11 December, Seria on the following day. Limbang was recaptured on 13 December and Bangar followed suit on the 14th. By the latter date, indeed, every town captured by the rebels had been freed. By 20 December, over 40 rebels had been killed, nearly 2000 taken prisoner and 1500 'soft core' rebels returned to their homes, all for the loss of only seven members of the security forces. Mopping-up operations were still necessary, some of the rebels having fled into the jungle, but these were brought to a speedy conclusion. Many of the rebels who fled towards the safety of Indonesian Borneo (Kalimantan) found their way blocked by hostile tribesmen, while reliable intelligence enabled British forces to locate other rebels still hiding within the sultanate. On 18 May 1963 top rebel leaders, including Affendi himself, were found in a secret hideaway; all were either killed or detained. This effectively brought the revolt to an end.

By that time, however, a more serious threat had arisen. While British forces were rounding up the stragglers, President Sukarno had been intensifying his campaign against Malaysia. He announced that volunteers were ready to 'liberate' Kalimantan Utara from 'colonialism' and backed up his declaration by sending guerrillas across the border. The first such incursion occurred on 12 April 1963 when a group of 30 Indonesian 'volunteers' crossed the frontier into western Sarawak and attacked a police station at Tebedu. A new offensive, openly sponsored by Sukarno, was about to begin.

The task of defeating Indonesian aggression, or 'confrontation' as it became known, fell to Major General Walker, who had been appointed Commander, British Forces Borneo, on 19 December 1962. The difficulties facing Walker were immense. He had to defend a 1500km (970-mile) land frontier which traversed wild and mountainous country; there was also a coastline 2400km (1500 miles) in length. Behind these frontiers he had to secure nearly 205,000sq km (80,000sq miles) of territory, most of which was jungle, and protect the diverse peoples – Malays, Chinese and the indigenous population – who lived in the country's towns, villages and kampongs. On top of this, he had to cope with an internal threat from the Clandestine Communist Organisation (CCO), a 24,000-strong body which drew its

Above: Characteristic defences at a forward base in Sarawak.

Top right: An infantry patrol of the Argyll and Sutherland Highlanders in a typical jungle setting.

Right: Major General Walter Walker (second left), the architect of victory in Borneo.

Left: A Royal Horse Artillery 105mm howitzer in action from a forward base along the border with Indonesia.

support mainly from the Chinese community. Moreover, the forces available to Walker were extremely limited. Sarawak and Sabah had no standing army and very few policemen; apart from a small irregular force, Walker had five battalions of British and Gurkha troops, plus a handful of helicopters and coastal minesweepers. With these meagre resources he was being asked to maintain control over a vast confusion of jungles and mountains, through which neither rail nor road-ways ran.

Walker's solution was to apply the counterinsurgency lessons he had learnt in Malaya. Upon his arrival in Borneo he issued a five-point directive listing the ingredients for success. These were: first, unified operations; second, timely and accurate information; third, speed, mobility and flexibility; fourth, security of bases; and fifth, domination of the jungle. A month later he added a sixth ingredient: winning the hearts and minds of the people.

These directives were put into effect, with the hearts and minds campaign receiving particular attention. Many of the indigenous tribes were already well-disposed towards the British, but Walker proceeded to gain the trust, confidence and respect of most of the population. Soldiers and policemen were sent into the villages and settlements in order to protect and advise the people. Medical and agricultural help was offered and some troops, notably small teams of men from the Special Air Service

ROYAL NAVY
W

(SAS), lived and worked alongside the villagers.

The success of this campaign made it very difficult for the guerrillas to secure food, shelter or intelligence and, conversely, increased the flow of intelligence to the security forces. Intelligence was also improved by building up the local police forces, notably the Special Branch, and by enlisting friendly tribesmen as irregular soldiers; a force of 1500 irregulars, known as the Border Scouts, acted as the eyes and ears of the security forces, giving early warning of guerrilla movements on both sides of the border.

Speed, mobility and flexibility were greatly enhanced by the availability of a fleet of 60 or so helicopters which were used to ferry troops and supplies around the jungle; most of these vehicles were deployed in forward positions, thus avoiding time-consuming journeys between the main and forward bases. Light aircraft, which operated from jungle clearings, were also used. So too were small naval vessels and hovercraft; British forces made good use of Borneo's numerous waterways.

Domination of the jungle was achieved by maintaining a permanent presence in contested areas. Forward bases were established all along the frontiers and from these, patrols would venture out into the jungle for long periods, replenishment being carried out by helicopters or light aircraft. Great care was taken to avoid tying troops up in static posts. Bases were well defended but the emphasis was on continuous patrolling and ambushing.

Walker also ensured that the three branches of the armed forces – Army, Navy and Air Force – did not fight separate wars. A joint headquarters was established and operations were carefully co-ordinated. He also made sure that the services' activities were co-ordinated with those of the Police and civil administration.

Top: Gurkhas manning a machine-gun post in the jungle. The Gurkhas' performance in Borneo further enhanced their reputation as superb jungle fighters.

Above: Gurkhas patrolling a waterway in Borneo.

Right: As well as making use of helicopters, artillery and boats, British forces in Borneo also used light aircraft such as the Beaver and the Auster which were capable of operating from jungle clearings. Shown here is an Auster overflying a Saladin armoured car of 4th Royal Tank Regiment.

Left: A soldier being winched up by a Royal Navy Wessex helicopter during operations in Sabah, August 1964.

Above: Gurkhas leaving for Brunei. The Gurkhas made an invaluable contribution to the British effort in Brunei/Borneo, each of the Gurkha battalions carrying out at least four six-month tours.

These methods soon began to bear fruit. Invariably, Indonesian guerrillas would be cut off before they had reached their target. Infiltrators would be discovered by friendly tribesmen or by SAS teams, troops would be dropped into the jungle by helicopter to intercept them and the guerrillas would be ambushed or tracked down by the security forces. The guerrillas did score some successes, but not many. By the end of 1963 it was clear that they had been contained. It was also clear that the Malaysian Federation, which came into existence on 16 September 1963, was not going to collapse so easily. Consequently, Sukarno decided to change his strategy. From December 1963, he threw Indonesian regulars into the conflict. Thus started the third and final phase of the confrontation.

In theory, Sukarno's escalation of the confrontation represented a grave new threat to the security forces. Indonesian regulars were

Right: A Wessex helicopter over South Arabia. In the Radfan, as in Borneo, helicopters enabled British forces to overcome many of the difficulties posed by the terrain.

Above: HMS *Hermes* and HMS *Victorious* off Aden, 1967. The Conservatives had proposed to retain the naval and air base at Aden, but the succeeding Labour Government announced in February 1966 that the base would be abandoned.

better trained and tougher than their guerrilla counterparts and with an army of some 300,000 men, Sukarno had plenty of troops on whom to call. In practice, however, victory remained elusive. For one thing, Walker by now had more manpower and equipment available to counter the Indonesian escalation. By the time he handed over to his successor, General Lea, in March 1965, these forces included 13 battalions of infantry, two regiments of engineers, two regiments of artillery, the equivalent of one battalion of SAS, two battalions of Police Field Force, 1500 Border Scouts, 40 fixed-wing aircraft, 70-80 helicopters, and an undisclosed number of coastal minesweepers, fast patrol craft and hovercraft. Four nations – Britain, Malaysia, New Zealand and Australia – were contributing to the allied cause.

As well as persevering with a successful strategy, the allies introduced tactical innovations. Forward bases were moved closer to the border and hill-top positions were strengthened. Artillery support for the infantry was provided by 105mm howitzers placed in single-gun emplacements along the entire frontier; when necessary, guns were picked up and moved, lock, stock and barrel, by Belvedere helicopters. SAS teams were sent over the border to locate Indonesian camps and identify likely infiltration routes. Later, these teams led 'killer' groups across the border in pre-emptive attacks on Indonesian infiltrators.

These tactics, coupled with Walker's six-point plan, stymied the Indonesians. By late 1965 they had been forced to abandon their forward bases, ceding control of the frontier to the allies. Sukarno then tried a variety of tactics, ranging from conventional assaults on allied bases to small-scale terrorist attacks, but these met with little success. As the stability and economy of Indonesia began to falter, Sukarno became discredited. In March 1966 he was removed from power by General Suharto, who subsequently put out peace feelers to Malaysia. On 11th August 1966 the two countries signed a peace agreement and Indonesia called off its confrontation. Thus ended what could easily have become an interminable and bloody conflict. As it was, Britain and her allies had achieved a decisive victory over the insurgents and had lost less than 100 men in the process. As the then Defence Secretary Denis Healey commented, Britain's campaign in Borneo was 'one of the most efficient uses of military forces in the history of the world'.

This success brought no respite for Britain's armed forces. By the time Britain began withdrawing her forces from East Malaysia (Sarawak and Sabah) in September 1966, her remaining major possession east of Suez – South Arabia (formerly Aden and the Aden Protectorates) – was in the throes of an insurgency. The origins of this conflict can be traced

back to the period 1959-63. In order to prepare Aden and the protectorates for independence, Britain had set up the Federation of South Arabia, which threw together the colony of Aden and the numerous sheikhdoms, emirates and sultanates of the interior, and had created the Federal Regular Army (FRA) and the Federal National Guard. At the same time, Britain insisted on retaining use of the important naval and air base at Aden, where Headquarters Middle East Command had been established in 1960. These twin policies were reflected in the Defence White Paper of July 1964, which stated that Britain would grant independence to South Arabia in 1968 but continue to maintain a military presence at Aden. These policies drew strong opposition, however, from Arab nationalists both inside and outside South Arabia. President Gamal Abdul Nasser of Egypt, who welcomed any opportunity to drive the British out of the Middle East, denounced the Federal government and its forces as puppets of British imperialism and called for the ejection of the British. Cairo Radio beamed a continuous stream of anti-British propaganda to South Arabia, as did radio stations from neighbouring Yemen after that country's monarch was overthrown by Egyptian-backed republicans in September 1962. Moreover, Nasser used the Yemen as a base from which to launch military attacks into South Arabia. In June 1963 nationalists from South Arabia formed the National Liberation Front (NLF). This organisation, based at Taiz in the Yemen and sponsored by Nasser, decided in October 1963 to use force to 'liberate' South Arabia from 'colonialism'.

The first overt act of violence occurred on 10 December 1963, when a grenade was hurled at Federal government ministers at Aden airport. This incident led the government to declare a state of emergency but further terrorist attacks did not take place until late 1964. Instead, the nationalists' opening move in the campaign against the British was a guerrilla war in the border region adjacent to the Yemen. During 1963, the nationalists had infiltrated men and weapons across the border into the Radfan, a wild and mountainous region inhabited by tough tribesmen such as the Quteibi. If the aim

Above: A Royal Air Force Belvedere delivers food and ammunition to troops of the 3rd Battalion, Parachute Regiment near Hajib in the Radfan, May 1964.

Top right: Soldiers of the Royal Northumberland Fusiliers keeping a wary eye on movements in the Crater district of Aden, 1967. As the name implies, the town was built inside the crater of an extinct volcano.

Right: Gunners of the Royal Horse Artillery in action from Thumier base camp, firing their 105mm howitzers at rebel positions in the Radfan mountains.

of the nationalists was to cause trouble for the Federation they had picked a very useful means of doing so. The Radfan tribes were fiercely independent and resented any interference by the Federal authorities. Encouraged by the nationalists, they became a law unto themselves, waylaying travellers and firing on government posts. In late 1963, therefore, the Federal government decided that a punitive attack against the Radfan had become necessary. After some hesitation, Britain's Middle East Command agreed to back this proposal.

The operation, carried out in January 1964, was a success. Three battalions of the FRA, with British air and ground support, managed to fight their way into the Radfan hills for the loss of only five men. As soon as the FRA withdrew from the area, however, the tribesmen reoccupied their old positions and resumed their old activities. Worse still, they gave passage to infiltrators from the Yemen.

By April 1964 the situation had begun to deteriorate. The Federal authorities, therefore, pressed for a second operation against the dissidents, but this time on a larger scale. Britain agreed to the request. A force of brigade strength, initially consisting of two FRA battalions, 45 Commando, Royal Marines, and one company of the 3rd Battalion, Parachute Regiment, supported by engineers, artillery, armour and strike aircraft, was assembled and sent into action on 29 April 1964. The outcome of this operation was by no means a foregone conclusion. There were believed to be 500 or more dissidents in the Radfan and the allies had no information as to their dispositions. Moreover, the dissidents were fighting on their own ground whereas the allies would have to fight their way into hostile and rugged terrain. Despite these difficulties, the operation was a complete success. By 5 May 1964, for the loss of only two killed and 10 wounded, the allies had established themselves in the Radfan. By 11 June they had captured their last objective,

Right: Members of the 3rd Battalion, Parachute Regiment negotiating typical Radfan terrain.

Bottom right: Anti-British demonstrations were an all-too-common sight in Aden. This photograph, taken in April 1967, shows demonstrators tearing down railings so as to set up a roadblock, while in the background car tyres have been used to start a street fire. The political sympathies of the protesters are indicated by the placard.

Below: Soldiers of the 1st Battalion, the Royal Sussex Regiment in the Radfan mountains, early 1965.

Radfan's highest point, the 1700m (5500 foot) Jebel Huriyah. The Radfan tribes were brought to heel, and although dissident activity continued for the next three years it was on a small scale only.

In the meantime, the nationalists had switched the main thrust of their campaign to the town of Aden, a bustling urban community of 220,000 people. In November 1964 the NLF began to launch terrorist attacks and these were steadily increased during 1965. Operating from safe houses in the Sheikh Othman, Maalla and Crater areas of the town, the terrorists used a variety of weapons, notably grenades, to attack British servicemen and their families. The terrorists also murdered and intimidated those who were associated with the Federal government. The latter technique was particularly successful. The populace became reluctant to co-operate with the security forces and the flow of intelligence was reduced to a trickle. The security forces were also hampered by political constraints like the 'no-shoot first' policy.

In spite of these problems, the security forces did make some progress during 1965. They were not able to obtain much co-operation from the local people, but they managed to make inroads into terrorist activities by carrying out house searches, cordon-and-search operations, road blocks, covert observation, and by continuous patrolling. However, this progress was nullified by political developments in Whitehall. On 22 February 1966 the Wilson government issued a Defence White Paper which indicated that, contrary to previous promises, Britain would not be maintaining a military presence in Aden after South Arabia became independent. This decision undermined the position of the Federal leaders, many of whom had only agreed to Britain's proposal for a Federation on the understanding that Britain would continue to protect them against external or internal threats. It also rendered the task of the security forces even more difficult. Intelligence virtually dried up, since few Adenis were prepared to risk their lives to help forces that were about to depart. Even pro-British Adenis decided that they had better mend their fences with the nationalists before the British forces were finally pulled out.

In the aftermath of the British government's decision, terrorist attacks increased in quantity and quality. The NLF's 'Cairo Grenadiers' became more sophisticated, using booby traps and small arms as well as grenades and mines. They also stepped up the tempo of their campaign, particularly after a rival organisation,

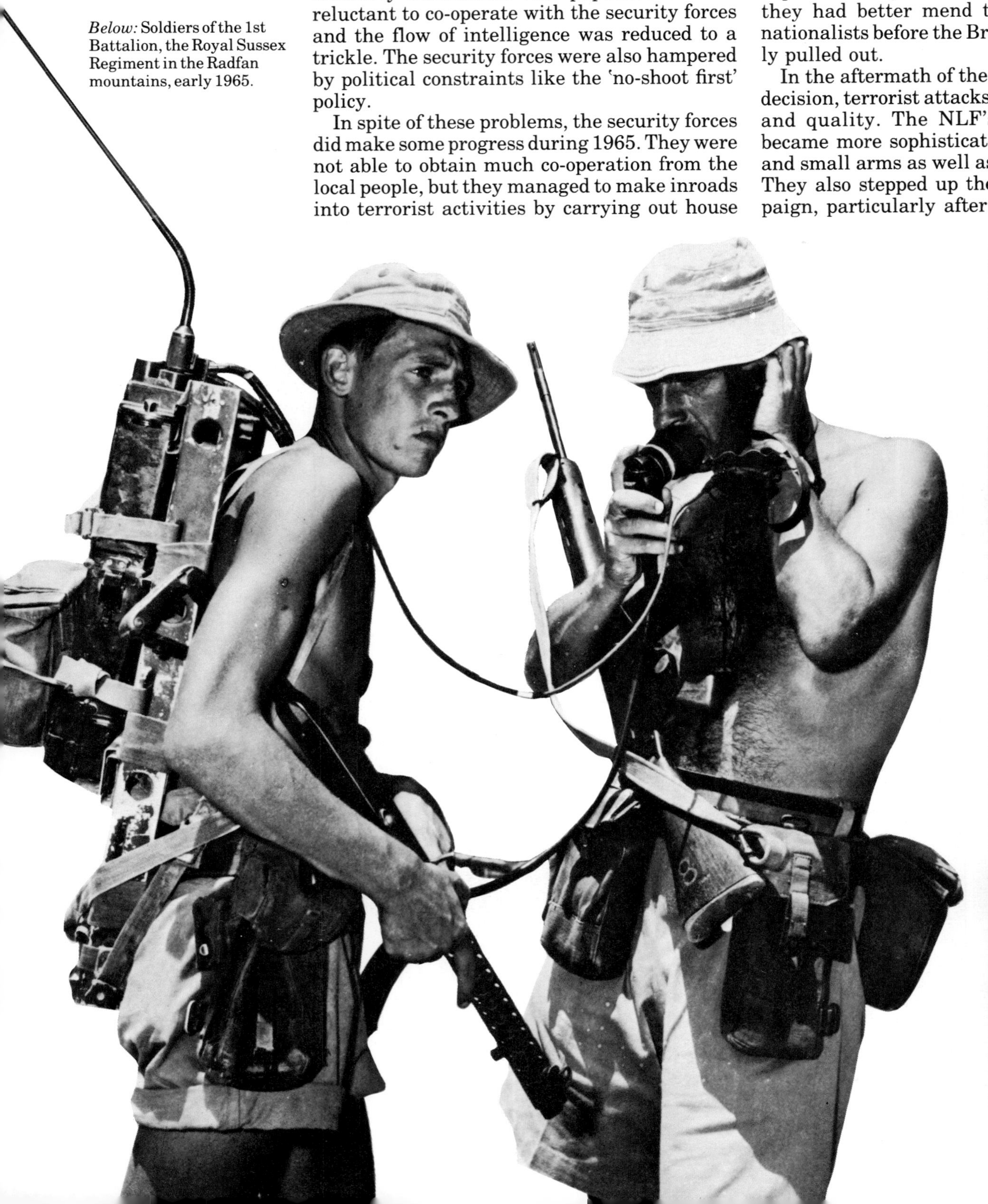

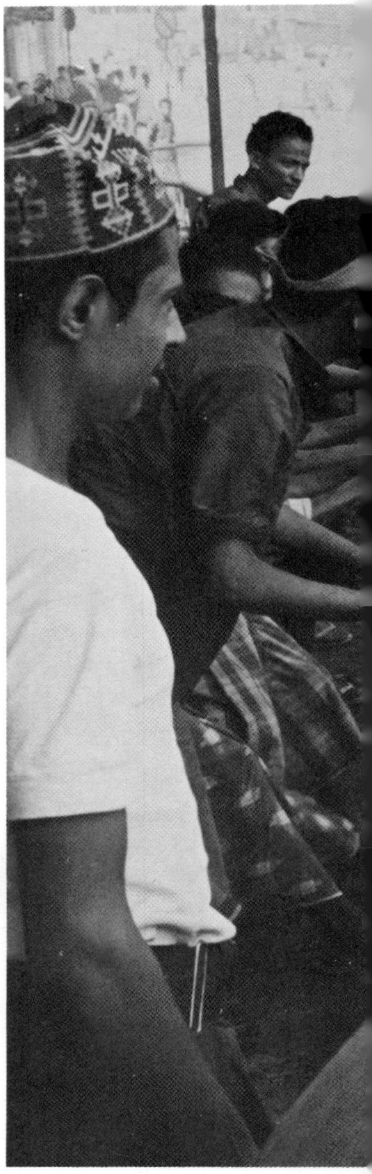

the Front for the Liberation of Occupied South Yemen (FLOSY), emerged in December 1966. This escalation of terrorism was reflected in a dramatic rise in British casualties. In 1964, casualties had totalled only two killed and 25 wounded while in 1965 the figures were six killed and 83 wounded. By 1966, the totals had risen to five killed and 218 wounded, and in 1967 to 44 killed and 325 wounded. British morale was not helped by the fact that half the fatalities incurred during 1967 resulted from two mutinies – by the South Arabian Police (formerly the Federal National Guard) in Champion Lines, and by the Aden Armed Police in the Crater district, on 20 June 1967. Order was soon restored in Champion Lines but the Crater district fell into the hands of dissidents and British troops were not allowed (for political reasons) to launch a swift counter-attack. However, British morale was lifted somewhat on 3/4 July, when Lieutenant Colonel Colin Mitchell's 1st Argyll and Sutherland Highlanders recaptured Crater without loss. British forces were also treated to the spectacle of an internecine conflict between the NLF and FLOSY; the two nationalist groups turned against each other (for the third time), just before Britain was due to withdraw. Nevertheless, when Britain finally pulled out of Aden on

01DC13
328
31BA89

Above: A soldier of the Royal Northumberland Fusiliers throws himself to the ground as a grenade explodes in Aden's Crater district, April 1967.

Left: An armoured car and an armoured personnel carrier of the Queen's Own Hussars moving through the Steamer Point district of Aden on 14 October 1967.

Right: The regimental flag is lowered as the Argyll and Sutherland Highlanders evacuate the Crater district on 26 November 1967. Three days later, the final withdrawal took place.

Below: Royal Marines of 45 Commando moving off into the Radfan mountains, May 1964.

29 November 1967, few servicemen were sad to see the back of the place.

Three months later, the Wilson government announced further withdrawals from the empire. In 1967, as an emergency measure, Wilson had announced that British bases in Malaysia and Singapore were to be abandoned by the mid-1970s. In January 1968 these plans were revised. Shaken by economic crises, Wilson announced that the withdrawal of British forces from east of Suez – the Far East and the Arabian (Persian) Gulf – would be brought forward. All commitments, except for a token presence in Hong Kong and Brunei (which had elected to remain under British protection rather than join Malaysia), would be ended by 1971. The effect of this decision, as Wilson himself said, was that apart from a few residual commitments, Britain would cease to maintain bases or garrisons outside the NATO area. However, as subsequent events were to show, residual commitments were not so easy to relinquish.

THE ALTERNATIVE–BRITAIN'S NATO COMMITMENT

In April 1981 the British White Paper on Defence stated plainly that 'without collective security through NATO there could be no effective defence of our own country'. It also noted that 'our forces make an outstanding contribution to the Alliance'. Britain was the only European member to make 'not only an independent contribution to the strategic nuclear forces of NATO, but also major contributions to the land and air forces of the Alliance in the Central Region, to its naval and maritime-air forces in the Channel and Eastern Atlantic, and to the protection of our own home base'. It is also well known that Britain played a leading part in the foundation of NATO and it might, therefore, be thought inevitable that NATO has been the key to British defence policy since 1949. The reality is rather different.

The British Foreign Secretary, Ernest Bevin, might perhaps be described as NATO's midwife. He brought Britain, France and the Benelux countries together in the Brussels Treaty of March 1948. This paved the way for an alliance of West European states and America which was achieved when the North Atlantic Treaty was signed in April 1949. But Bevin's, and Britain's, interests were not confined to Europe. The Middle East and Far East were considered equally important and absorbed more of Britain's resources than NATO. The Soviet threat in Europe was seen as a long-term one involving subversion rather than open aggression until they had fully recovered from the devastation of the Second World War.

The invasion of South Korea by the North in June 1950 destroyed that theory and the West began to rearm frantically. The British programme would have cost £4700 million in three years, effectively doubling defence expenditure. This was more than the British economy, and the British public, were able to stand. In 1951 Winston Churchill returned to power; in the following year the NATO meeting at Lisbon agreed 'goals' which would have provided 96 divisions in Central Europe within 90 days of mobilisation. The British contribution was to be 18 divisions, no mean feat when the Army only had 22 divisions world-wide, including reserves.

Churchill knew that Britain could not afford such a programme and he had also learnt something of the American Strategic Air Command's plans for a war with Russia, which entailed the early use of nuclear weapons on a wide range of targets. In these circumstances he doubted whether the conventional forces required by the Lisbon Goals would be able to influence the war's outcome. A study by the Chiefs of Staff, known as the 'Global Strategy Paper', confirmed Churchill's doubts. The Paper recommended that NATO should make it clear that Russian aggression would be immediately

Previous page: Soldier of 1st Battalion, the Staffordshire Regt with Carl Gustav 84mm Medium Anti-tank Weapon. Lighter anti-tank weapons are crucial to the viability of infantry on the European battlefield.

Below: Since NATO adopted the 7.62mm round, the General Purpose Machine Gun, seen here in the hands of a soldier of the Royal Anglian Regiment, has been a major element in British infantry fire power.

Above: The P1127, predecessor of the Harrier 'jump-jet', on trials with HMS *Ark Royal*.

Above left: The first Chief of the Defence Staff, Earl Mountbatten of Burma, visiting British troops in Borneo, at a time when such overseas responsibilities were being challenged by the NATO commitment.

punished by nuclear strikes against Soviet territory. All the NATO countries, even including the United States, were worried about the economic consequences of their defence programmes. The British idea was taken up by the Americans under the name 'Massive Retaliation' and then became declared NATO strategy. Spending on conventional armaments was rapidly reduced.

The full implications of the Global Strategy Paper for British defence policy were not realized until after Duncan Sandys' White Paper of 1957. By then Britain had also suffered the humiliation of the Suez episode in 1956. It is often claimed that Suez disillusioned Britain with the idea of a world role but this is very far from the case. The 1957 defence review confirmed Britain's reliance on nuclear weapons to deter aggression in Europe. The British army and air force units in Germany were reduced in size and it was no longer planned to send two Territorial divisions to Germany in wartime because it would take three months to get them ready. Manpower reductions were made in the rest of the world but a strong central reserve was to be based in Britain with a fleet of aircraft to fly it to trouble-spots around the world. The total saving in manpower made it possible to plan the end of conscription and Britain was to rely on all-regular forces from the end of 1962. Generally speaking this reduction in the size of Britain's armed forces was not accompanied by a slimming of her overseas commitments. It was, however, hoped that as the colonies received their independence, British forces would no longer be tied down in long counter-insurgency campaigns.

The Sandys White Paper closed an unusual period in the history of British strategy, and required some adjustment to Britain's role in NATO. In both world wars Britain had been forced to raise a mass army by conscription. This was common enough in continental Europe, but contrary to traditional British strategy. Nevertheless Britain played a major part on land in both wars and by retaining conscription after 1945 kept the capacity to do so in future. But Britain had still been obliged to maintain her dominant fleet and a major air force. The costs had been crippling in both wars and remained severe in peacetime. By ending conscription Britain was swinging away from the 'continental commitment' and moving closer to its traditional strategy. The conti-

Left: Cold War antagonism, symbolised by British troops erecting barbed-wire fences around the Soviet War Memorial in West Berlin, to keep West German demonstrators away after the building of the Berlin Wall, August 1961.

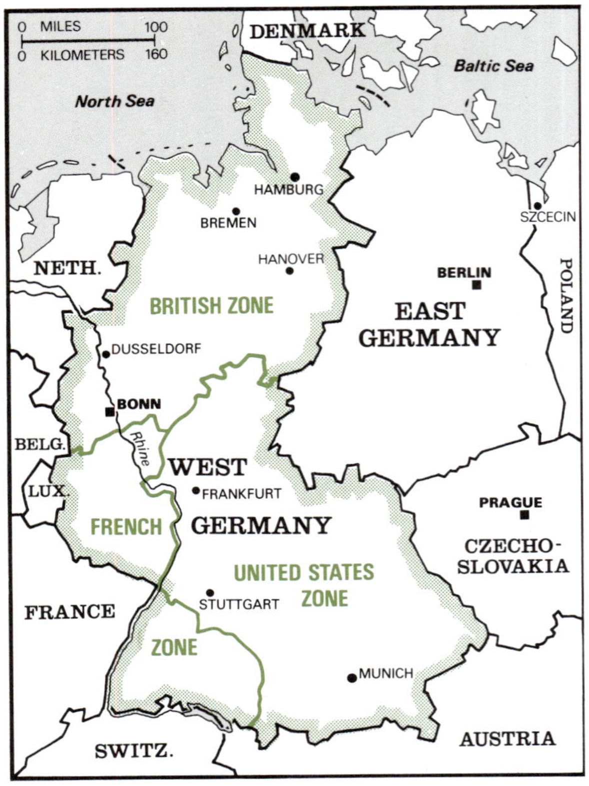

Maps: (Left) the post-war occupation zones in Germany; (Right) approximate peacetime locations of BAOR formations today. Note that most of 2nd Infantry Division is based in the UK in peacetime.

nental members of NATO possessed not only large peacetime armies but strong reserves which would be quickly available in war. To maintain her position as the leading European member of NATO, Britain had initially tried to match up to this traditional yardstick of European influence. The Sandys White Paper abandoned the attempt and rested Britain's claim to European pre-eminence on its possession of nuclear weapons.

Despite Sandys' efforts, defence spending continued to absorb a large proportion of government spending. A comprehensive review of defence policy was undertaken by the new Labour government, with Denis Healey as Secretary of State for Defence. It became increasingly clear that Britain had to choose between NATO and her 'east of Suez' commitments. The east of Suez role was more attractive to the government, opposition, the armed forces and probably, the nation as a whole. It was generally believed that the British presence in the area made a major contribution to its stability and gave Britain a unique place in world affairs. Within the North Atlantic alliance, Britain's position was less significant. France and Germany were far more important land powers and Britain's naval, air and especially nuclear contributions were eclipsed by the United States. However, events suggested

Below: Centurion tanks of the British garrison in Berlin on the annual Allied Forces Day Parade, 17 May 1969.

Above: Air defence of the United Kingdom. A practice scramble for a Phantom F-4 aircraft.

Below: Minesweepers of the Standing Naval Force Channel (STANAVFORCHAN), peacetime symbols of NATO cooperation.

that Britain's claim to be the policeman of the Indian Ocean was wishful thinking. World affairs were increasingly settled without British intervention. Experiences such as the Indonesian 'Confrontation' also warned that it was impossible to limit British commitments in the way defence planners desired. Lastly the British government was trying to join the European Economic Community. EEC members were likely to look at British defence policy for proof that the country was fully committed to a European future rather than an imperial past.

Financial pressure finally resolved the conflicting arguments. After the devaluation of sterling in 1967 it was announced in January 1968 that the British military presence east of Suez would end in 1971. The strategic reserve maintained in Britain to reinforce her garrisons in the east would be earmarked for NATO.

It is obvious that NATO's increasing priority in British defence policy arose almost by default and the NATO role too suffered its share of cuts in 1967 and 1968. It was not long before Britain's continuing economic problems forced the government to consider the range of Britain's NATO commitments. It was pointed out that Britain devoted a higher proportion of her Gross National Product (GNP) to defence than most of her allies. In particular Britain spent 5.8 per cent of her GNP on defence, compared to West Germany's 4.1 per cent and France's 3.8 per cent. This time Roy Mason was the Secretary of State for Defence charged with reconciling the conflicting demands of the Treasury and the defence community. His White Paper, published in March 1975, stated that:

'Britain's defence forces had to be concentrated on those areas in which a British contribution to collective defence would be most effective in ensuring Britain's security and that of her Allies. This meant that NATO – the linch pin of British security – should remain the first and overriding charge on the resources available for defence; that our commitments should be reduced as far as possible to avoid overstretching our forces; and that general purpose forces should be maintained as an insurance against the unforeseen.'

The areas where Britain could best contribute were the Central Region of NATO, the Eastern Atlantic and Channel Areas, the defence of the United Kingdom itself and NATO's nuclear deterrent. This meant that Britain would almost entirely abandon her capability to operate in the Mediterranean, NATO's Southern Flank. Specialist reinforce-

Above: Hawk T Mk1 advanced jet trainers of the RAF. 72 Hawks are currently being equipped with Sidewinder air-to-air missiles to supplement Britain's air defence.

Below: Test firing of a Polaris missile from HMS *Resolution*. Polaris missiles have been the most important part of Britain's nuclear deterrent since 1968.

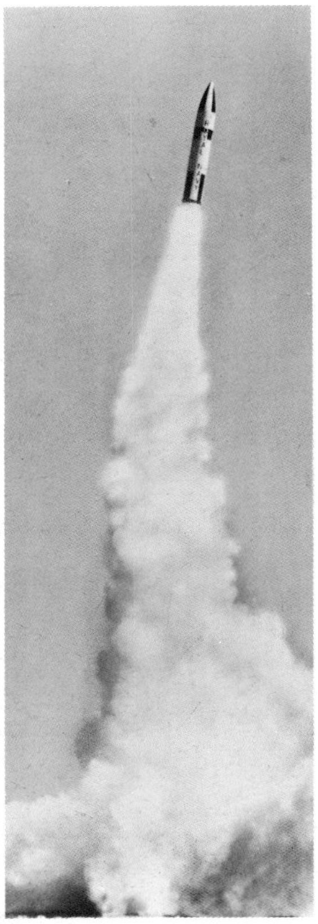

ment capabilities, basically the amphibious and airborne forces, would be severely cut.

Even these limitations did not end the succession of defence cuts. The soaring costs of new equipment could not be met as long as Britain's economic problems remained. In June 1981 John Nott introduced to Parliament a White Paper entitled *The United Kingdom Defence Programme: The Way Forward*. Previous reviews had tended to allocate resources or cuts among the three services on a basis of more or less equal shares. The government had no intention of abandoning any of the four main roles outlined in Mason's White Paper but it was necessary to reconsider how these roles should be carried out. The first decision was to modernise the nuclear deterrent which otherwise would have effectively to be abandoned by the end of the century, as Britain's Polaris submarines reached the end of their service life. The defence of the UK base was strengthened and the British forces on NATO's Central Front were considered essential to the cohesion of the alliance. This meant that the 'most complex and difficult issues concerned the future shape of Britain's maritime contributions'. It was decided that it would be more cost-effective to emphasise submarine and air forces at the expense of the surface fleet.

It is only too easy to present British defence policy since 1945 purely in terms of retreat in the face of financial pressure. This can be misleading. The cost of modern weapons has grown so much since 1945 that even the superpowers have been forced to cut their cloth to suit their pockets. Defence policy has rarely been a major issue in British politics and, underneath the parliamentary rhetoric, the general tendency of British policy has been remarkably continuous, whichever party was in office. Economic pressures have forced governments to face realities and take decisions which they would otherwise have avoided for lack of a national debate on defence. It is, therefore, significant that the conclusion of all governments, whatever the pressures they faced, has been that NATO represents the unavoidable commitment which is essential to the defence of Britain. For a country which traditionally prided itself on its freedom from permanent alliances, this is a remarkable turn of events.

Britain fulfils its commitment to NATO in a wide variety of ways. It has always contributed fully to the political structure which provides the guidelines for the alliance's strategy and foreign policy. NATO's first Secretary-General was Lord Ismay, who had held the post of Military Secretary to the British War Cabinet during the Second World War. Ismay was at NATO from 1952-57 and his experience of the British Cabinet system was crucial in developing the Secretary-General's role. The Foreign Secretary is a member of the North Atlantic Committee. Britain is naturally represented in the Nuclear Planning Group and also on a large number of committees dealing with matters ranging from economic affairs to the challenges of modern society.

In the military structure Britain has a permanent representative on the Military Committee, which also meets at chief of staff level. Field Marshal Montgomery was the first Deputy Supreme Allied Commander-in-Chief (Deputy SACEUR) and one of SACEUR's deputies has always been a senior British officer. Other senior NATO commands which are held by British officers include the Commander-in-Chief Channel (CINCHAN); the Commander-in-Chief Eastern Atlantic; the Commander-in-Chief of Allied Forces Northern Europe (AFNORTH); the Commanders-in-Chief of the Northern Army Group (NORTHAG) and the 2nd Allied Tactical Air Force (2 ATAF) which are both part of NATO's Central European region.

Britain supports NATO with a wide range of forces including a nuclear contribution, which can be divided into two elements, British nuclear forces themselves and the bases Britain provides for American nuclear-capable forces.

British scientists played an important role in the development of nuclear technology and worked with the Americans on the 'Manhattan' Project which led to the first atomic bombs. However, in 1946 the American Congress passed the McMahon Act which prohibited sharing American nuclear 'know-how' with other countries. This was a considerable setback, but the government was apparently convinced that Britain could not continue as a major power without atomic weapons. Thus in January 1947 Clement Attlee's Labour Cabinet decided to develop a British nuclear bomb. An atomic device was tested in the Monte Bello Islands in the Pacific on 3 October 1952 and an H-bomb at Christmas Island in May 1957. By this stage the success of the British weapon programme impressed the Americans so much that they decided to amend the McMahon Act and resume the exchange of information on nuclear matters.

However, there is more to a nuclear capability than building the bombs themselves. It is also necessary to have a delivery system which can hit the enemy and can survive his attacks. These aspects have caused Britain the greatest difficulty. Design work began on three types of

bomber, the Victor, Vulcan and Valiant, in 1947 but their development was not given the highest priority until 1952 and the V-bombers did not enter operational service until 1957. In the meantime Britain had only the Lincoln bomber, an up-grading of the wartime Lancaster, which did not have the range to operate against Russia. As a stop-gap, a number of American B-29s were transferred to the RAF.

Britain's nuclear armoury was also increased in March 1957 by an Anglo-American agreement to station Thor IRBMs (Intermediate-Range Ballistic Missiles) in Britain. A 'dual-key' system was introduced by which an American key activated the warhead while a British key fired the missile. Sixty Thor missiles were deployed in British bases from 1959-63. At this time the British deterrent

Above: A Ferret scout car of a BAOR recce regiment on exercise in Germany in 1962.

Left: The Handley Page Victor, which served with the RAF as strategic bomber, strategic reconnaissance aircraft and tanker.

Below: Abbot 105mm self-propelled guns, which replaced the wartime 25-pounders as part of the Army's modernisation programme in the early sixties, are fired on exercise in UK by 2nd Field Regt, RA.

force, like the American, was not committed to NATO command, but remained entirely under national or joint Anglo-American control. However, NATO was entirely dependent on the Anglo-American threat of nuclear retaliation to deter a Soviet attack as its conventional forces were little more than a 'tripwire' to trigger the nuclear response. The British nuclear contribution was probably at its most significant in the early 1960s. A total of over 140 V-bombers was available and they could fly faster and higher than any bomber in front-line service anywhere in the world. It was calculated that, together, the V-bomber force and the Thors formed about a third of the total Western nuclear deterrent which could be expected to survive a surprise attack.

This was an impressive achievement but it represented the peak of British effectiveness. The United States had embarked on a very large missile-building programme which meant that the proportion of the Western deterrent provided by Britain was drastically reduced by the end of the decade. Furthermore the British weapon systems were facing obsolescence. The Thor missiles were withdrawn from service in 1963. The 1957 Defence White Paper admitted that the days of unarmed bombers were numbered. They were dependent on vulnerable airfields and it was becoming increasingly difficult to penetrate modern air defences. The search for a successor began a very unhappy period for British defence planning, with a succession of expensive projects having to be cancelled.

The first step was to improve the V-bombers' chances of survival. By adopting the Blue Steel stand-off bomb and flying low-level, rather than high-level, missions it was possible to extend the V-bombers' usefulness in the strategic nuclear role into the late 1960s. It was first planned to replace them with the British-built Blue Streak, a liquid-fuelled rocket operating from a fixed base. When the government finally accepted the weakness of such a system and cancelled the project in April 1960, they had to choose between building a British submarine-

Right: The Anglo-French Lynx helicopter, armed with Sea-Skua anti-ship missiles.

Left: Volvo Over-Snow vehicle and men of the Royal Scots serving with the ACE Mobile Force in Norway, 1973.

or air-launched missile from scratch or buying an American weapon. A British system was not only too expensive, it would not be ready in time. The American Skybolt system, an air-launched ballistic missile, was chosen because it could be fitted to the V-bombers and would be available before the alternative, the submarine-based Polaris. Unfortunately the Skybolt lost favour with the Americans and late in 1962 they cancelled the programme. The British government's embarrassment was considerable but in December Prime Minister Harold Macmillan met President Kennedy at Nassau. Macmillan asked for the Polaris system. At first the Americans wanted to sell Polaris only as part of a NATO nuclear force. The final agreement was very much a compromise. The Americans would provide Polaris missiles to carry British nuclear warheads and help in designing submarines. The missiles would be used 'for the purposes of international defence of the Western Alliance in all circumstances' except 'where Her Majesty's Government may decide that supreme national interests are at stake'.

The Nassau Agreement led to the integration of the British nuclear deterrent in the NATO system. Britain already assigned Valiant and Canberra bombers to SACEUR for strikes within the European theatre. However, the bulk of the British nuclear force had remained independent of NATO although its targets were co-ordinated with the American Strategic Air Command. The Nassau Agreement provided that the whole of the V-bomber force and the Polaris submarines when completed would become part of a 'NATO nuclear force targeted in accordance with NATO plans'. But another objective of the agreement was the development of a multilateral NATO nuclear force. Such a force would have been jointly manned by several NATO nations and controlled by those nations acting within NATO. The idea was discussed but there was little enthusiasm for it in Europe and discussions ceased in 1964. The Polaris force was thus left with two roles and two sets of targets, provided by SACEUR and the British government. However, it remains in British hands to decide which role the submarines should adopt and the actual command system is entirely in British hands. Thus the Polaris fleet remains an independent nuclear deterrent, even if British governments have sometimes preferred for domestic political reasons to emphasise its NATO role.

In recent years the value of an independent British deterrent has been increasingly challenged. The Polaris system will not out-last the century. It has been urged that Britain should abandon nuclear weapons altogether, either on moral grounds or because the British force is too small to act as a credible deterrent. Others have called for the cheapest possible nuclear force

Bottom right: Sea Vixen day and night fighter of the Fleet Air Arm makes its approach to HMS *Ark Royal.*

Below: British carrier task force based on HMS *Ark Royal* on exercise with the Brazilian Navy.

Left: A Phantom fighter-bomber is launched from HMS *Ark Royal*.

Top right: British paratroops about to jump from a Hercules aircraft.

Below: HMS *Ark Royal*, the last British strike carrier.

and sought the answer in the cruise missile, either based in special submarines or on a range of submarines, surface ships, land bases or aircraft. Eventually in July 1980 it was decided to buy the American Trident submarine-launched ballistic missile. Only a submarine-based system, it was argued, could provide invulnerability. Cruise missiles were cheaper individually than ballistic missiles but more of them would be required to guarantee the same level of threat, so the whole system would not have been cheaper. The strategic justification for retaining a British nuclear system is to provide a 'second centre of decision' within NATO. Thus even if the Soviet Union imagined that the United States might not risk nuclear war to defend Europe, they would still have to take account of a significant force in purely European hands.

NATO's theatre nuclear capability includes a number of American forces based in Britain. Even before NATO existed, Britain provided bases for American B-29 bombers which provided the West's ultimate guarantee against overwhelming Soviet conventional forces. Once nuclear weapons were made available to SACEUR in the mid-1950s, an important element was, and still is, aircraft based in the

Above: HMS *Abdiel*, exercise minelayer and support ship for mine-countermeasures forces.

Top left: The American M109 self-propelled gun in British service. The M109 is the standard medium gun on NATO's Central Front.

Centre left: HMS *Dreadnought*, the first British nuclear-powered submarine.

Below: HMS *Resolution*, the first British Polaris submarine.

United Kingdom. The Americans deployed F-104s and then F-111s. British aircraft such as the V-bombers, Canberra, Buccaneer and now the Tornado have also been deployed in this role. When these in turn were threatened with obsolescence, NATO was also concerned by Soviet deployment of the SS-20 missile. As a counter, NATO decided in December 1979 to deploy GLCMs (Ground-Launched Cruise Missiles) and the Pershing II missile in Europe. Britain agreed to provide bases for 160 cruise missiles which began arriving at Greenham Common, an RAF base used by the Americans, in November 1983. Despite the controversy generated by the decision, it clearly involved no change in Britain's role in NATO's theatre deterrent.

Britain's conventional contribution to NATO is best analysed in terms of the NATO commands which it supports. The British element in Allied Forces Central Europe consists of the British Army of the Rhine (BAOR) and RAF Germany. The major formation in BAOR is 1st British Corps, which was formed in 1951. Originally it consisted of three armoured divisions and an infantry division. Today, after several changes in organisation, it consists of the 1st, 3rd and 4th Armoured Divisions in Germany, with the 2nd Infantry Division based in Britain but committed to Germany in wartime. Its strength is approximately 55,000 men. The RAF in Germany has varied considerably in strength. At its peak in 1955 it briefly included 35 squadrons of aircraft. At its lowest during the reconstruction of airfields and conversion of units to new types of aircraft in 1969-70 only five squadrons were stationed in Germany. Today there are eleven squadrons of fixed-wing aircraft; two of Buccaneers and four of Jaguars in the strike-attack role, two Harrier squadrons for offensive support, one Jaguar reconnaissance squadron and two Phantom air-defence squadrons. Two squadrons of helicopters are deployed, one of Chinooks and the other of Pumas.

The size of the British force in Germany is determined by the Paris Agreement of October 1954. It was these agreements which made possible the rearmament of West Germany and its admission to NATO. Desirable though this was on purely military grounds, the memory of German militarism was too recent for it to be generally welcomed on the continent. A firm

28
XV228

Left: Nimrod MR Mk 2, a maritime reconnaissance aircraft which makes a vital contribution to NATO's ability to patrol the north-east Atlantic.

Right: The Carl Gustav anti-tank weapon.

Below: HMS *Ark Royal*, showing (bow to stern) Phantom, Wessex, Buccaneer, Sea King and Gannet aircraft.

British commitment was required to reassure the rest of the alliance. The Paris Agreement guaranteed that Britain would maintain a force equivalent to four divisions and a tactical air force on the mainland of Europe. These forces are not to be withdrawn against the wishes of the majority of the Brussels Treaty powers, except in the case of an acute overseas emergency. At the time the British force in Germany was, in theory, 77,000 men but this was shortly reduced to its present establishment of 55,000.

1st British Corps' operational doctrine has developed through several stages, mirroring either changes in NATO's plans or new British thinking and equipment. At first NATO tried to match the Soviet Union's conventional strength but, as already related, the Lisbon goals overtaxed the alliance's resources. When this became obvious a German contribution seemed essential, although this was likely to create new strategic problems. NATO's earliest plans had talked of the Rhine as a suitable obstacle on which to base the defensive battle. The Germans naturally wanted the battle to be fought further to the east and NATO's battle line has moved closer to the Inner German Border. In the British sector first the Weser and then the Leine Rivers have been chosen as defence lines and current doctrine would fight the battle as close to the border as possible.

In the 1950s NATO tried to compensate for its manpower deficiencies by employing tactical nuclear weapons. However, experience on exercises and other studies suggests that the nuclear battlefield is even more expensive in manpower than a conventional one. NATO as a whole has not satisfactorily solved this problem. The British approach has been to emphasise the professionalism of its forces and the quality of its equipment as counters to the threat of being outnumbered from across the border.

Although the tactical doctrines of the NATO armies are broadly similar and matters such as deployment lines have to be properly co-ordinated, there are various national characteristics. These are determined by variations in the ground to be defended, the equipment available and in the military traditions of each army. The British Army differs from most of its allies in being a volunteer, not a conscript, force. It also contains a higher proportion of non-mechanised infantry and engineers and less artillery than other European field armies.

1st British Corps would be deployed in war in a vital sector of NATO's front, on the North German plain. Its doctrine for a battle would employ reconnaissance forces using the CVR(T) family of vehicles, backed by artillery, engineers and armour, to identify the main enemy axes and, where possible, disrupt their advance. Behind this screen a strong defensive position would be prepared in the greatest possible depth, using natural obstacles strengthened by demolitions and minefields. Within this main defensive position battle groups, formed of the Chieftain or Challenger main battle tanks and of mechanised infantry in armoured personnel

Right: NATO's Standing Naval Force Atlantic (STANAVFORLANT) usually has a British component. Here HMS *Bachante*, centre right, is shown with American, Canadian, Norwegian, Dutch and West German vessels.

carriers with all-arms support, would absorb the enemy attack. Having disrupted the enemy's plans, the corps would launch counter-attacks, either from its own resources or with allied assistance. The support of the allied air forces would be vital. Although the aim is to fight a conventional battle for as long as possible, the corps must be aware that nuclear weapons could be used at any time. To fight this sort of battle effectively 1st British Corps requires considerable reinforcement from the United Kingdom, which would more than double its effective strength.

Britain has always been famous as a naval power and even today, despite the military and political importance of the British forces in Germany, it is at sea that Britain makes her most substantial contribution to the Alliance. Most of the forces which would have to defend the Eastern Atlantic in wartime would be British. The British Commander-in-Chief Fleet is also NATO's CINCHAN and C-in-C Eastern Atlantic. His headquarters for all three posts is located at Northwood in the suburbs of London, where it is co-located with an equivalent RAF headquarters. In wartime the tasks of these forces would be immense. They would have to provide a safe environment for Britain's Polaris submarines. They would also have to secure the Atlantic and Channel for the passage of reinforcements and supplies from the United States or the United Kingdom to the continent in order to sustain the land battle. To do this NATO forces would try to hold the so-called 'choke points', such as the Greenland-Iceland-United Kingdom Gap against the Soviet Navy. The Royal Navy's submarines and surface vessels, with RAF aircraft, would have a crucial role. In addition the Royal Navy would supply Anti-Submarine Group 2, based on 'Invincible'-class anti-submarine carriers, with air-defence destroyers and anti-submarine frigates. This contribution frees the American carriers for

Below: HMS *Brecon*, the first of a new class of mine sweeper/minehunters, commissioned in 1980 and designed to counter the latest generation of naval mines.

Main picture: The Chieftain main battle tank, with its 120mm gun, was the most powerful in service with NATO during the sixties and seventies.

their primary air-defence and strike-attack roles. The 1981 decision to reduce the size of the Royal Navy's surface fleet has inevitably caused disquiet in NATO's navies. In peacetime the Royal Navy contributes ships to the Standing Naval Force Atlantic and the Standing Naval Force Channel. Besides demonstrating the solidarity of the alliance in peacetime, the training of these forces helps to discover and remove the problems of inter-allied co-operation which might arise in the far more testing conditions of wartime.

The defence of the United Kingdom itself is obviously a vital task for British forces, but it is of considerable significance for NATO itself. Because of its geographical position the United Kingdom is a vital staging-post and base area for NATO. However, a base is little use unless it is secure. After a period of neglect following the 1957 White Paper, which was possibly too concerned with the nuclear threat and the impossibility of defence against it, the defences of Britain have been greatly improved. Air defences are based on seven squadrons of Phantom and Lightning interceptors, with

Left: Avro Vulcan, showing the delta-wing, first used by these aircraft, and the white paint scheme used in the aircraft's early service when high-altitude operations were envisaged.

Far left: A free-fall parachute display team jumps from an RAF Hercules.

Right: M109 self-propelled 155mm gun in service with 27th Medium Regt, RA in BAOR. The M109 can fire tactical nuclear weapons.

Bottom left: Sea King helicopter with dipping sonar.

Main picture: The Avro Vulcan, the longest serving V-bomber, shown in low-level operations camouflage.

airborne-early-warning and tanker aircraft in support and backed up by Bloodhound and Rapier surface-to-air missiles. At sea the threat of mining is most serious and has perhaps not received the attention it deserves. It is most unlikely that Britain would be threatened with a full-scale invasion but land forces would be required to guard key sites against saboteurs and airborne forces. Thirty per cent of the Army's mobilised strength would be devoted to home defence.

Outside these main areas of deployment, Britain provides certain specialist reinforcement forces which play important roles in NATO's order of battle. Three forces are assigned to SACEUR. First, there is the infantry battalion group and Harrier and Puma squadrons that Britain contributes to the Allied Command Europe Mobile Force (AMF). The AMF has several national contingents and can be deployed at the shortest notice. It demonstrates allied solidarity in the event of a crisis and is particularly suited to operations on the flanks of NATO.

Second, there is the United Kingdom Mobile Force (UKMF); a brigade-sized force with its own air element. It is well-suited to deployment on NATO's Northern Flank and often exercises there. However, the units of this force must also meet contingencies outside the NATO area, such as the Falklands operation. Finally, three Jaguar squadrons and a Harrier squadron, together with US air force units based in Britain, form SACEUR's Strategic Reserve (Air).

The other British reinforcement force is assigned to the Supreme Allied Commander, Atlantic (SACLANT) and consists of the United

Left: The guided missile destroyer *Sheffield*.

Right: HMS *Resolution*, Polaris submarine, which is Britain's contribution to SACEUR's theatre nuclear forces.

Below: HMS *Opportune*, a conventional patrol submarine, preparing to take part in the Queen's Silver Jubilee Review in 1977.

Kingdom/Netherlands Amphibious Force. In the event of a crisis on the Northern Flank this would be one of the first forces deployed. The British element is based on the Royal Marines' 3rd Commando Brigade, which is trained and equipped for arctic warfare. This training, and that of part of the UKMF, is particularly significant because few other forces in NATO have the skills to reinforce the outnumbered Norwegian forces in the event of war.

NATO has no capability to operate outside the North Atlantic and Western European area, even though it is increasingly clear that the member states' national interests are not confined to that region. The problem is a very contentious one in NATO and it is possible that NATO will never develop such a capability. However, if it does, the other chapters of this book make it obvious that the experience and skills of British forces would make their contribution essential. Within Britain itself, a continuing debate on the nature of Britain's role in the North Atlantic Alliance is likely. The validity of the British nuclear deterrent will no doubt be challenged and, particularly within the armed forces themselves, the struggle between the proponents of 'continental' and 'maritime' strategies will continue. The quarrel is age-old, even if the arguments have been dressed in new forms. One of the lessons of British history seems to be that Britain cannot afford to do without either a maritime or a continental capability and that Britain has never been able to afford both. Only NATO is capable of squaring the circle, by helping Britain to concentrate on one role and by making good the deficiency elsewhere itself.

PROBLEMS AT HOME

Previous page: British troops in the Falls Road area of Belfast, August 1969. Burnt-out vehicles and littered streets bear witness to the ferocity of the rioting which necessitated the troop-commitment.

Top centre: Ferret armoured cars of the 17th/21st Lancers form a roadblock outside Belfast, June 1970. The soldiers are checking vehicles as they pass, hoping to curtail terrorist movement and build up intelligence.

Top right: As a British sniper armed with a Lee-Enfield bolt-action rifle stands guard, a local civilian, hands in the air, makes sure that he is not mistaken for a terrorist. Photograph taken in the Bogside, Londonderry, August 1971, during an Army search for arms caches.

Bottom right: A British Army patrol, made up of men of the Light Infantry, crosses a side-street off the Shankhill Road, Belfast, October 1969. Although the soldiers are wearing protective 'flak vests', they are well bunched up: IRA snipers were not yet a major threat.

Below: A teenage rioter, spattered with blood from a head injury, is arrested by an Army snatch squad, Belfast, 1971.

About ten years ago, a retired British general gave a lecture on the subject of insurgency and the challenge presented to a democratic society by the then-current upsurge of urban guerrilla warfare. In the course of this lecture he asserted that the British had been both sensible and remarkably fortunate in so ordering their affairs that since the end of the First World War only one person had been killed during or as a result of civil disturbance, 'the present situation in Northern Ireland excepted'.

Even leaving aside the very obvious point that there seems to be something blatantly dishonest in pressing a claim by disregarding all the evidence that contradicts it, the observation is incorrect. The war that led to the creation of the Irish Free State in 1921-22, subsequent sectarian rampages in Northern Ireland, the campaign of 1939 and the 1956-62 Border Campaign, were all conducted in whole or in part on British soil, and the fact that all involved the Irish was the constant proof of Britain's continuing and fragile relationship with Ireland – and the truth of Oscar Wilde's witticism that of the far-flung parts of the British empire, Ireland was the one part not flung far enough.

In fact, in historical terms the crux of the Anglo-Irish problem has always been that Ireland was too close to a more powerful, populous and wealthy neighbour that sought to control her because of the potential threat she posed to her security. Nevertheless, the campaign that has been fought in Northern Ireland since 1969 has its causes in reasons very different from those that plagued Anglo-Irish relations from the sixteenth to the early-twentieth centuries. Put in its most simple terms, the essential problem of Northern Ireland is that within the province there are two communities whose attitudes and aspirations are antagonistic and mutually exclusive. The political aspirations of the minority cannot be accommodated within the British political system any more than the parliamentary

democracy within the Republic of Ireland can accommodate those of the majority: both the British and the Irish dimensions of the Northern Ireland problem fail to meet the political aspirations of both communities within the province.

Herein lies the basis of any attempt to detach the Irish problem from the mainstream of British life in the manner that the lecturer of 1973 divided affairs. In a sense, the discounting of the Irish dimension is not unfair because Ireland most definitely is very different from the other societies that share the British Isles with her. In Ireland, and particularly in Northern Ireland, politics is not primarily concerned with social issues such as full employment, housing, education and welfare, but with questions of the nature and legitimacy of the state itself. In the case of Britain, politics for some 30 years after the end of the Second World War was concerned with social and economic rather than political matters because in that time there was a very large measure of agreement within society about the role of the state and its objectives. Moreover, Britain and Ireland differ not just in the nature of their politics but in their views on how objectives are to be achieved. Ireland has a long-established and honourable tradition of violence as part of the political process. In Irish history violence has been if not the normal then certainly the frequent means of bringing about change, but on mainland Britain direct action has generally held little attraction to a society that evolved a tradition of gradual change, dissent and peaceful protest. Herein lies the key to any understanding of military operations by the British armed forces in Britain since 1969. The armed

Smithwicks
draught
Smithwicks
draught
have a pint today
Smithwicks
draught
have a pint today
32

CLEARWAY

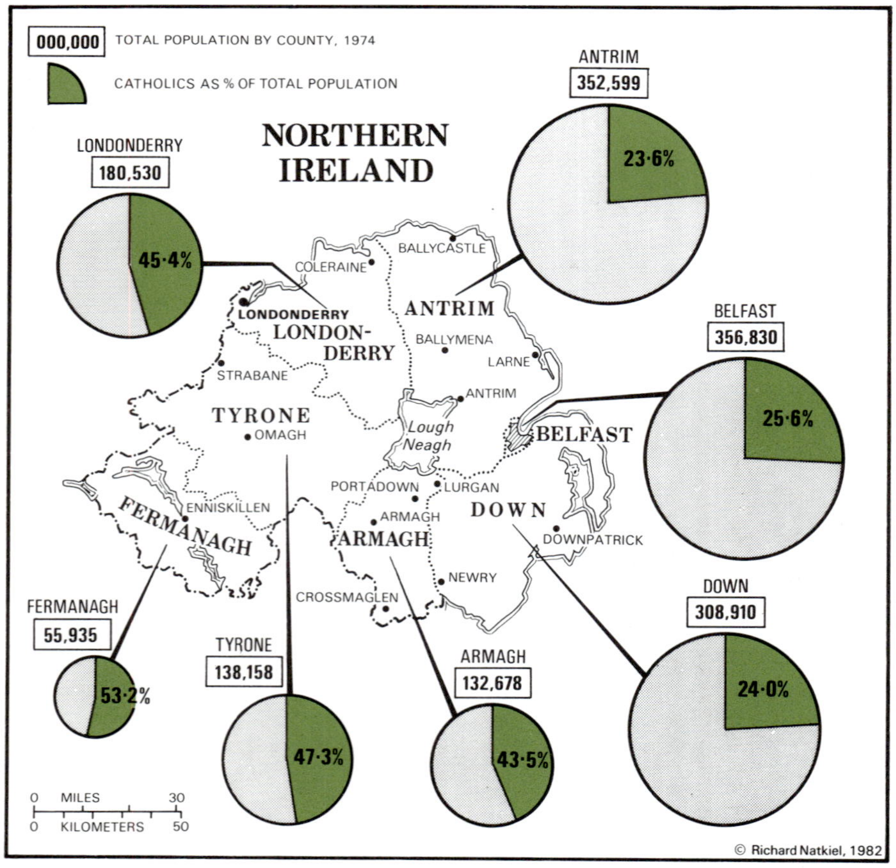

forces, apart from individual secondment and very specialist but routine services such as bomb disposal, have had little involvement in internal security duties on the mainland. Security in Britain, even in dealing with 'imported' violence from Ireland or the Middle East, has been mainly a police matter: Northern Ireland, on the other hand, has involved a major military commitment with regard to internal security duties, partly alongside the Police but more latterly in its support.

The record of British military operations inside the United Kingdom since 1969 has, therefore, been dominated by the campaign in Northern Ireland, although it would be wrong to imagine that it is only the Army that has been involved. The RAF may have been restricted to a minimal support and transport role in Ulster, but the Royal Navy has been responsible for safeguarding the coastline of the province (which is half as long again as the Anglo—Irish border) against infiltration and smuggling by terrorist organisations. This commitment in the 1970s usually involved no more than a couple of minesweepers and a number of light inshore patrol craft – the security forces obviously have to rely more on sound intelligence than on a physical naval presence for the security of Northern Ireland from the sea – but

Above: During a curfew in the Falls Road, July 1970, women and children try to break through the Army barricades to deliver milk and bread to the local population. The imposition of curfews, some of which lasted for days rather than hours, were the major factor in alienating the Catholic community from the security forces.

Above right: Ulster Loyalist para-military personnel man roadblocks in Londonderry, 1971, in response to the continued existence of IRA-held 'No-Go' areas in the city. The formation of Protestant groups deepened the sectarian divide.

Map: Northern Ireland, showing the breakdown of population by religion. The figures are for 1974.

it does illustrate a level of inter-service response which is often ignored. Even so, the main emphasis of the commitment has been military and it is the Army which has borne the brunt of the campaign. British regular units were first deployed in early August 1969 when the government of Northern Ireland (Stormont), headed by Major James Chichester-Clark, was obliged to ask the British government (Westminster) of Harold Wilson to provide troops to assist the civil power in the restoration of order. This request came as the culmination of months of rising sectarian strife that had stemmed from a campaign of protest and civil disobedience on the part of the minority Catholic community and a counter-campaign of violence and intimidation against the demonstrators on the part of Protestant extremists and sections of the Police and Police Reserve ('B'-Specials). Stormont's request was met by Westminster with some reluctance, the result being that British troops were deployed in Londonderry on 14 August and in Belfast on the following day. But while the aim of this initial commitment of forces was the restoration of order this, involving very different things in the two main cities of the province, reflected the ambiguity of the British position in Northern Ireland. In Belfast British troops had to be committed to the protection of Catholic areas from a Protestant rampage, but in Londonderry the Army had to go to the support of a beleaguered police force exhausted by days of incessant rioting and in danger of being overwhelmed by an enraged Catholic community. The subsequent visit of Home Secretary James Callaghan confirmed this ambiguity. He was cheered in the Catholic Falls Road area of Belfast and the Bogside in Londonderry as the guarantor of the minority's security against further Police-Protestant attack: he was also lauded in the Protestant Shankill Road area of Belfast as the representative of law and order against a recalcitrant Catholic population. The ambiguity within the British position was to become obvious in the course of the next 11 months.

Initially the British Army was deployed to keep two warring communities from one another's throats, and it was welcomed by both in this role. In conscious imitation of the situation in which it had found itself in Cyprus in the 1950s, the Army sought to separate the two communities physically by the creation of peace lines. Its objective in doing this was to try to calm the situation and to prevent further sectarian fighting, but in settling upon this policy the Army created safe areas for the Catholics that were proofed not just against Protestant attack but normal policing. This was to have an obvious and disastrous repercussion. Before the summer of 1969 the Police had had a firm grip over the Catholic population that had been shaken only in the last four months before the commitment of British troops. It had a very fair idea of Catholic para-military forces and members, and in all truth in the summer of 1969 there were precious few of either. The Police and Protestant attacks on the Catholic community had prompted a taunt that IRA stood for 'I Ran Away', and it has been alleged that in August 1969 the IRA had fewer than 30 weapons in the whole of Belfast and less than

£300 in funds. The IRA leadership, for some time anxious to get away from the simplistic 'British out' attitude that had failed to win Catholic support during the Border Campaign, had been surprised by the speed with which events developed in the summer. It had expected the campaign of protest and civil disobedience to take much longer to produce a crisis of which it might take advantage than proved to be the case, and the hesitation of the official leadership of the IRA in meeting the crisis that confronted the nationalist movement in late 1969 resulted in the organisation splitting into Official and Provisional factions in December 1969/January 1970.

The creation of safe areas provided the two wings of the IRA with the chance to build up control over the Catholic population and to prepare it to support a campaign of violence against the authorities. This the two IRA factions, which were bidding against one another as well as preparing for the struggle against the Protestants and the British, attempted to do by cajolery, intimidation and self-fulfilling rhetoric. The general IRA claim was that the Army was nothing more than the instrument of Protestant ascendancy which, of course, it was in the sense that it was operating in support of the civil power, and the civil power was Chichester-Clark's Stormont government. It mattered not that in the immediate aftermath of the deployment of British troops in Londonderry and Belfast, Westminster forced Stormont to commit itself to a programme of long-overdue reform: the damage was in the continued existence of an administration that was sectarian in appeal and composition and which was naturally distrusted by the minority. As it was, the Army slowly drifted into a series of abrasive exchanges with the Catholic community, the initial fund of mutual goodwill on the part of both the Army and the Catholics being unable to withstand the friction that exists between a 'force of occupation' and the population with which it has to deal. The most obvious points of conflict even by the spring of 1970 were the seemingly daily street riots in which the hooligan element confronted a hopelessly ill-organised Army that was untrained and not equipped for crowd-control duties of the kind it was now called upon to perform. With the IRA not directly involved in these confrontations, but willing them on because it knew that it stood to gain from a polarisation of attitudes within the community, the Army gradually found itself in an increasingly impossible situation. This was ironic in view of the fact that the Army's first armed action was not against Catholics or the IRA but Protestant extremists who fought the security forces in October 1969 in protest against a proposal to disarm the Police. It was in the course of these battles that the first policeman was killed during the present campaign.

The Army's main problem in this situation was that it lacked an operational headquarters and, crucially, it had no intelligence organisation or sources within the province. Moreover, because of the collapse of police authority in many areas, the Army was not operating in support of the civil power because in effect there was no civil power to support. What was to compound these problems was that over the next three years, as the Army's commitment deepened and it began to organise itself across the whole of the province, it was always one step behind the growth and development of the IRA factions and it was constantly on the defensive, obliged to react to events over which it clearly had no control. This, of course, was politically very damaging and provided the IRA factions with domestic and international credibility.

In the first five years of the campaign the size of the military presence in the province fluctuated considerably before settling down for a long period at the 12/13 battalion level. Because of a quiet strengthening of the garrison during the spring disturbances, four battalions were in Northern Ireland in July 1969. This rose to eight in August, and this proved to be the general establishment level during the winter months of both 1969-70 and 1970-71. But initially because the summer was the traditional time for sectarian demonstrations and then because after the spring of 1971 the IRA campaign of violence began to gather momentum, the Army found itself forced to commit no fewer than 17 battalions in Ulster at such peak periods as July 1970 and August 1971. At the same time it was obliged to build up a part-time defence force for service within (but not outside) the province. The latter, the Ulster Defence Regiment (UDR), was established by an Act of Parliament in December 1969, and initially consisted of an administrative headquarters at Lisburn and seven battalions, one for each of the counties with the seventh in Belfast. In December 1971 to January 1972 three more battalions were raised by dividing ones already in existence, and the following September an eleventh was raised by the same process. The establishment of the UDR was then set at 11,050 all ranks from the province, plus 1532 seconded personnel from the regular Army.

On 1 October 1975 the total strength of the UDR, excluding its permanent staff, was 7735 all ranks, but from the start the organisation suffered from two serious weaknesses. First, its Catholic members, who accounted for about one in seven of its total strength in the early days, were intimidated into leaving the organisation by the IRA, thereby enabling the latter to claim that the UDR was a sectarian force. Second, the UDR naturally recruited well in areas away from where it was needed. In those areas where the IRA secured some measure of control over the population, enlistment in the UDR was poor. In any case in 1971-73, when the struggle was at its most intense and was mainly concentrated in urban areas, most of the UDR was committed in rural areas. Six whole battalions and part of another were deployed under the command of the 3rd Infantry Brigade because the Army, conscious of the past excesses of a now-disbanded sectarian police reserve, deliberately kept the UDR clear of major built-up areas. In this way the Army could avoid the charge of using a Protestant para-military force against the Catholic community but at the same time give the UDR an important role.

Right: A major feature of British Army involvement in Northern Ireland in the early 1970s was riot control. Here, in the Little Diamond area of Londonderry, soldiers advance behind shields against a stone-throwing mob, many of whom appear to be teenage children.

Bottom right: 'Bloody Sunday', Londonderry, 30 January 1972: a para snatches a suspect. Thirteen people died as British forces, opposing a huge Civil Rights demonstration, responded to sniper fire.

Below: The face of terrorism in Northern Ireland: men of the IRA, anonymous behind dark glasses, march in public through the Upper Falls, April 1971.

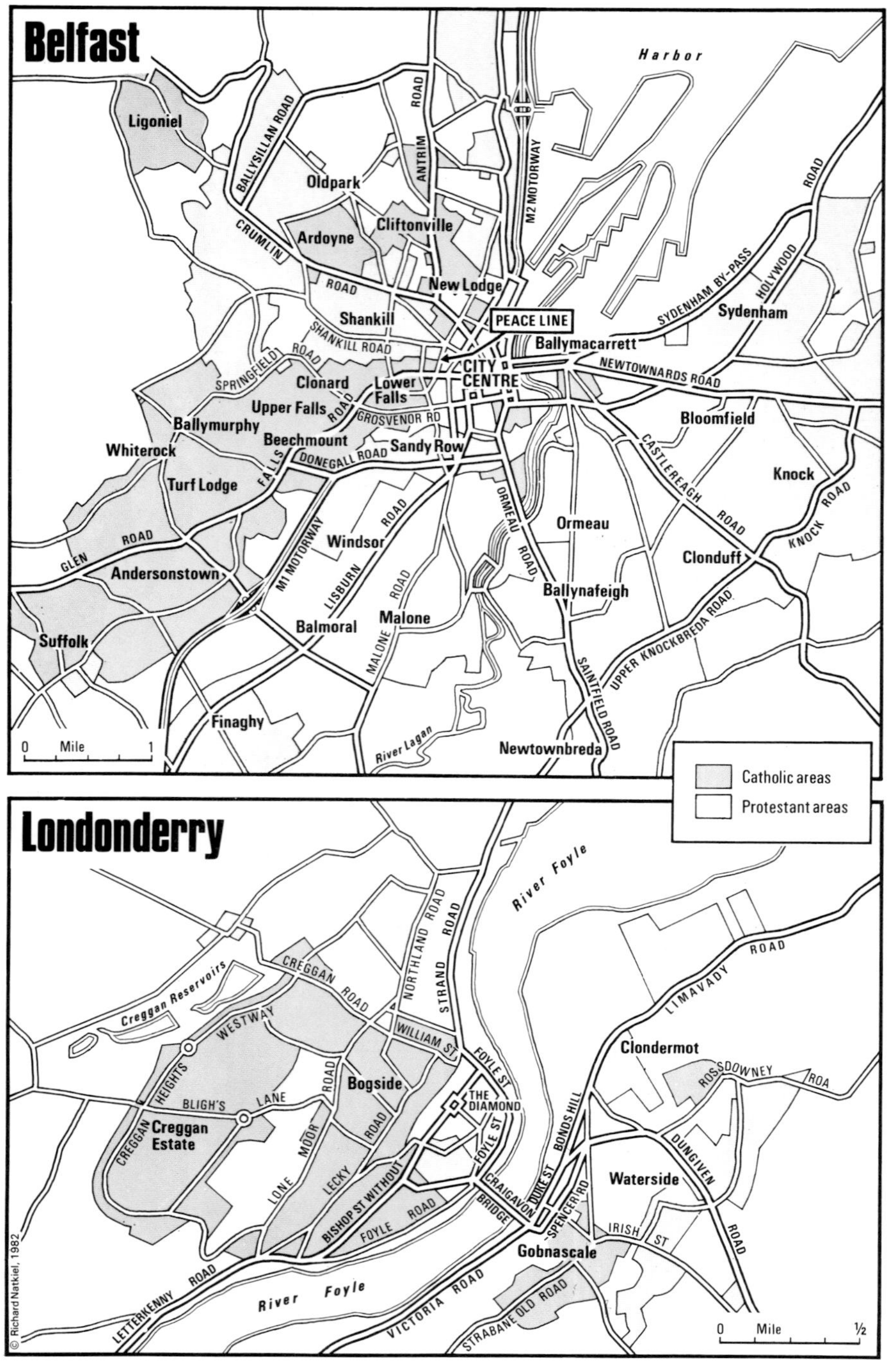

As the Army set about organising itself for a long campaign, it built up a normal garrison of four battalions in Londonderry with the 8th Infantry Brigade, and an establishment of six battalions in Belfast with the 39th Infantry Brigade. That left the 3rd Infantry Brigade in Lurgan with just three infantry battalions (plus reconnaissance and support elements) and responsibility for the remainder of the province, for 433 of the 485km (269 of the 301 miles) of border with the Republic, and for 242 of the 285 border crossing-points. Without the UDR, the 3rd Infantry Brigade could never have hoped to function effectively, and even with the part-time battalions it still had less than one soldier for every square mile of its area of responsibility. The impossibility of the task confronting the 3rd Infantry Brigade can be gauged by the fact that an estimated 14 battalions would have been needed to seal the border effectively, and that was more than the normal garrison of the province as a whole.

Before 1974 the UDR was by no means immune to loss, but it was not until 1974-75 that IRA attention was switched to the countryside in a deliberate attempt to develop a dual urban-rural campaign. In previous years IRA campaigns had been deliberately concentrated in the cities as the republican factions waged a struggle to bring down Stormont, to destroy British resolve, and thereby lead to the creation of an all-Ireland socialist republic. In this period the initiative, as we have seen, lay initially with the IRA, but even in the successes that it was able to register in this period, there were two weaknesses that proved vital to the success of the security forces in establishing such a stranglehold on the IRA that both of its factions were willing to observe ceasefires in 1975 – a sure indication of weakness. First, the power of the republican movement was in its ability to make Ulster ungovernable but not in being able to offer anything to the Protestant *majority*. Any success that the IRA enjoyed could only be partial and negative because it could never command the support of a majority of the population of Northern Ireland. In the

Right: An IRA-manned checkpoint, Creggan Estate, April 1972. The existence of the 'No-Go' areas – finally taken out in Operation Motorman on 31 July 1972 – was a constant challenge to the writ of the security forces.

Left: Map showing the streets of Belfast and Londonderry: the battleground for the Army since 1969.

Below right: A wall-sign marks the entrance to the 'No-Go' area in the Bogside, Londonderry. Beyond this point the security forces could not patrol and normal policing broke down.

Below: Suspects are rounded up and marched away by British paras, Londonderry, 30 January 1972. The fire-fight known as 'Bloody Sunday' certainly quietened a potentially volatile situation, but the 13 deaths caused many people to query the Army's tactics.

final analysis, the IRA lacked the means to persuade or coerce the Protestants, and the British government had no inclination to attempt either course with regard to a community that used the occasion of the border referendum of 8 March 1973 to demonstrate its implacable resolve to remain within the United Kingdom. There were very real limits to the success that any republican campaign of violence might achieve, though this was not immediately realized by many parties of the conflict. Second, in organising themselves for an armed struggle, both wings of the IRA adopted a standard military establishment of companies and independent detachments, battalions, brigades, and command headquarters complete with general, administrative and quartermaster branches.

This was a conventional organisation of forces of the kind that the IRA had adopted at the time of the Anglo-Irish and Irish civil wars, but it was one that had absolutely no place in the fierce and unremitting struggle that unfolded in the years between 1970-74.

Owing to the unpreparedness of the Army and the effectiveness of IRA security within Catholic safe areas – both of its factions recruited heavily in 1969 and 1970 and their efforts went unmonitored by an increasingly ineffective Royal Ulster Constabulary (RUC) – the IRA was able to command success in 1970, 1971 and in the first half of 1972. Even though it was able to maintain a high (if declining) level of violence in 1973 and 1974, after 1972 the republican cause suffered militarily as an increasingly effective intelligence effort on the part of the security forces bit more deeply into its strength. In the opening phase of the campaign, much of the IRA's success was the result of the ineffectiveness of the security forces' intelligence effort, and Sean MacStiofan, Chief of Staff of the Provisional IRA, subsequently claimed that throughout 1970 the Army could have wiped out the organisation without its being able to offer any form of effective resistance: he also claimed that by the time the Army did make a move it was too late to achieve success, because by then the Provisional IRA was too well established. The fact of the matter was that in 1970 the Army could not move against MacStiofan's organisation because it did not have an inkling of who to look for. The Army found that the RUC was of little use to it. The Police Special Branch had no records of any kind on Protestant extremists, and it had very few records even on the Catholic community. Most of its information was entrusted to that most fallible of memory banks, the human

Above: A patrol of the Royal Welch Fusiliers, ignoring the anti-Welsh graffiti, keeps a careful eye out for trouble, Strabane, 1971.

brain, and British military and police personnel sent to Northern Ireland to support the hopelessly undermanned organisation were frequently amazed and appalled by the lack of professionalism of the RUC and its Special Branch. Moreover, the Army distrusted the security of the Police, and had good reason to suspect that information that came in would find its way to Protestant para-military forces.

One of the legacies of this distrust was the refusal of the Army to accept co-location of headquarters and intelligence services with the Police, although all post-1945 British counter-insurgency operations showed this to be essential. The Police, on the other hand, had little liking either for the Army or the situation in which it found itself from 1969-71. It was demoralised by its own failures of 1969, the reforms imposed upon it in 1969 and 1970, its losses, the restrictions placed upon its operations, and the barrage of criticism to which it was subjected. With regard to the Army, the RUC resented what it saw as amateurism on the part of military units that would leave the province before they had time to reap the consequences of their errors. Most Army units were rotated through Northern Ireland on four-month tours, and certainly in the initial stages of the campaign there were instances of the military treating the Police in a somewhat cavalier manner and both sides compromised the other's sources as a result of poor co-ordination and lack of professionalism. Moreover, the Army itself did not make too impressive a job of organising its own intelligence services. The three local military headquarters developed without the intelligence services being placed in charge of the intelligence establishments within the individual brigades; they were, therefore, unstandardised and hence a source of duplication, waste, and lack of co-ordination not simply within the brigades themselves but also with the Police. This organisational situation was far from perfect even in 1976, but in spite of that the Police and Army had managed to put their separate and combined acts together in a very satisfactory manner long before that time. A very high degree of integration and liaison was achieved by virtue of the Army providing the RUC and Special Branch with military police, intelligence and ordnance personnel for support operations. It also provided intelligence personnel in clerical support, and again army intelligence provided or trained personnel for

Right: A tracker dog, carefully trained to sniff out explosives, is used in the Strabane rural area by the Royal Welch Fusiliers. Rural operations have been a central feature of the campaign in Northern Ireland, although they tend to have been over-shadowed by more dramatic events in the cities.

liaison duties with Army units. Such personnel operated under Police and not Army command.

An increasingly effective co-ordination between Army and Police was paralleled by the success that both had in dealing with the IRA. Much of this success stemmed from routine surveillance and police work at which the Army slowly became proficient, but most importantly from interrogation successes and the infiltration of the IRA or the turning of insurgents. One event was of supreme importance. After a mounting campaign of murder and mayhem, punctuated by ceasefires as both the IRA factions briefly recoiled from the prospect of civil war in mid-1972, the Provisional IRA on the afternoon of 21 July 1972 detonated 22 bombs within one mile of Belfast city centre, killing nine people and injuring 130. 'Bloody Friday', as it became known, provided the pretext for the largest single operation carried out by the British Army since the end of the Second World War. Operation 'Motorman', the breaking down of the Catholic 'no-go' areas, was carried out on 31 July by no fewer than 27 battalions, the British intention being to operate so obviously and in such overwhelming strength that terrorist organisations would be forced to flee rather than stand and fight as the Army broke into the Catholic safe areas. Though the IRA did take on the Army in a number of fire-fights and terror-bombed the village of Claudy on the day of 'Motorman' itself in an attempt to divert attention from its set-back, the general aim of the security forces in carrying out 'Motorman' was fulfilled.

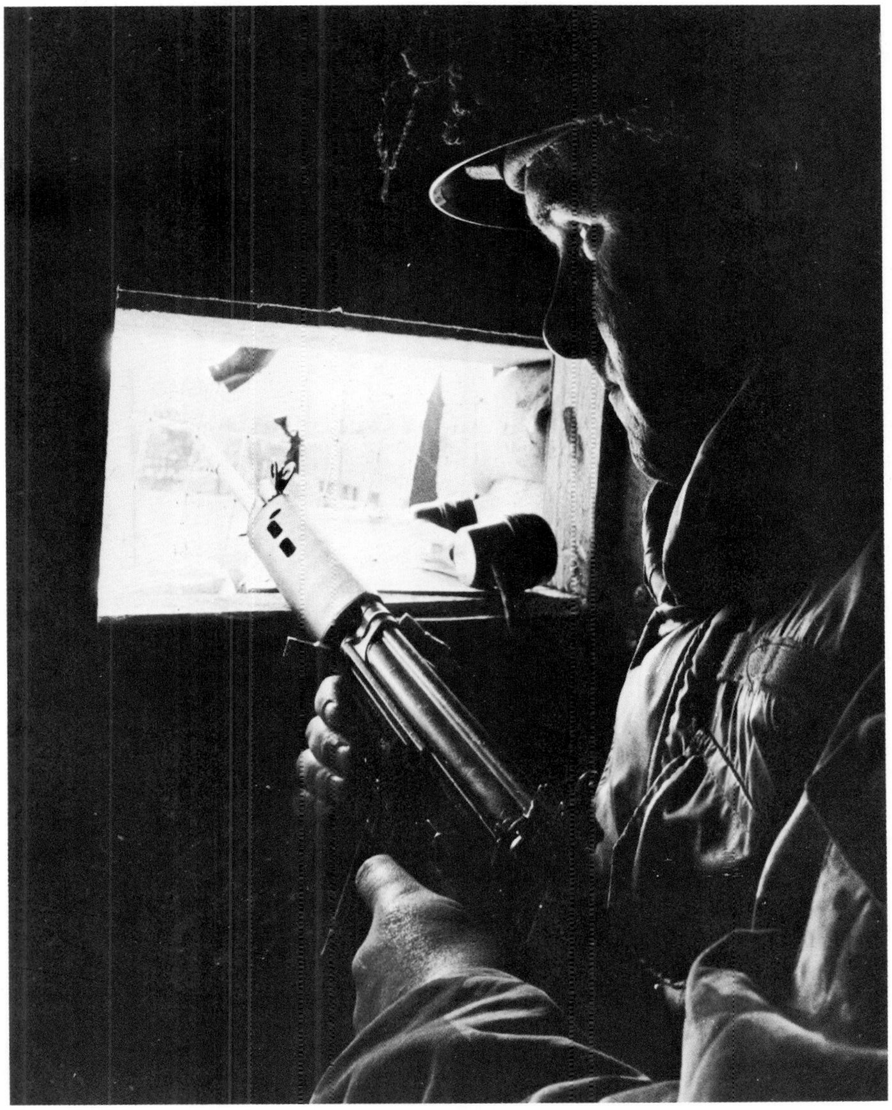

Above: A British Army sentry, 7.62mm SLR in hand, looks out from his fortified post, Belfast, 1973. The protection of Police and Army posts has been an essential part of the security forces' task.

Bloody Friday and 'Motorman' did more than provide the security forces with a local or temporary initiative: together they formed a watershed in the campaign. For more than two years before Bloody Friday the IRA had been able to make most of the running in the campaign. The security forces had only contributed to their own embarrassment by such actions as the introduction of internment and detention without trial on 9 August 1971; the use of in-depth interrogation of prisoners that technically constituted torture; and the 'Bloody Sunday' incident in Londonderry on 30 January 1972 when 13 Catholics were shot dead in the course of a riot. The subsequent suspension of Stormont and the imposition of direct rule by Westminster on 24 March 1972 only aggravated the situation in that it inflamed Protestant opinion against the British government and thereafter forced it to divide its attention between two hostile forces. However, Bloody Friday destroyed much of the IRA's credibility. There was no way in which indiscriminate bombing of Belfast centre could be portrayed as defensive and in the interests of the Catholic community; and the support of the Catholic community was beginning to wilt as a result of two years of mounting terrorism. Already the greatest forced evacuation of people to have taken place in Europe since 1945 had occurred in Belfast as families caught on the 'wrong' side of the sectarian divide sought sanctuary in their own ghettoes, and Bloody Friday was the sticking point for many Catholics – particularly when 'Motorman' broke, or at least substantially weakened, the IRA's grip over the minority. Denied the right to conduct rigorous interrogation of suspects, the security forces resorted to what was known as 'screening'. This was a seemingly random questioning of people picked from the streets; a surprising amount of casual information was acquired from routine interrogations but the real bonus was that genuine sources could be disguised and protected by the sheer scale on which screening was carried out. The security forces carried out so many questionings that the IRA security and debriefing teams were simply overwhelmed when they tried to find the sources of leaks.

The period after 'Motorman' saw the time of maximum success for the security forces in destroying successive IRA orders of battle, particularly in the Belfast area. Throughout 1973-74 the security forces proved able to destroy IRA command headquarters and military formations almost as quickly as they could be organised, such was their success in infiltrating the IRA and the effectiveness of screening. By these means the security forces were able to make major inroads into IRA strength and slowly to reduce the level of insurgency within the province. In fact, it would hardly be an exaggeration to say that by the end of 1974 the security forces had broken the back of the IRA effort, the Official faction having been a spent force for some time (in part because it had lost in its battle with its republican rival) and the Provisional wing being harassed to defeat. As already noted, the willingness of the IRA to observe ceasefires was a clear indication of which side held the initiative; ceasefires are rarely suggested by winners.

Nevertheless, the success of the security forces in destroying successive IRA orders of battle was flawed because the process had to be repeated against one organisation after another. The security forces were able to destroy IRA military structures, but they could not prevent them making good their losses. The inability to stem the flow of recruits to the terrorist organisations was not a direct failing of the security forces but the result of the much deeper political division within society that prevented any possibility of reconciliation across the sectarian divide, and this forestalled any chance of the emergence of a secular attitude that could be the basis of political settlement. By 1974-75 the security forces had broken the back of a major campaign of violence within Northern Ireland, and the ending of internment and detention in December 1975 deprived the IRA and Catholic community in

Top right: The aftermath of the Warrenpoint bomb attack by the terrorist INLA group, in which 18 soldiers were killed, August 1979. Lord Mountbatten was assassinated on the same day.

Bottom right: An Irish Army patrol moves alongside the Belfast-Dublin railway in County Louth, Republic of Ireland, April 1976.

Right: The Reverend Ian Paisley, Loyalist leader of the Ulster Democratic Unionist Party, holds out a Declaration pledging Ulster's link with Britain, February 1981.

general of one of their most potent propaganda weapons against the British government. But the security forces could not end a political campaign by military means. Without a political settlement the success of the security forces could not be completed. The best single chance of a settlement was lost when the power-sharing experiment of December 1973 to May 1974 collapsed with the Protestant strike against it. This left the Army and Police with a lingering campaign that was much more difficult to combat than the previous one.

In the aftermath of the reverses of 1972-74 the IRA recast its tactics and organisation even as it resplit in the same manner as it had in 1970. In the years of defeat, pressure within the Provisional IRA grew for a switch of emphasis from military to political means. The subsequent split resulted in the formation of the Irish Republican Socialist Party and its military wing, the Irish National Liberation Army (INLA), by hard-line militants who were led by Seamus Costello, a defector not from the Provisional IRA but the Official wing. At the same time the INLA and the Provisionals both sought to secure themselves against infiltration and betrayal by adopting the cell (called the 'active service unit') as the standard operational unit.

The idea was to have up to four members in a unit that could come together for specific operations but who would (or could) be otherwise unknown to one another. At the same time the IRA tried to maintain a level of violence within Britain itself, but made particular efforts to step up its activities in the countryside of Northern Ireland. Its main area of operations tended to be in South Armagh, an area that was predominantly Catholic and difficult to patrol because of its narrow lanes, hedgerows and open border with the Republic. South Armagh was good soldiering country in which the IRA, because it held the tactical initiative, could hope to gain compensation for the reverses it had incurred in the urban areas. In fact, the IRA had always paid some attention to the rural areas and particularly South Armagh, no doubt in part because of the stress laid upon mutually supporting urban and rural operations by the high priest of urban insurgency, Carlos Marighela.

By January 1976 the security forces had lost 49 dead in South Armagh, almost all of them in the immediate area of Crossmaglen. Such was the extent of the IRA's control over this particularly difficult area that on one notable occasion a battalion operation was needed to serve two summonses on individuals in Crossmaglen. Matters came to a head when 10 Protestants and five Catholics were murdered in two separate incidents in South Armagh (the latter by UDR men) around the turn of 1975-76. Thereafter the British government committed the 22nd Special Air Service (SAS) Regiment to South Armagh in an active combat role, and by the end of 1976 the grip of the Provisional IRA had been eased if not broken. Given the political impossibility of the situation, the border area could not be brought under total control and, indeed, the republican military units remained with so many options with regard to the timing, location and form of attacks that the surprising feature of operations in the area since 1976 is not how many or how destructive they have been but how relatively few have been carried out. The area still provides a rich return for the republican cause, none more so than in August 1979 when 18 British soldiers were killed in one single attack at Warrenpoint near Newry, on the same day that Lord Mountbatten was murdered by the INLA just south of the border.

Since the end of internment, however, the Army has gradually assumed a low profile in Northern Ireland. Its maximum involvement came in 1972, and since 1975 the Army has played an ever smaller role as responsibility for security has been increasingly turned over to the Police. Over the years the standard garrison of about 14,500 troops has been reduced to one of about 11,000, and while the Army still provides the RUC with specialist support, patrols in the rural areas, support for routine policing where necessary and at vehicle and personnel checkpoints, the process of returning the problem of Ulster to its people – 'Ulsterisation' – has resulted in a corresponding reduction of the Army's role in Northern Ireland, even though apparently it is one without end.

It is not just in Northern Ireland that the

Right: IRA men in combat jackets, balaclavas and berets attend the funeral of hunger striker Bobby Sands in May 1981. Although the hunger strikers had little effect upon British Government policy towards Northern Ireland, they did draw world attention to the IRA cause.

Below right: SAS back-up team, disguised in civilian clothes and balaclavas, fires CS gas into the Iranian embassy as their colleagues go in to rescue the hostages, 5 May 1980.

Below: The Princes Gate embassy siege, May 1980: the SAS goes in to rescue the hostages, in full view of an enthralled TV audience. The success of the SAS operation was a tremendous morale-booster to a country weary after 11 years of terrorist attack.

threat of terrorism has been faced, for the mainland itself has had its share of incidents, some of which have necessitated military involvement in support of the Police. By far the most dramatic was the Iranian embassy siege of 30 April to 5 May 1980. This one episode, culminating as it did in complete victory for the counter-terrorist forces, marked the climax of seven years of preparation on the part of the Counter Revolutionary Warfare (CRW) Team which the elite 22 SAS had organised for just such an eventuality. This was not the first time that this unit had been used inside the United Kingdom, and it was by no means the first time that there had been a major 'non-Irish' incident within Britain, but the embassy siege was the first occasion on which the British were able to have a clear run against any terrorist organisation within their border and, of course, it was an incident that was seen live on television – with an outcome to the obvious satisfaction of most of the population.

After 1969 Britain was unfortunate in that the parties to the Arab-Israeli dispute seemed intent on resolving their differences in other people's countries, and Britain – and particularly London – seemed to be in the front-line of the battle. With various governments being involved in this struggle it was particularly difficult for the British to try to counter the 'in-and-out' operations that were carried out on their soil, the effective response to the assailants who shot the Israeli ambassador in London in June 1982 (one was shot and two others captured, tried and imprisoned) being an obvious, isolated and very fortuitous exception to the general pattern of enforced helplessness. As a general rule, Arab and Israeli terrorists experienced relatively little difficulty in carrying out their operations, and hence, in part, the importance of the Iranian embassy episode. Coming less than one month after and in stark contrast to the abortive American attempt to rescue their people from Teheran, the Princes Gate episode served as a timely demonstration that neither the British nor the democratic process as such were easy push-overs for terrorist organisations.

The Iranian embassy siege was not the first time that the CRW Team had been used in Britain. Its debut had been in January 1975 when it disarmed a hijacker at Stansted airport, and it had followed this by being deployed to, but not used in, the capture of a Provisional IRA active service unit in the Balcombe Street siege in the Marylebone district of London in the following December. Subsequently the SAS was alleged to have played a minor supporting role in May 1977 when the Dutch ended an attempt by South Moluccan separatists to promote their rather forlorn cause with a hijacking of a train in Holland. It was certainly involved in a more substantial supporting role in October 1978 when it advised the West German anti-terrorist squad, *Grenzschutz 9*, during the latter's attack on a *Lufthansa* airliner that had been hijacked to Mogadishu. But the Iranian embassy siege was the first time that the SAS was put under the spotlight in Britain. After a six-day siege, at the end of which the group of six Iraqi terrorists killed the Iranian press attaché, the CRW Team stormed and cleared the embassy, killing most of the terrorists and saving all the remaining hostages but one. It was an action that ended the obscurity with which the SAS had always deliberately tried to conceal its activities, but in terms of deterrence the episode would seem to have had a salutary effect on terrorist groups that might otherwise have tried their hand in Britain.

For Britain remains vulnerable to terrorist attack, whether Irish or international in origin, and it is only through displaying a willingness to use elements of her armed forces in support of the Police to counter such attacks that security may be maintained. The fact that the armed forces contain units of proven capability in such operations indicates a depth of military expertise that can only develop from high professionalism. This in turn has become the hallmark of the modern British services, displayed in a host of simultaneous commitments beyond the home islands since the late 1960s.

RESIDUAL RESPONSIBILITIES

In June 1976 the Soviet Ministry of Defence published a survey of 'Imperial Aggression' since 1945. Not surprisingly in view of her Army's almost continuous involvement in colonial campaigning, Britain was awarded prime place. It could be argued that the Soviet assessment was essentially a reflection of the past rather than a guide to the present, since Britain had seemingly renounced a global role in January 1968, but despite the pace of decolonisation throughout the 1960s and the reorientation towards European affairs in the 1970s, the fact remains that Britain has yet to escape completely from the residual responsibilities of a former imperial power.

In a sense, the apparently radical redirection of British defence policy during the period of Labour government from 1964-70 was rather less than the watershed it appeared at the time, for despite antipathies towards colonial involvement, the Cabinet moved to divest a world role only slowly. In December 1964 Prime Minister Harold Wilson stated that Britain 'could not afford to relinquish a world role', while policy as defined by Secretary of State for Defence Denis Healey's successive reviews diluted rather than reduced the substance of British commitments. The defence review of February 1966, for example, envisaged British servicemen remaining in the Arabian (Persian)

Previous page: Santa arrives by river in a 7½ ton Scimitar of Alamein Troop, Royal Scots Dragoon Guards, at an outpost in Belize, December 1976.

Left: A briefing for a helicopter pilot with the British contingent of UNFICYP.

Right: British troops, wearing the distinctive blue beret of UN peacekeeping forces, pictured by a petrol tanker on Cyprus.

Below: A British patrol of UNFICYP along the 'Green Line' on Cyprus.

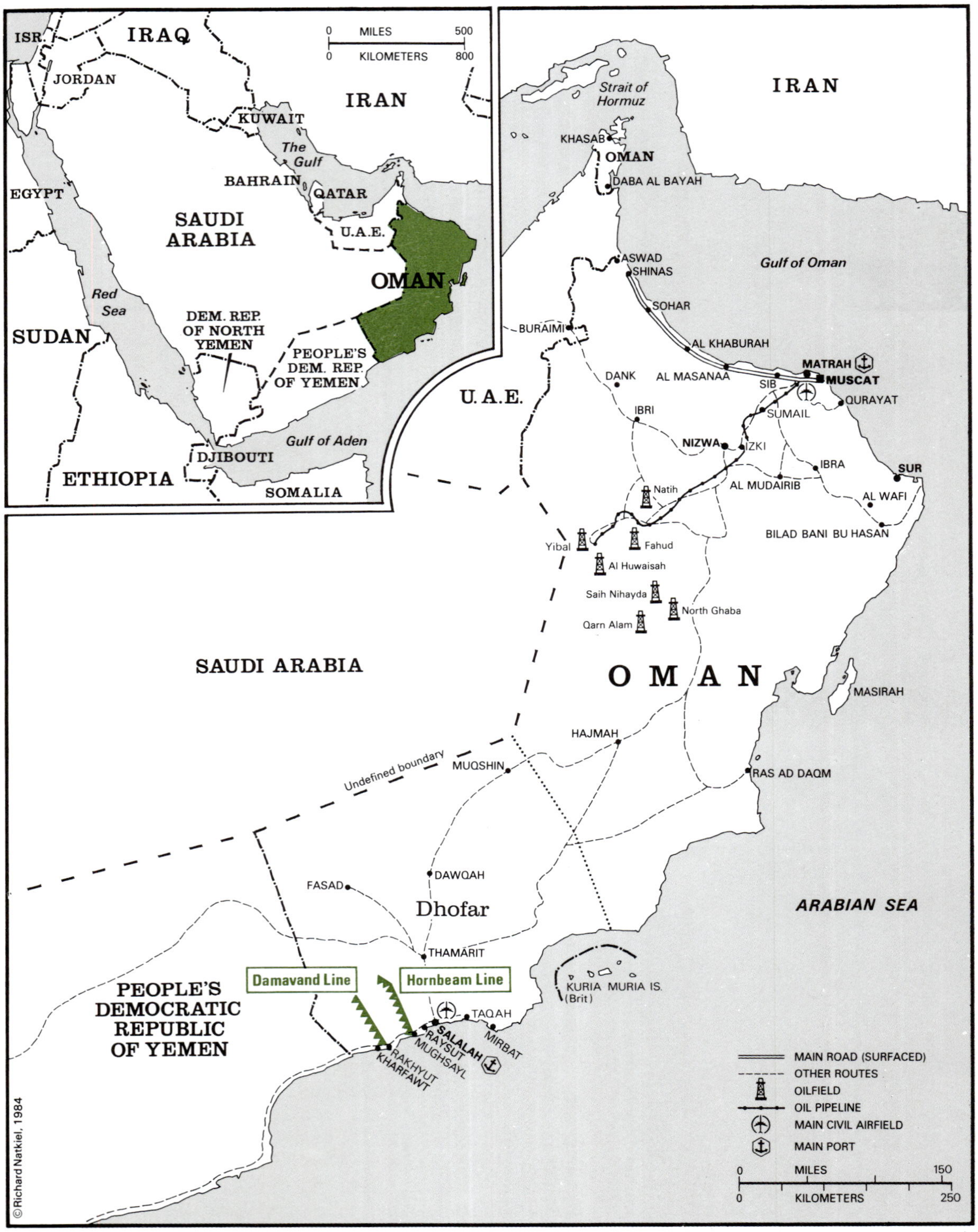

Left: Map of Oman and the Dhofar, showing the defensive lines that prevented PFLOAG infiltration from South Yemen.

Right: Men of the 2nd Battalion, the Parachute Regiment with Anguillans on 21 March 1969, two days after the 'invasion' of the West Indies island.

Below: British troops of the Royal Engineers moving into Nicosia during the communal troubles on Cyprus, 1 January 1964.

Gulf even though Aden was to be abandoned by 1968, while the supplementary Defence Paper of July 1967 envisaged a British presence east of Suez until at least 1973. It was, of course, the economic crisis and devaluation of sterling in November 1967 which finally prompted the abandonment of a role east of Suez by 1971. There was something of a stay of execution when the Conservative government returned to power in 1970, after which defence agreements were concluded with four Gulf States and a Five Power Agreement signed to maintain some forces in Malaysia and Singapore. Similarly, although a coup in Libya in 1969 led to Britain withdrawing from its last permanent African base there in March 1970, the Heath government did renew the Simonstown agreement with South Africa. All of this implied a degree of muddle and uncertainty about Britain's position in the world, and this was reflected in the experiences of the armed forces. Despite a growing orientation towards NATO and European defence, British service personnel continued and still do continue to be regularly involved in operations within remaining colonies, former colonies and those territories for which Britain has remained nominally responsible.

In terms of colonies, for example, British troops were required to assist the civil police in Hong Kong when riots broke out in May 1967. Carefully orchestrated by the communist Chinese, the disturbances escalated into an even more serious situation when five policemen were killed by machine-gun fire from across the Chinese border on 8 July. British and Gurkha troops from the garrison were at once

moved up to the border, where they faced an ugly series of incidents in which Chinese guards would rush across the frontier and surround British outposts, knowing that they were under strict orders not to open fire. Hong Kong itself was racked by bomb explosions which killed two servicemen, and it was not until November 1967, when an agreement on border exchanges was signed by London and Peking, that the violence finally died down.

Another colony which frequently required military intervention was Bermuda. In April 1968 150 men of the Royal Inniskilling Fusiliers (soon to be renamed the 1st Royal Irish Rangers) were landed from HMS *Leopard* to aid the civil power during pre-election riots, while in July 1969 Royal Marines were deployed as a precaution during a black power conference. A state of emergency was declared in March 1973 after the murder of the British governor and again on 2 December 1977 when the execution of the governor's murderer and another killer resulted in widespread rioting. Eighty men were flown in from Belize and a further 150 from Britain before the state of emergency was lifted on 9 December. In similar fashion, a frigate was sent to the Cayman Islands in April 1970 when there were demonstrations there against the colonial administration.

Other colonies had difficult passages towards independence, with British forces having to be deployed to ensure a smooth handover of power. In the case of Mauritius, for example, two companies of the 1st Battalion, King's Shrop-

shire Light Infantry (soon to be renamed the 3rd Battalion, The Light Infantry) were airlifted from Singapore in January 1968 when gang warfare between Moslems and Creoles erupted into race riots prior to independence. There had been similar riots in May 1965, when a company of the 2nd Battalion, Coldstream Guards had restored order on the island. In the 1968 riots, one company of troops remained after independence in March and did not leave until December.

But the British response was not always so immediate or effective, as the example of Rhodesia serves to show. When Ian Smith's white minority government issued its Unilateral Declaration of Independence (UDI) from Britain in November 1965 there were immediate Commonwealth demands for military action. But it was estimated that up to 25,000 troops might be required to subjugate Rhodesia, and only two British battalions were immediately available. Moreover, because of a shortage of transport aircraft only one of these could be airlifted at a time; there were no guarantees that over-flying rights would be granted by Rhodesia's neighbours and obvious doubts about the ability of a single battalion to overcome Rhodesia's efficient armed forces. It was possible, of course, that some Rhodesians would be loath to fire on British troops, but the opposite also applied, for the British might display reluctance to fight against 'kith and kin'. A land operation from Zambia was out of the question in view of the time it would take to organise and, amid reluctance by the Chiefs of Staff and Cabinet to authorise military action, Wilson settled for economic sanctions instead. A company of the 1st Battalion, Gloucestershire Regiment was despatched to Bechuanaland in December 1965 to guard a new BBC transmitter designed to broadcast to Rhodesia, and the Royal Navy soon became involved in the attempted blockade of the rebel state (the Beira patrol), but it was apparent that on this occasion at least there was a limit to Britain's ability to intervene.

This lack of firm military action did little to enhance the country's credibility, particularly as the government showed no such unwillingness when the rebel state was small and its

Above: Preventing Guatemalan infiltration into Belize means coming to terms with the jungle.

Top left: A member of 'D' Squadron, 22nd SAS Regiment shares tea with a villager at Al Rawdah, Wadi Hissan, in the South Arabian Federation, 8 December 1964.

Right: A British Scorpion light tank in Belize.

Left: A British patrol fords a river in Belize, the former British Honduras.

armed forces insignificant. In February 1967, for example, Anguilla declared its 'independence' from the 'associated state' of St Kitts and Nevis in the Caribbean. Administratively linked with distant St Kitts since 1822, Anguillans always felt neglected and wished to remain a colony rather than become independent in association with their neighbours. Royal Marines from HMS *Salisbury* escorted police reinforcements to Anguilla in February 1967, but the police were later expelled by the islanders. Two years of fruitless negotiation resulted in a further declaration of 'independence' in January 1969, while on 11 March of the same year the islanders mobbed the British Parliamentary Under-Secretary at the Foreign and Commonwealth Office, William Whitlock, when he visited Anguilla: he left hastily amid a fusillade of undirected shots. The Labour government of the time seized upon wildly exaggerated reports that Anguilla had fallen into the hands of the Mafia and that the islanders were armed to the teeth. At 0315 hours on 19 March a force of 315 men of the 2nd Battalion, Parachute Regiment, airlifted from Britain to Antigua in company with 47 London policemen, stormed ashore at Anguilla from the frigates *Rothesay* and *Minerva*. They were met only by the flashbulbs of an amused and incredulous international press, and subsequently discovered only 39 weapons and a

Above: One of the RAF Harriers, which proved such a deterrent to Guatemalan aggression, on a jungle air strip in Belize, 1981.

Above right: A group of Patriotic Front guerrillas moving into Assembly Point *Papa* in Rhodesia, December 1979.

Above, far right: A Hercules transport and Puma helicopter, marked with the distinctive cross of the Commonwealth Monitoring Force, flying over the Rhodesian bush, 1980.

Right: A guerrilla who shot himself in the foot, about to be taken to hospital by British troops of the CMF, February 1980.

rusting Napoleonic cannon on the entire island. The paras were withdrawn in September 1969, although Royal Engineers continued to work on modernising the island until two years later. By that time Anguilla had won a notable victory in being restored to colonial status by the special Anguilla Act of 1971. Since 1976 it has been a 'dependent territory' of Britain, while St Kitts and Nevis moved to full independence in September 1983.

An operation which threatened to rival Anguilla for ridicule occurred on Espiritu Santo eleven years later. The island seceded from the Anglo-French condominium of the New Hebrides in May 1980, the situation being aggravated by the dislike of French settlers for the Anglophone Vanuaaka Party, destined to form the new government on independence in July 1980. Rather like Anguilla, it was rumoured that Jimmy Stevens' Nagriamel movement which controlled Espiritu Santo had close links with dubious American businessmen. Typical of the British and French rivalry which had plagued the condominium's past, the French sent 55 paramilitary *gendarmes* to Espiritu Santo on 11 June without informing the British authorities, who immediately requested their withdrawal. A joint Anglo-French force was then put together and 200 Royal Marines despatched to the New Hebrides, where they met up with 100 French paratroopers of the 11th Parachute Division from New Caledonia. On 24 July the French paras and an equal number of British Marines restored authority on Espiritu Santo without encountering any opposition. The New Hebrides proceeded to independence as the Republic of Vanuatu on 29 July and the British and French forces withdrew on 18 August when they were replaced by troops from Papua New Guinea.

It was not only colonies that caused problems, for there were also former possessions or protectorates for which Britain retained some responsibility, and since the mid-1960s two in particular – Oman and Belize – have necessitated lasting military commitments. Oman had enjoyed British protection since 1798 and had in fact received military assistance as early as June 1957, when the Sultan, Said bin Taimur, faced a rebellion in the interior by the country's religious leader, Imam Ghalib bin Ali. A troop of the 15th/19th King's Hussars and a company of Cameronians had helped to stabilise the situation in the vicinity of the rebel stronghold on the Jebel Akhdar ('Green Mountain') and, in the following year, Britain helped to organise the Sultan's Armed Forces (SAF). In November 1958 'D' Squadron of the 22nd Special Air Service (SAS) Regiment arrived to find routes to the top of the Jebel Akhdar and in January 1959, by which time 'A' Squadron of 22 SAS had also been deployed, the British spearheaded the assault that retook the mountain and restored the sultan's authority. They withdrew in March 1959.

In 1962, however, rebellion erupted in the Dhofar region of Oman, largely as a result of frustration with the backward nature of Oman as a whole and Dhofar in particular. The rebel leader, Musallim bin Nuffl, had in fact come into contact with Western oilmen and had recognised what benefits might be derived from the new oil revenues which Oman was receiving but not utilising. Dhofar had certainly been neglected by the sultan, with only a single dirt-track road connecting Salalah and Mirbat and only a jeep track connecting Salalah and Thumrait (the 'Midway Road'). About the size of Wales, Dhofar was sparsely populated by 150,000 people, most of whom inhabited the narrow costal strip which the annual monsoon, sweeping in from the Indian Ocean between June and September, transformed into verdant and heavily wooded terrain. Behind the coast lay the mountains of the *jebel* and beyond them the vast desert of the 'Empty Quarter'.

176

Left: A Ferret Scout Car of Britain's UNFICYP contingent on Cyprus.

Below: 'Winning hearts and minds' in Belize.

By 1965 the rebels, now known as the Dhofar Liberation Front (DLF), had enjoyed only limited success, but they became a serious threat when the withdrawal of British troops from Aden in November 1967 opened the way for the Marxist People's Democratic Republic of the Yemen (PDRY) to emerge as Oman's neighbour. By 1968 Nuffl had been ousted and Ahmad Al Ghassani was leading the newly formed People's Front for the Liberation of the Occupied Arabian Gulf (PFLOAG), based upon the old DLF. Ghassani was backed by the Chinese (until 1971) and by the Soviet Union, receiving increasingly sophisticated weapons such as the RPG-7, 82mm RCL, Shpagin heavy machine gun, 122mm rocket launcher and the ubiquitous AK-47. Despite its Marxist ideology, PFLOAG seemed to enjoy the support or at least the acquiescence of many tribesmen in Dhofar, although the use of intimidation cannot be ignored.

The rebellion was, however, never to be exported beyond Dhofar because of the region's isolation from the rest of Oman and the grievous blow dealt PFLOAG by the bloodless coup in July 1970 in which the sultan was deposed by his son, Qaboos bin Said. Qaboos immediately launched a major programme of modernisation, while the SAF was greatly expanded, its Omani and Baluchi troops (the latter recruited from Pakistan) amounting to some 9600 regulars by 1974. Assisted by about 500 British personnel on secondment or contract, the SAF rapidly became capable of major operations. The pressure on PFLOAG, which at its height mustered 2000 hard-core activists and 4000 part-time militia in 1970-71, was greatly increased by the assistance given to Qaboos by the Shah of Iran and King Hussein of Jordan. An Iranian battlegroup amounting eventually to 2500 men arrived in Dhofar in December 1973, while Jordan sent engineers and, between February and September 1975, the 91st Special Forces Battalion. Jordanian pilots also flew alongside British pilots and Jordan sold Oman a squadron of Hunter jet fighters to supplement the sultan's existing squadron of BAC 167 Strikemasters.

An essential feature of the strategy to defeat PFLOAG after 1970 was the promotion of social and economic development in Dhofar, the campaign being directed by a special Dhofar Development Committee, with military operations being followed up by Civil Aid Department teams. It was quickly realised that a nomadic people would not accept resettlement, but the key to control was water and it became the practice to sink wells. These then became a natural focus for resettlement, and shops (with goods at first given *gratis*), clinics and schools could be gradually introduced. Efforts were also made to develop cattle breeding. As PFLOAG was rent by internal divisions and purges, so guerrillas began to defect, Qaboos' amnesty in 1970 alone resulting in 200 surrenders. These dissidents then became the nucleus of the *firqa*, a kind of sophisticated Home Guard organised by the British SAS. The contribution of the *firqat* (who numbered 3000 by 1975) was immense through their local knowledge and influence over fellow tribesmen. By April 1974 a total of 814 guerrillas had defected to the security forces.

Above: A British Puma helicopter in Belize.

In military terms, the solution to the insurgency was to interdict PFLOAG's supply route from the PDRY. In April 1972 an SAF battalion was dropped by helicopter onto cliffs at Sarfait under which the supply route had to pass, but the sheer escarpment and the early loss of the dominating 'Capstan' feature led to the position being virtually under siege for the next three years. It did, however, absorb much enemy attention and was regularly shelled from inside the PDRY. PFLOAG was still a force to be reckoned with, as its full-scale attack on Mirbat in July 1972 proved, although in this case the attack by 200 guerrillas was beaten off by just ten SAS men with Omani and *asker* (local militia) assistance.

The next attempt to close off infiltration came with the consolidation of a line of pickets between Mughsayl and the sea known as the 'Hornbeam Line'. Extending for 56km (35 miles), the line cut cross the guerrilla supply route about 80km (50 miles) from the PDRY frontier, and although not entirely proof against infiltration, it did prevent PFLOAG's animal-borne supplies from penetrating further east. Pressure was then increased again by the Iranians creating the 'Damavand Line' (named after an Iranian mountain) to the

Below: A patrol moving through a Belizean village.

Above: Patriotic Front guerrillas, armed with Soviet AK-47 assault rifles, pose at one of the CMF assembly points in Rhodesia, 1980.

Left: Major General John Acland (left front), commanding the CMF, with Mr Joshua Nkomo (second from left), leader of the ZAPU/ZIPRA wing of the Patriotic Front, at an assembly area in Rhodesia, January 1980.

north of Rakhyut between December 1973 and November 1974. The pressure now exerted was perhaps reflected in PFLOAG's change of name to the People's Front for the Liberation of Oman (PFLO) in 1974 and its reduction to about 600 hard-core activists.

The creation of obstacles to infiltration now enabled the security forces, commanded at all levels of the SAF by British seconded or contract officers, to clear the areas thus isolated systematically. The first to be tackled was the area between the Hornbeam and Damavand Lines, the Iranians capturing Rakhyut in February 1975. By July the average number of guerrilla defections had doubled from 14 to 29 a month and it was intended to drive a third line of obstacles through to the sea at Dhalqut as soon as the monsoon ended. In the event, intended diversions around Sarfait in October were so successful that the original plan was abandoned in favour of a concerted drive towards the PDRY. It was feared that PDRY artillery fire might interfere with the operation and reports had also been received of SAM-6s being landed in Aden. As a result, air strikes were authorised by the Hunters on Hauf inside the PDRY. These air attacks continued from 17 October until 21 November. A total of 91 guerrillas surrendered in November and a further 107 in December, the war being declared officially over with the capture of the last guerrilla village of Dhalqut on 2 December 1975. The PDRY continued to fire shells into Sarfait until April 1976, but to little effect. In all a total of 35 British servicemen had been killed in the course of one of the most successful counter-insurgency campaigns of modern times. The PDRY, which signed a treaty with the Soviet Union in 1979, remained a threat and British advisers were still serving in Oman in the early 1980s, but there was no denying the reality of a success based upon the methods of counter-insurgency so laboriously perfected by British forces since 1945.

Belize, or British Honduras as it was known prior to June 1973, was more of a long-term commitment, being at risk well before its eventual independence in September 1981 through the claims of its neighbour Guatemala to sovereignty over the country. First settled by British seamen in 1638, rights of settlement along the Belize River had been ceded to Britain by Spain in 1667. The colony was recognised by Spain again in 1763, 1783 and 1802, although it was also attacked by the Spanish on frequent occasions between treaties. Both Mexico and Guatemala subsequently claimed to have inherited a Spanish sovereignty over British Honduras, but this has never had much standing in international law. The United Nations – no friend of colonialism – has continued to vote overwhelmingly for Belize's right to self-determination on every occasion upon which the issue has been raised in the General Assembly since 1945. Mexico recognised the existence of Belize in 1826 and Guatemala accepted a delimited frontier in 1859 but later claimed the convention to be invalid.

The Guatemalan claim was revived in 1936, and after temporary suspension during the Second World War, raised again soon after. In February 1948 it appeared that Guatemala might actually invade, and as a result HMS *Sheffield* was despatched to the colony, followed by HMS *Devonshire* carrying the 2nd Battalion, Gloucestershire Regiment. Nothing materialised, but it was decided to retain a company of British troops in Belize as a deterrent, this being drawn from the garrison battalion at Jamaica until 1962 and thereafter from Britain.

By that time there was a growing nationalist movement in Belize, represented by the People's United Party (PUP), and in 1963 Britain announced that she would introduce self-government. Guatemala immediately broke off diplomatic relations with Britain, although negotiations were opened and the dispute referred by both parties to the United States for mediation in 1965. The plan put forward by an American lawyer, Bethuel Webster, was decisively rejected by the PUP in May 1968, however, since it proposed an association of Belize and Guatemala which amounted to virtual domination by the latter. In January 1972 there was a concentration of Guatemalan forces on the frontier, allegedly for an anti-guerrilla drive. The aircraft carrier HMS *Ark Royal* was at once diverted from a cruise off the United States far enough south to fly off two Buccaneer aircraft to 'show the flag' over Belize. This was not deemed sufficient deterrent and in February *Ark Royal* led a naval task force south for 'manoeuvres' while the 2nd Battalion, Grenadier Guards reinforced the garrison. Guatemala protested to the Organisation of American States (OAS), but an OAS representative confirmed that the doubling of the permanent garrison to two companies could not be regarded as provocative.

Negotiations resumed in February 1975, by which time PUP was demanding full independence and no surrender of Belizean territory or seabed oil deposits. The talks broke down and, with the quadrupling of Guatemalan frontier forces in November 1975, Britain reinforced the garrison to a strength of 1000 men and sent HMS *Zulu* and six Harrier 'jump-jets'. This had the desired effect and the Harriers were withdrawn when negotiations resumed in April 1976. But once again Guatemalan internal politics took on a threatening aspect and the Harriers, additional troops and HMS *Achilles* returned on 5 July 1977. Further negotiations over the next four years reached an agreement on Guatemala recognising Belize's independence in return for access to the sea in March 1981, although this led to riots against the PUP in Belize and a brief state of emergency. The Guatemalans subsequently repudiated the agreement and Belize was granted independence in September 1981 without Guatemalan claims being reconciled. The British garrison was retained for 'an appropriate period' and by 1984, amid speculation that it was to be withdrawn altogether in the near future, still consisted of 1500 men, four Harriers, four Puma helicopters and a guard-ship.

British forces have not just been involved in colonial-type commitments since the late-

06CC65

A watchful patrol of the Queen's Dragoon Guards in East Beirut, 1983.

1960s, however, for operations have also taken place in other countries of the world. In August 1982, for example, a platoon of the Staffordshire Regiment was flown, in civilian clothes with weapons concealed, from Gibraltar to the Gambia to guard RAF Hercules while British residents were evacuated following a coup. More frequently, British forces have assisted in the wake of natural disasters such as the earthquakes in El Salvador (May 1965), Sicily (January 1968) and Iran (September 1968), the floods in Hong Kong (June 1966), Tunisia (September 1969) and East Bengal (November 1970), and the hurricanes in Belize (September 1978) and St Lucia (August 1980). In September 1970 Army medical teams were also flown to Jordan after King Hussein had requested medical support during the fighting between the Jordanian Army and the Palestine Liberation Organisation.

By the end of the war in Oman in 1975 it could, therefore, be seen that the balance of distribution of British servicemen had shifted decisively from a position in 1965-66 where some 28.4 per cent were serving outside Britain and Europe to that of 1974-75 where the equivalent figure, drawn from a smaller overall manpower total, was only 9.8 per cent. The return of a Labour government to power in 1974 also led to a new round of defence cuts aimed at trimming £4.7 billion from the defence budget over a period of ten years. The Mason Defence Review of March 1975, therefore, sought to withdraw all remaining forces from Singapore and Malaysia, the Indian Ocean and the Mediterranean east of Gibraltar, while reducing the garrison at Hong Kong. But Britain still found it difficult to reduce her global commitments to levels commensurate with her resources; a state of affairs which was not eased by her growing involvement in international peacekeeping efforts which required the deployment of troops on the ground.

The first such deployment had been to Cyprus in December 1963, when President Makarios' attempt to alter the constitution agreed between Britain, Greece and Turkey upon Cyprus' independence in 1960 had resulted in Turkish opposition and communal violence. Having retained two Sovereign Base Areas in Cyprus since 1960, British troops were able to move at Makarios' request to separate Greek and Turkish communities in Nicosia and Limassol, establishing the 'Green Line' (so-named from the colour of the chalk used to mark it on British maps) with the assistance of reinforcements flown in from Libya and Britain. It was a difficult role and one gladly handed over to the United Nations' UNFICYP force on 2 March 1964. It is not usual for permanent members of the Security Council to contribute to UN peacekeeping forces, but the presence of British bases on Cyprus made it inevitable on this occasion. Britain, therefore, continued to deploy a contingent of its Cyprus garrison in UN colours. In November 1967 there was further communal violence and troops of the 1st Battalion, Royal Green Jackets on UN duty at the Turkish village of Kophinou were ordered to hand over their weapons by members of the Greek National Guard. All refused to do so and two British soldiers were manhandled by the Greeks. The trouble subsided, but there was violence again in the wake of the National Guard coup against Makarios in July 1974, when the Turkish government in Ankara seized the opportunity to invade the northern half of the island. The UNFICYP role since 1974 has been to attempt to restore normality, for instance by escorting Greek farmers while they reopen fields in disputed areas, and by 1983 some 817 men from the 3500 British troops on Cyprus were still seconded to UNFICYP, responsible for 1300sq km (500sq miles) of territory, including a 40km (25 mile) length of the 'Green Line'.

The second occasion upon which British troops intervened in a peacekeeping role was in the former British colony of Rhodesia, where Britain had enjoyed so little influence at the time of UDI in 1965. Still nominally responsible for the affairs of Rhodesia, Britain organised a conference in London in December 1979 which reached agreement on implementing a ceasefire between the Patriotic Front guerrillas and the multi-racial government of Bishop Muzorewa. When Lord Soames proceeded to Rhodesia as governor, the first elements of a Commonwealth Monitoring Force (CMF) went with him. In all, 159 Australians, 75 New Zealanders, 51 Kenyans, 24 Fijians and 1100 British troops were deployed to supervise the ceasefire and to receive guerrillas at 39 rendezvous points and 14 assembly areas. Deploying on 26/27 December 1979, the CMF handled 20,634 guerrillas by 9 January and there were almost 50,000 in the assembly areas by the time the teams left on 16 March 1980. The CMF also assisted in the election that led to Rhodesia's independence as Zimbabwe on 18 April. A number of British personnel then remained behind as the British Military Advisory and Training Team (BMATT) to attempt to weld a unified army out of former rivals and enemies in the new state. At its height BMATT had 167 men and a smaller number were still there in 1984.

In a sense, Rhodesia/Zimbabwe was precursor to a new kind of peacekeeping force, created in response to the inability of the UN to act in certain crises because of the exercise of the veto in the Security Council. Thus 'multinational forces' have entered the international arena. The first was the Multi-National Peacekeeping Force deployed to Sinai in 1979 to police Israel's disengagement under the terms of the Camp David agreement of the previous year. Consisting of men from 11 different countries with a total strength of 2418, the force arrived in Sinai on 25 April 1982. Britain provides a staff headquarters unit of 35 men at El Gorah, where ceasefire violations between Israel and Egypt are reported by the mutual consent of both countries. Rather different was the Quadripartite Multi-National Intervention Force (MNF) in the Lebanese capital of Beirut. This was requested by the Lebanese government as an inter-positional force designed to separate Moslem and Christian areas, not by mutually agreed diplomacy but by actual military presence. Each contingent had a

Above: Members of the Queen's Dragoon Guards liaise with members of UNIFIL, 1983.

Below: Lieutenant Colonel John Cochrane, Royal Irish Rangers (second from right), the first commander of the British contingent of the MNF, with Lebanese on the roof of the Regie Hadath in Beirut.

Above right: A deceptive calm in a Beirut street as a British patrol of the MNF passes by in their Ferret scout cars.

separate bilateral agreement with the Lebanese government, by which its troops were stationed in Beirut, and each was answerable only to its own ambassador, with no formal coordinating headquarters. Out of 5910 men from the United States, France, Britain and Italy, the British contributed 71 men of the Queen's Dragoon Guards, equipped with Ferret scout cars, and a headquarters and signal section of 29 men. They arrived in February 1983 and were stationed at Regie Hadath in east Beirut's Christian sector for nine months before being relieved by 115 men of the 16th/5th Queen's Royal Lancers and support units. In the wake of renewed inter-communal violence, however, they (together with the US, French and Italian members of the MNF) were withdrawn early in 1984. Multi-national forces have advantages in being quickly deployed if requested, but the Beirut force also showed the potential disadvantages of a force originally intended only as a temporary expedient being drawn into a wider conflict.

Despite the gradual constriction of her commitments, therefore, Britain's forces since the late-1960s have continued to play a substantial role world-wide. In 1984 there were still commitments to two peacekeeping forces (Cyprus and Sinai), advisers in ten countries (Ghana, Kuwait, Mauritius, Nigeria, Oman, Saudi Arabia, Sudan, Swaziland, Uganda and Zimbabwe) and defence agreements with eight (Bahrein, Belize, Cyprus, Kenya, Oman, Qatar, Sri Lanka and the United Arab Emirates). Although Brunei became fully independent in December 1983, the Gurkha battalion deployed there since 1962 will remain. Of Britain's 14 remaining colonial possessions (Anguilla, Bermuda, the British Antarctic Territory, the British Indian Ocean Territory, the British Virgin Islands, the Cayman Islands, the Cyprus Sovereign Base Areas, the Falkland Islands and their dependencies, Gibraltar, Hong Kong, Montserrat, Pitcairn, St Helena and its dependencies and the Turks and Caicos Islands), a total of six – the British Antarctic Territory, Cyprus base areas, the Falkland Islands, Gibraltar, Hong Kong and St Helena's dependency of Ascension Island – still have a military presence. All this is in addition to Northern Ireland, NATO and even the provision of an honour guard to the UN force policing the armistice line in Korea.

Such a continued strain on resources may yet prove too much for Britain's economy to bear. This was shown to particular effect in April 1982, when the Argentinian invasion of the Falklands colony occurred. The legacy of residual commitments, manifested in the need to fight an unexpected and expensive war as well as to increase the garrison once the Falklands had been liberated, still persists.

THE FALKLANDS WAR

By the late 1970s Britain's defence commitments appeared to have settled down into a stable pattern. The long period of strategic uncertainty, characterised by a political reluctance to face the realities of declining world power, had gradually given way to policies which reflected a new orientation towards Europe. Such a reassessment had been occasioned principally by the need to save money, but despite the cuts of the 1960s and 1970s, defence spending continued to be high. When the Conservatives entered office in 1979, a large gap was already opening up between what was needed to satisfy existing defence commitments and what the country could actually afford.

The government responded with a defence review, presented to Parliament on 25 June 1981 by Secretary of State for Defence John Nott. Entitled *The United Kingdom Defence Programme: The Way Forward*, it aimed to close the gap by ridding the armed forces of much of their remaining global capability and tying them more firmly to the NATO area. As both the Army and RAF had been already redeployed to a largely European role in the late 1970s, the main weight of Nott's revision fell inevitably upon the Navy. In future, it was announced, Britain would deploy only two instead of three aircraft carriers and the destroyer/frigate fleet would be cut from 59 to 'about 50' vessels, dedicated to countering the Soviet threat in the eastern Atlantic and Channel. With fewer ships in commission, the size of the Royal Fleet Auxiliary (RFA), responsible for resupplying the fleet at sea, could be reduced, dockyards run down or closed and up to 10,000 sailors made redundant. The financial savings would be considerable.

The full impact of these changes soon became apparent. The amphibious assault ships HMS *Fearless* and *Intrepid* were ordered to be mothballed, the recently completed aircraft carrier HMS *Invincible* was offered to the Australians

Above: Flagship of the Task Force, the anti-submarine carrier HMS *Hermes*.

Right: Assault ship HMS *Fearless*, saved from the scrapyard by the Falklands crisis.

Far right: Valiant class submarine HMS *Conqueror* sails alongside the *Leander* class frigate HMS *Penelope*. Both ships participated in the Falklands War.

Previous page: Scots Guards 'walking wounded' move towards a casevac Scout helicopter on Goat Ridge, after the battle for Tumbledown. An SAS soldier (right), identified by his M16 rifle, inadvertently enters the picture.

Left: Rear Admiral John Forster 'Sandy' Woodward, commander of the Falklands Task Force.

and the anti-submarine carrier HMS *Hermes* was earmarked for reduction. At the same time a whole range of naval-support facilities were run down, while the ice-patrol ship HMS *Endurance* – Britain's only naval vessel on permanent duty in the South Atlantic – was ordered home at the end of her current tour (March 1982) and was not to be replaced. The last vestiges of global capability were fast disappearing.

Britain still retained a small number of overseas possessions and Nott's review, by implying that the government was no longer interested in their protection, left them potentially vulnerable to rival claims. This was particularly the case in the South Atlantic, where British rule over the Falkland Islands, lying 770km (480 miles) north east of Cape Horn, had long been disputed by Argentina. The islands had neither strategic nor economic value – unlike their dependencies of South Georgia and the South Sandwich group to the south east, which gave Britain access to the untapped resources of Antarctica – and diplomatic talks, conducted on a regular basis since 1965, had created an impression that Argentinian demands would be satisfied in the long-term. But the 1800 people of the Falklands, most of whom were of British stock, opposed any transfer of sovereignty and deadlock ensued. By early 1982, frustrated by the delays and aware of British military weakness in the region, the Argentinian ruling junta, led by General Leopoldo Galtieri, resolved to decide the issue by force of arms.

The original intention appears to have been to mount an operation sometime between June and October 1982, after *Endurance* had returned to Britain, but events began to slide into crisis in mid-March when Argentinian scrap-metal workers landed at Leith in South Georgia to dismantle an old whaling station. Their contract had been officially approved, but when they neglected to seek local permission for their landing from British representatives in

Left: Type 42 destroyer HMS *Sheffield* shows her lines. While on radar picket duty to the south of Port Stanley on 4 May 1982, she was hit by an Exocet missile and set ablaze.

Right: Type 42 destroyer HMS *Coventry*, sister-ship to *Sheffield*. She was lost on 25 May 1982, hit by bombs from Argentinian A-4 Skyhawks.

Below: Type 21 frigate HMS *Ardent*, hit by bombs and rockets fired by an Argentinian Aermacchi MB.339 attack plane on 21 May 1982. She burst into flames and had to be abandoned.

Bottom: Royal Fleet Auxiliary stores ship *Resource* at anchor in Falkland Sound, June 1982, indicative of the enormous back-up needed by the Task Force.

South Georgia and insisted on raising the Argentinian flag, *Endurance* was sent to investigate, carrying 23 Royal Marines from the Falklands garrison. Argentinian marines then arrived to protect the workers and Galtieri decided to exploit the confrontation. In late March elements of the Argentinian fleet were diverted from exercises off the coast of Uruguay to attack the Falklands.

The invasion began at 0430 hours (local time) on 2 April, when 150 Argentinian marine commandos landed by helicopter at Mullett Creek, a few miles south-west of the Falklands capital Port Stanley, and marched to attack the Royal Marine barracks (fortunately unoccupied) at Moody Brook, to the west of the town. At 0615 the main Argentinian force began to come ashore at Yorke Bay to the east and the British garrison, numbering only 79 Royal Marines, was caught between two converging groups. As the Marines fell back towards Government House they succeeded in delaying the invaders, killing at least two, but by 0925, with an estimated 2500 Argentinians ashore, Governor Rex Hunt had to accept the inevitable and authorise surrender.

Twenty-four hours later a similar battle took place at Grytviken, South Georgia, defended by the 23 Marines from *Endurance*. Commanded by a lieutenant, this small force held out for about two hours, killing four Argentinians, destroying a helicopter and damaging a corvette before surrendering. The bravery of these men and their colleagues at Port Stanley (all of whom survived to be repatriated) may have been a cause for British pride, but photographs of their surrender hammered home the fact that Britain had suffered a humiliating defeat.

Even so, Galtieri had miscalculated, believing that Britain lacked the resolve to respond to his *fait accompli*, and he was undoubtedly shocked by the nature and speed of the reaction. Diplomatically Britain still retained considerable influence, and this was fully exploited to ensure widespread condemnation of Argentinian actions. As early as 3 April the United Nations Security Council adopted Resolution 502, demanding an immediate Argentinian withdrawal and calling upon both sides to seek a peaceful solution to the crisis. Six days later the EEC agreed to impose trade sanctions upon the aggressor and many Commonwealth countries followed suit. By the end of the month even the United States, caught between two allies and hitherto intent upon an 'even-handed' policy of mediation, had been persuaded to support the British position.

Of far more significance, however, was the decision, finalised on 2 April, to send a task force to the South Atlantic to liberate the islands should other policies fail. If Galtieri had stuck to his original plan, this might have been a difficult decision to execute, for a significant number of ships would no longer have been available because of the Nott review. As it was, *Invincible, Hermes* and *Fearless* were all in home waters and, accompanied by nine destroyers and frigates as well as a number of RFA supply ships, they left Britain on 5 and 6 April, sailing towards Ascension Island in mid-Atlantic. Once there, they were to join ships of the First Flotilla (another seven destroyers and frigates) which had been diverted from Exercise 'Spring Train' in the Mediterranean. Air support was to be provided by 22 Sea Harrier V/STOL (vertical/short take-off and landing) fighter aircraft on board the carriers. On 7 April, as the task force began to take shape under the command of Rear Admiral J F 'Sandy' Woodward, it was announced that a 200-nautical-mile Maritime Exclusion Zone (MEZ) would be imposed around the Falklands from 0400 hours GMT on the 12th. By then, three nuclear-powered submarines, ordered to the South Atlantic in late March when the South Georgia crisis first developed, would be on station to deter Argentinian naval movement within the specified zone.

Naval and air forces alone could never re-occupy the islands and a military contingent was essential. It was centred upon 3rd Commando Brigade under Brigadier Julian Thompson, and its normal constituents – 40, 42 and 45 Commando, Royal Marines, with supporting arms – were reinforced for the purposes of the task force by 2nd and 3rd Battalions, Parachute Regiment (2 and 3 Para) from 5th Infantry Brigade. Together with artillery, engineers and light armour (four Scorpion and four Scimitar light tanks from two troops of the Blues and Royals), as well as elements of the Special Air Service (SAS) and its naval equivalent the Special Boat Squadron (SBS), they boarded a variety of transports in early April. Some units travelled south from Britain in naval vessels, but the sheer number of men involved required the provision of extra transport capability. On 4 April an Order-in-Council authorised the Ministry of Defence to requisition civilian ships and among the first was the P and O liner *Canberra*, hastily modified to carry 40 and 42 Commando, plus 3 Para and supporting units. She set sail on 9 April, to be followed four days later by the ferry *Norland* with 2 Para aboard. These ships represented a process of requisition and charter, known as STUFT (ships taken up from trade), which was eventually to affect 50 merchant vessels. It was one of the most remarkable aspects of the Falklands campaign, helping to create an almost continuous supply and transport chain between Britain and the South Atlantic, a distance of 12,870km (8000 miles), supported only as far as Ascension by C-130 Hercules and VC-10 air transports.

The aim of the task force was to exert increasing pressure upon the Argentinians, preparatory to a campaign of liberation under the codename Operation 'Corporate'. The process began on 21 April when Task Force 317 – the destroyer *Antrim*, frigate *Plymouth*, *Endurance* and RFA *Tidespring*, with SAS, SBS and Marines on board – approached South Georgia. Initial attempts to establish covert reconnaissance teams ashore were thwarted by the appalling weather – on 22 April, for example, an SAS Mountain Troop had to be evacuated from the Fortuna Glacier to the north of Leith, with the loss of two Wessex helicopters – but the size and deployment of the Argentinian garrison was observed. Preparations for a landing were being made when, early on 25 April, the Argentinian submarine *Santa Fé* was spotted on the surface, sailing away from Grytviken. She was engaged by helicopters from Task Force 317 (which by now included the destroyer *Brilliant*) and hit by AS-12 air-to-surface missiles. As she limped back into harbour, the British decided to exploit their success. A scratch force of 75 Marines, SAS and SBS was landed by helicopter close to

A386
FORT AUSTIN

Grytviken at 1445 hours and, after a display of naval gunfire designed to demoralise rather than kill, the main body of Argentinians surrendered. Early the next morning (26 April) a small detachment at Leith followed suit, leaving the British with 156 prisoners and possession of the island for no loss of life.

But South Georgia was of only marginal strategic value, for although its reoccupation undoubtedly dealt a blow to enemy morale, it did little to solve the problems facing the British in their main task of liberating the Falklands. As Woodward's battle group sailed into the MEZ in late April, it entered an area in which Argentinian forces were potentially strong. The Argentinian Navy, with its one aircraft carrier, one cruiser, eight destroyers, three corvettes and (after South Georgia) three diesel-powered submarines, may have been outnumbered by a task force which was eventually to involve 39 warships, but its existence posed a constant threat, particularly to the British carriers. If they had been damaged or lost, the task force could not have continued to operate, for without its integral air cover it would have been dangerously vulnerable to attacks by the Argentinian Air Force. As it was, despite British confidence in the combination of Sea Harriers and shipborne surface-to-air missiles (SAMs), the task force faced a formidable total of nine B62 Canberra bombers, 82 A-4 Skyhawk fighter-bombers, 10 Super Etendard strike aircraft and 47 Mirage III or Dagger interceptors/ground attack machines, all of which enjoyed the advantage of operating from mainland bases. Finally, with an estimated 10,000 Argentinian troops on the Falklands, supported by 15 IA-58 Pucara counter-insurgency aircraft and a host of light machines and helicopters, it was obvious that the islands themselves were not going to be easy to retake.

Woodward's first priority was to establish at least a degree of naval and air control, for without this a landing could be suicidal. On 30 April, therefore, he imposed a Total Exclusion Zone (TEZ) around the Falklands, through which neither air nor sea craft would be allowed to pass, and began a policy of steady pressure upon the enemy garrison. At 0423 hours on 1 May a Vulcan bomber, having flown 5550km (3450 miles) from Ascension, dropped 21×454kg (1000lb) bombs onto Stanley airfield. Only one of the bombs actually hit the runway – Argentinian C-130s continued to use it throughout the war – but the fact that Britain was willing and able to carry out such a difficult attack deeply affected the enemy. The raid, which took over 15 hours and 17 in-flight refuelling operations to complete under the codename 'Black Buck I' (a further four such raids were to be completed before the end of the campaign), was followed at dawn by Sea Harrier low-level attacks. The Argentinian air response was effectively contained, with two Mirages and a Canberra being shot down.

Almost immediately, however, the scale of the fighting intensified as a naval threat to the task force materialised. As early as 26 April two Argentinian battle groups – one containing the carrier *Veinticinco de Mayo* and the other the cruiser *General Belgrano* – began to converge on the exclusion zone from north and south respectively. In the event the carrier group remained within range of shore-based air cover, but the *General Belgrano*, with two destroyer escorts, continued to skirt the southern fringes of the TEZ. When the ships approached to within 60 nautical miles of the task force, HM Submarine *Conqueror* was authorised to attack. At 1500 hours on 2 May, actually out-

Above: RFA stores ship *Fort Austin* at anchor, showing her helicopter flight decks to advantage. Full helicopter hangar and maintenance facilities exist on board and up to four Sea Kings can be carried for the movement of stores.

Left: Flight deck of HMS *Hermes*, taken from half way up the 'ski-jump', looking aft. Harrier 'jump-jets' and Sea King helicopters are on show.

Right: RFA tanker *Tidespring* refuels the requisitioned P&O liner *Canberra* during the journey towards the South Atlantic. The two helicopter landing pads, hastily added in early April 1982, may be seen on *Canberra*'s deck, together with stores.

Left: Wasp helicopter from HMS *Endurance* over Grytviken harbour, South Georgia, late April 1982. The conning tower of the Argentinian submarine *Santa Fé* – damaged by missiles from the same Wasp on 25 April – dominates the scene.

Right: A close-up of the *Santa Fé*. Caught on the surface and hit by AS-12 missiles early on 25 April, she limped into harbour and ran aground.

Centre right: Lieutenant Commander Alfredo Astiz (left) of the Argentinian Navy signs the surrender document for South Georgia on board the Type 12 frigate HMS *Plymouth*, 26 April 1982. He is watched (L to R, opposite) by Captains N J Barker of *Endurance* and D Pentreath of *Plymouth*.

Bottom right: Map showing the position of the Falkland Islands, together with the extent of the MEZ/TEZ. The relative proximity of Argentinian air bases is clear.

Below: Map showing the British operations on the Falklands, 15 May-8 June 1982. Note the distance of the landing beaches at San Carlos from the main Argentinian positions at Port Stanley.

side the TEZ, she fired a pattern of Mark 8 torpedoes, two of which struck the *General Belgrano*. Her steering wrecked, the cruiser gradually listed to port and sank, with the loss of 368 of her crew. It was a stunning blow to the Argentinian Navy and when, on 3 May, the patrol boat *Comodoro Somellera* was destroyed by helicopters within the TEZ, it was clear that the British held the upper hand. Thereafter, the Argentinians were to keep their major surface vessels safely in port.

If the naval threat to the task force had been countered, that from the air force had not, as events on 4 May were to show. At about 1000 hours Super Etendards, flying low and fast to escape radar detection, launched two Exocet sea-skimming missiles towards the carrier *Hermes*, stationed some 60 nautical miles to the south of Port Stanley. One failed to find a target but the other homed in on HMS *Sheffield*, a Type 42 destroyer on radar picket duty ahead of the carrier. The missile hit amidships and, although the warhead itself may not have exploded, the impact was enough to start fires which soon ran out of control. Twenty sailors died and *Sheffield* had to be abandoned. To the British forces and the public at home, the war was suddenly very real.

The loss of *Sheffield* highlighted certain weaknesses of the task force. Ship-borne radars were clearly inadequate, at least against Exocet; there were insufficient Sea Harriers to protect the ships and no early-warning aircraft with the fleet; Sea Dart SAMs on board *Sheffield* had failed to stop the incoming missile and, once hit, the destroyer had burned with frightening speed and intensity. In response, Woodward was forced to change his deployment, withdrawing the carriers to the east, beyond the range of enemy air attack, and using other ships to police the TEZ. Some success was achieved – on 9 May, for example, the Argentinian intelligence trawler *Narwal* was attacked and her crew captured – but the price continued to be high. On 12 May the destroyer *Glasgow* came under sustained attack from Argentinian Skyhawks, and although three were shot down, the ship was so badly damaged that she had to withdraw from the task force. By then it was obvious that Britain was engaged in a war of attrition which, far from home and with winter approaching, she would have difficulty in winning. Despite the lack of guaranteed air and naval supremacy, a landing on the Falklands was essential if the campaign was to be concluded quickly.

The problems were daunting. According to the accepted 'rules of war', the British needed a 3:1 advantage in men and equipment to take on an enemy force in prepared positions, and this

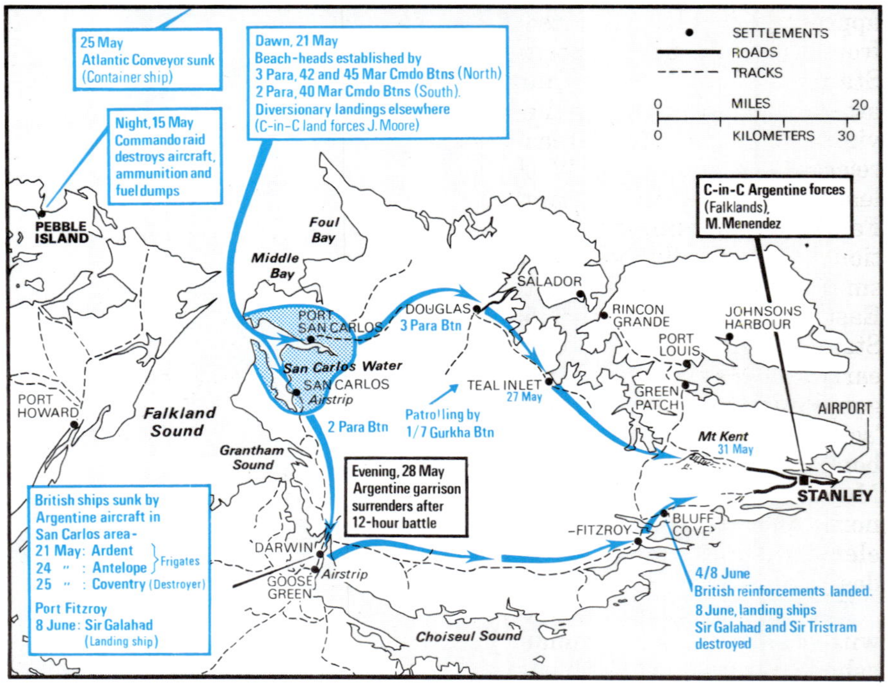

they did not have. Even when 3rd Commando Brigade was followed to the South Atlantic on 12 May by Brigadier Tony Wilson's 5th Infantry Brigade (by now comprising 2nd Battalion Scots Guards, 1st Battalion Welsh Guards and 1st Battalion 7th Gurkha Rifles, plus supporting arms) on board the requisitioned Cunard liner *Queen Elizabeth II*, the recently appointed land commander, Major General Jeremy Moore, could only equal the forces of the Argentinian garrison. In addition, a landing site with good beaches and deep-water approaches had to be selected, far enough away from the main enemy positions around Port Stanley to preclude an immediate counter-attack yet close enough to the town to make it a viable objective. Some areas could be quickly rejected – a landing on West Falkland would lead nowhere, while the southern part of East Falkland (Lafonia) was too exposed – and attention was gradually focused upon San Carlos, a small settlement on the northwestern coast of East Falkland, about 80km (50 miles) from Port Stanley. SAS and SBS teams, put ashore as early as 1 May, provided the necessary intelligence and the enemy garrison as a whole was 'softened up', chiefly by air attacks and naval bombardments but also, on the night of 14/15 May, by an SAS raid on Pebble Island, off the north east coast of West Falkland, in which eleven aircraft (including six Pucaras) were destroyed.

The landings began at 0400 hours on 21 May, with 2 Para and 40 Commando (the latter led ashore by a troop of the Blues and Royals) secur-

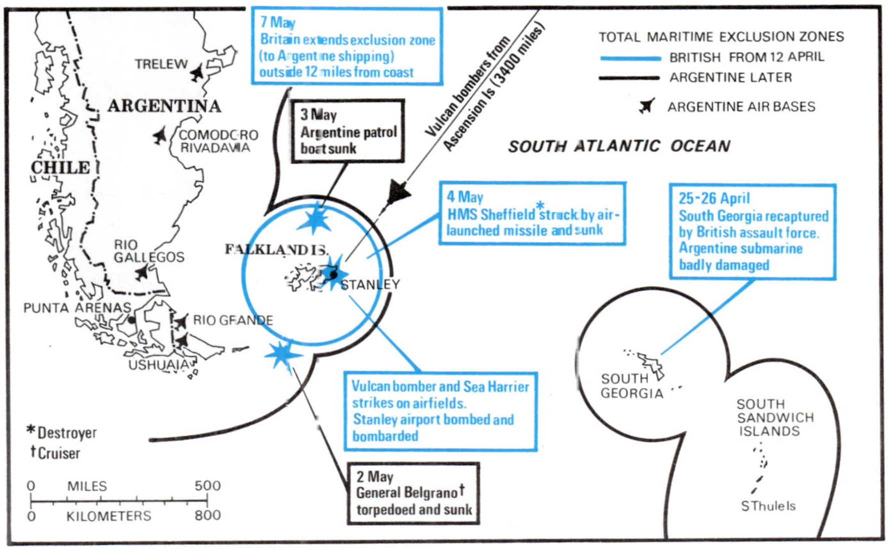

ing Blue Beach One and Blue Beach Two to the north of San Carlos settlement, on the British right. The troops immediately pushed inland to take the high ground of the Sussex and Verde Mountains, protecting the beach-head from attack by a small enemy garrison known to be at Goose Green to the south. Meanwhile, 45 Commando landed on Red Beach One at Ajax Bay, also on the right, and 3 Para, accompanied by the rest of the Blues and Royals and followed, at 1000 hours, by 42 Commando, came ashore on Green Beach One, east of Port San Carlos on the left. Once these units were ashore, priority was given to 105mm guns and Rapier SAMs of the Royal Artillery, the latter being rushed forward to set up an air-defence screen. By midday, for the loss of only two helicopters and three men, 3rd Commando Brigade was established ashore in a beach-head covering some 26sq km (10sq miles) and was frantically digging-in, expecting an immediate enemy response.

Fortunately for the British, the Argentinian commander on the Falklands, General Mario Menendez, decided not to send his troops (many of whom were unreliable conscripts) to oppose the landing, preferring to leave that task to the air force. The first air attacks were mounted at about 0930 on 21 May, heralding a conflict which was to last for five days with substantial losses on both sides. The Argentinians – perhaps mistakenly – concentrated upon the invasion fleet and, as wave after wave of Skyhawks and Mirages pressed home low-level attacks, they succeeded in causing considerable damage. On 21 May the frigate *Ardent* was hit by bombs and abandoned, the frigate *Argonaut* was badly damaged and the destroyers *Antrim, Broadsword* and *Brilliant* were all hit. Three days later *Ardent*'s sister-ship *Antelope* exploded spectacularly in San Carlos Water; on 25 May the destroyer *Coventry* was lost and the requisitioned Cunard containership *Atlantic Conveyor*, loaded with supplies and Chinook heavy-lift helicopters, fell victim to an Exocet. Many other ships were hit, often by poorly fused bombs which failed to explode, and by 25 May the task force was reeling.

By then, however, the Argentinian Air Force had been very badly mauled, losing about a third of its Skyhawk/Mirage fleet to a combination of Harriers and air-defence weapon systems. Just before the San Carlos landings, the task force had received an additional 20 Harriers (six Sea Harriers and 14 RAF GR3 variants), enabling forward air patrols to be mounted on a regular basis, and it was these that caught many of the enemy aircraft flying towards or away from the invasion fleet. In ensuing air-to-air battles the Argentinian machines proved no match for the Harriers, the pilots of which used the unique variable-thrust engines of the V/STOL design to gain remarkable manoeuvrability, enabling them to fire cannon and AIM-9L Sidewinder missiles to devastating effect. Moreover, those Mirages and Skyhawks which did manage to reach San Carlos Water met such a hail of SAMs and machine-gun fire that few survived. The damage to British ships was certainly severe but by 25 May, with no Harriers lost in aerial combat, a measure of air supremacy had been achieved.

3rd Commando Brigade was now free to break out from the beach-head, and late on 27 May 3 Para and 45 Commando left San Carlos to march across the northern part of East Falkland towards Argentinian positions around Port Stanley. At the same time 2 Para, commanded by Lieutenant Colonel 'H' Jones, prepared to secure the southern flank of the

Below: As a Sea King approaches to pick up the injured, *Sheffield* burns, 4 May 1982. The impact-point of the Exocet and the already-raging fires may be seen, together with the rather puny fire-fighting capability remaining once the ship had been hit. Twenty sailors died in the action.

advance by mounting a night attack upon the Argentinian garrison (estimated to contain about 500 men) at Darwin and Goose Green on the narrow isthmus connecting the two portions of the island. This began at 0235 hours (local time) on 28 May and initially slow but steady progress was made. On the east coast of the isthmus 'A' Company advanced as far as the slopes of Darwin Hill, while on the west coast 'B' Company fought through prepared enemy defences towards Boca House.

But at first light the tempo of the battle changed. The paras, short of ammunition and denied air support because of poor weather, were pinned down in exposed positions by Argentinian machine guns and artillery. The situation was especially bad around Darwin Hill, where 'A' Company, reinforced by 'C' Company and Jones' TAC HQ, could make little headway. As casualties mounted, Jones rushed forward against a particularly troublesome enemy position. He was shot down by a sniper but his act of exceptional bravery (for which he was to be awarded a posthumous Victoria Cross) helped to break the deadlock. Argentinian defences in this sector crumbled in the face of fierce close-quarter attacks, enabling Jones' successor, Major Chris Keeble, to turn his attention to the west, where 'B' Company was still pinned down in front of Boca House. He sent 'D' Company along the shoreline to outflank the Argentinian position and by 1115, after a co-ordinated two-company assault, success was achieved. 'B' and 'D' Companies were immediately directed to swing east towards Goose Green, while 'A' and 'C' Companies consolidated their hold on Darwin Hill and cleared Darwin settlement. 'C' and 'D' Companies linked up during the afternoon and took School House, to the north of Goose Green, while Harriers swept in through clearing skies to destroy Argentinian artillery positions. By nightfall 2 Para, having suffered 17 dead and 35 wounded, had the enemy contained.

Early next morning (29 May) Keeble offered surrender terms and, to his relief, these were accepted. It was only as some 1200 Argentinians emerged to lay down their arms that the true nature of the paras' victory became apparent. A battalion of 450 fighting men had taken on and defeated a defending force about three times its number. It was a remarkable achievement which gave the British troops a moral ascendancy they were not to lose.

No less remarkable was the concurrent advance by 3 Para and 45 Commando, for by 30 May they had reached Douglas and Teal Inlet after a march of about 50km (32 miles) over

Above: 'Bomb Alley', San Carlos Water, 22 May 1982. Argentinian bombs explode amidst the invasion fleet – (L to R) requisitioned ferry *Norland* and assault ship HMS *Intrepid.*

Below: A Sea Harrier FRS1 of No 809 Naval Air Squadron prepares to land on the container ship *Atlantic Conveyor.* The 'open hangar', made up of stores containers, shelters Chinook and Wessex helicopters. Only one Chinook was to survive when the ship was hit by an Exocet and sunk on 25 May 1982.

Above: A Sea King helicopter, orange flotation bags inflated and crew taking to a rubber dinghy, lies ditched in calm seas. The first Task Force loss was a crewman on a Sea King from *Hermes*, ditched in this manner on 23 April.

Below: Type 42 destroyer HMS *Coventry* lies blazing after being bombed by Argentinian aircraft to the north of Falkland Sound, 25 May 1982. She was abandoned with the loss of 17 crew.

exceptionally difficult terrain in deteriorating weather conditions. On 31 May 3 Para pushed on to secure Estancia House and high ground to the north east, while elements of the SAS and 42 Commando, in a dramatic heliborne operation, established positions on top of Mount Kent, only 19km (12 miles) from Port Stanley. The remainder of 42 Commando moved up to occupy Mount Challenger by 5 June, while 45 Commando dug in to the west of Mount Kent, leaving a disgruntled 40 Commando to guard the San Carlos beach-head.

Meanwhile 5th Infantry Brigade had arrived at San Carlos on 1 June, bringing with them Major General Moore to assume overall command. He decided to use Wilson's three battalions, with 2 Para temporarily attached, to open up a southern route of advance, through Fitzroy and Bluff Cove. 1/7th Gurkhas marched to relieve 2 Para at Goose Green on 2 June, whereupon the paras spearheaded a rapid advance by helicopter, first to Swan Inlet and then, on 4 June, to Fitzroy, only 32km (20 miles) from Port Stanley. Wilson now faced the problem of reinforcing this advance and, with the shortage of helicopters caused by the loss of *Atlantic Conveyor*, he decided to move the Guards round by sea. On the night of 5/6 June, in appalling weather conditions, the Scots Guards were offloaded from *Intrepid* at Bluff Cove, to be followed 24 hours later by the Welsh Guards on board *Fearless*. Unfortunately only two companies could be landed before *Fearless* had to return to the safety of San Carlos at dawn and the remaining Welshmen were transferred to the landing ship RFA *Sir Galahad*. Early on 8 June she sailed round to Fitzroy, where her sister-ship *Sir Tristram* was already offloading ammunition, only to find that no-one was expecting her. Confusion led to delays and the Guards were still on board at 1310 hours when two Mirages and two Skyhawks suddenly attacked. Denied air cover (a Harrier combat air patrol had been diverted to protect the frigate *Plymouth*, badly damaged by bombs at about the same time), the landing ships were extremely vulnerable. *Sir Tristram* was wrecked and *Sir Galahad* set ablaze: 51 servicemen, including 33 Welsh Guards, were killed.

Left: Members of 3 Para on board a landing craft leave *Intrepid* to go ashore at Green Beach, Port San Carlos, 21 May 1982. Delayed by difficulties of disembarkation, 3 Para landed at 0930 hours, cleared Port San Carlos and moved against Argentinian positions around Fanning Head.

Below left: A Royal Marine aims his Blowpipe SAM from the shelter of a timber sangar overlooking San Carlos Water, late-May 1982. Blowpipe is heavy and of only limited use against fast jets, although on East Falkland it proved of value against Pucaras and helicopters.

Below: A landing craft, painted in a distinctive camouflage pattern, delivers stores to Green Beach Two, San Carlos, late-May 1982.

But Moore refused to allow the tragedy to disrupt his final assault on Port Stanley. Since 4 June all available helicopters had been used to ferry artillery and supplies to the front-line. By the 11th five batteries, each of six 105mm guns, had been deployed in an arc to the west of Mount Kent with enough ammunition to provide each gun with 1200 rounds. The projected offensive against the series of rock features protecting Port Stanley was to enjoy the benefit of massive artillery support in an effort to neutralise defensive positions which the 8400-man enemy garrison had spent two months preparing.

The first phase of the offensive was carried out by 3rd Commando Brigade on the night of 11/12 June, with the overall aim of seizing hills to the east of Mount Kent. In the south, 42 Commando worked stealthily around Mount Harriet, attacking from the east in a move which took them to within 90m (100 yards) of

Left: The hulk of the *Sir Galahad* lies in Fitzroy Cove, the bodies of 33 Welsh Guardsmen still on board. She was later towed out to deep water and sunk as a war grave.

Right: Chinook helicopter 'Bravo November' – the only survivor from *Atlantic Conveyor* – lifts supplies forward on East Falkland.

Top, far right: The British commanders, (L to R) Brigadier Wilson, 5th Infantry Brigade; Brigadier Thompson, 3rd Commando Brigade; and Major General Moore, land force commander.

Bottom right: Map: The Battle of Goose Green, 28/29 May 1982.

Below right: A sapper from 59 Independent Commando Squadron, Royal Engineers, lifts a Spanish C3B anti-tank mine. The indiscriminate laying of mines by the Argentinians poses problems which persist to the present day.

Below: Fire-fighters on board the *Sir Tristram.* Although badly damaged, she was later salvaged.

the summit before the Argentinians reacted. Thereafter the fighting was hard but the objective was secured for the loss of only one Marine killed and 13 wounded. Casualties were heavier to the north, where 45 Commando seized Two Sisters for the loss of four dead and eight wounded after fierce fighting against well-protected Argentinian machine guns and snipers.

The toughest battle of the night belonged to 3 Para, even further to the north on Mount Longdon. Their attempt at a silent approach ended abruptly when one of the paras stepped on a mine and for nearly 10 hours they were forced to fight for the mountain inch by inch. 'A' Company was pinned down by extremely accurate sniper fire (the Argentinians, unlike the British, had ample stocks of night-vision equipment) and, as 'B' Company tried to relieve the pressure, the battle devolved into a series of section firefights. Using anti-tank missiles, grenades, close artillery support and even bayonets, the paras gradually gained the upper hand, but the cost was high. By dawn on 12 June 3 Para had lost 23 dead (including Sergeant Ian McKay, whose bravery in tackling a machine-gun nest was to earn the second Victoria Cross of the campaign) and 47 wounded. The night's

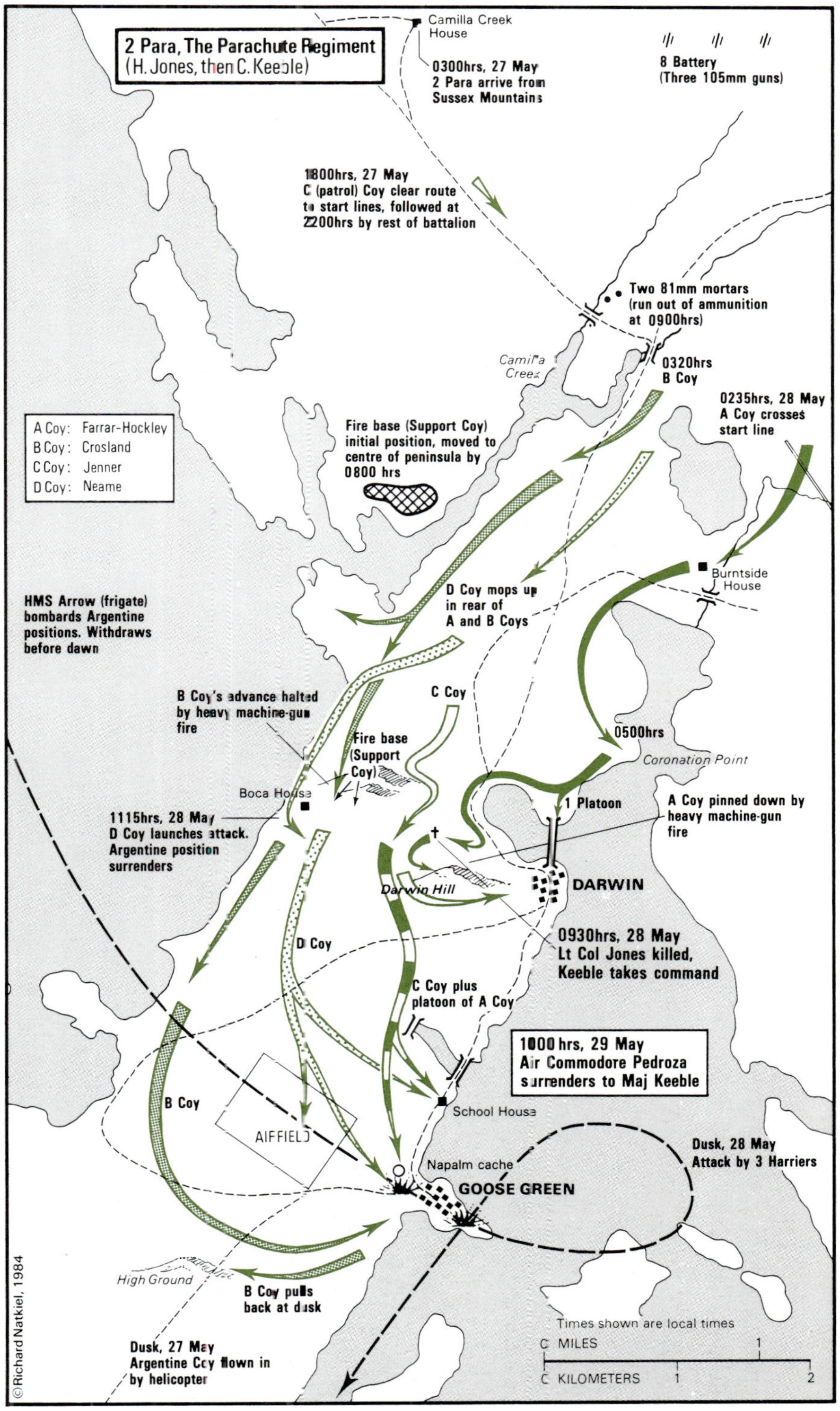
2 Para, The Parachute Regiment
(H. Jones, then C. Keeble)
Camilla Creek House
0300hrs, 27 May
2 Para arrive from
Sussex Mountains
8 Battery
(Three 105mm guns)
1800hrs, 27 May
C (patrol) Coy clear route
to start lines, followed at
2200hrs by rest of battalion
Two 81mm mortars
(run out of ammunition
at 0900hrs)
Camilla Creek
0320hrs
B Coy
0235hrs, 28 May
A Coy crosses
start line
A Coy: Farrar-Hockley
B Coy: Crosland
C Coy: Jenner
D Coy: Neame
Fire base (Support Coy)
initial position, moved to
centre of peninsula by
0800 hrs
Burntside House
D Coy mops up
in rear of
A and B Coys
HMS Arrow (frigate)
bombards Argentine
positions. Withdraws
before dawn
C Coy
B Coy's advance halted
by heavy machine-gun
fire
0500hrs
Fire base
(Support
Coy)
Coronation Point
Boca House
1 Platoon
A Coy pinned down by
heavy machine-gun
fire
1115hrs, 28 May
D Coy launches attack.
Argentine position
surrenders
Darwin Hill
DARWIN
D Coy
0930hrs, 28 May
Lt Col Jones killed,
Keeble takes command
C Coy plus
platoon of A Coy
1000 hrs, 29 May
Air Commodore Pedroza
surrenders to Maj Keeble
B Coy
School House
AIRFIELD
Dusk, 28 May
Attack by 3 Harriers
Napalm cache
GOOSE GREEN
High Ground
B Coy pulls
back at dusk
Times shown are local times
0 MILES 1
0 KILOMETERS 1 2
Dusk, 27 May
Argentine Coy flown in
by helicopter
©Richard Natkiel, 1984

Left: LCM9s from HMS *Fearless* return to UK, carrying the Scimitar and Scorpion light AFVs of B Squadron, the Blues and Royals. Landed at San Carlos on 21 May, the AFVs proved useful in the infantry support role, particularly at the battle for Wireless Ridge on 13/14 June 1982.

Right: The image of the Falklands Task Force: two Royal Marines, faces streaked with camouflage cream and carrying belts for the 7.62mm GPMG, prepare to confront the enemy, May 1982.

Below: Sea King helicopters pick up troops in the typically desolate terrain of East Falkland. The shortage of helicopters with the Task Force, particularly after the loss of *Atlantic Conveyor*, was keenly felt.

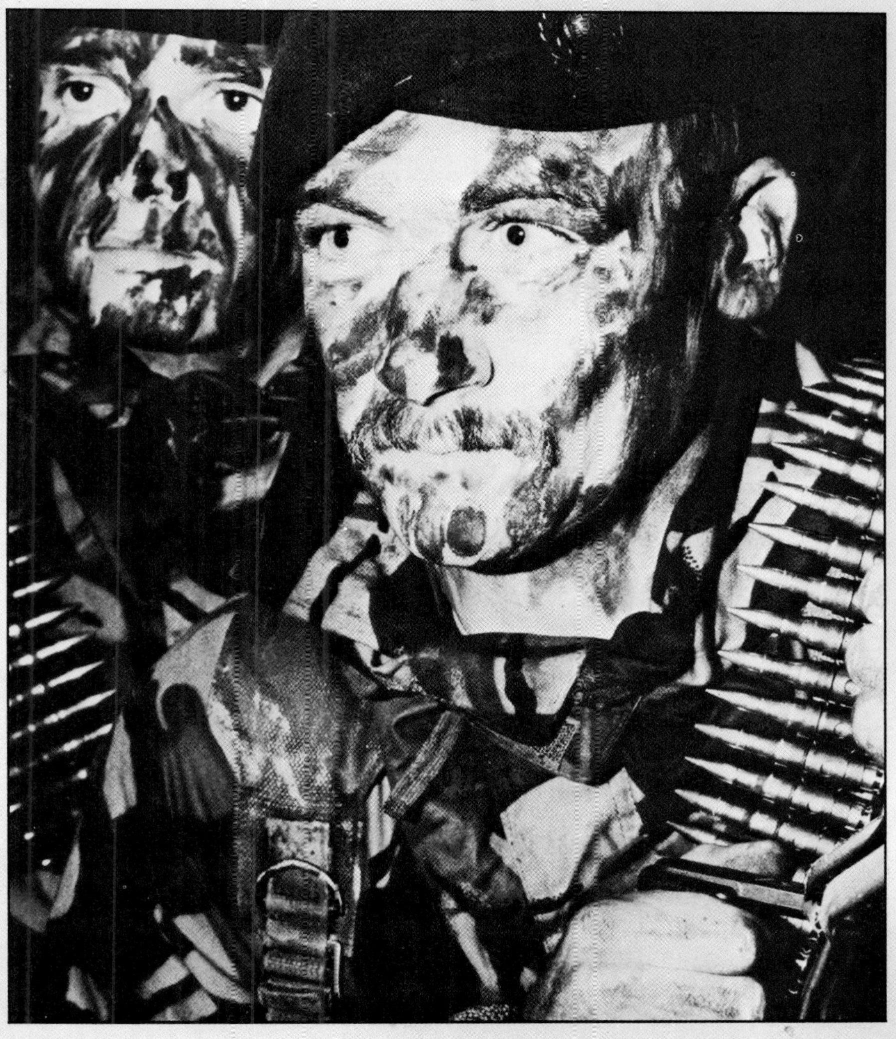

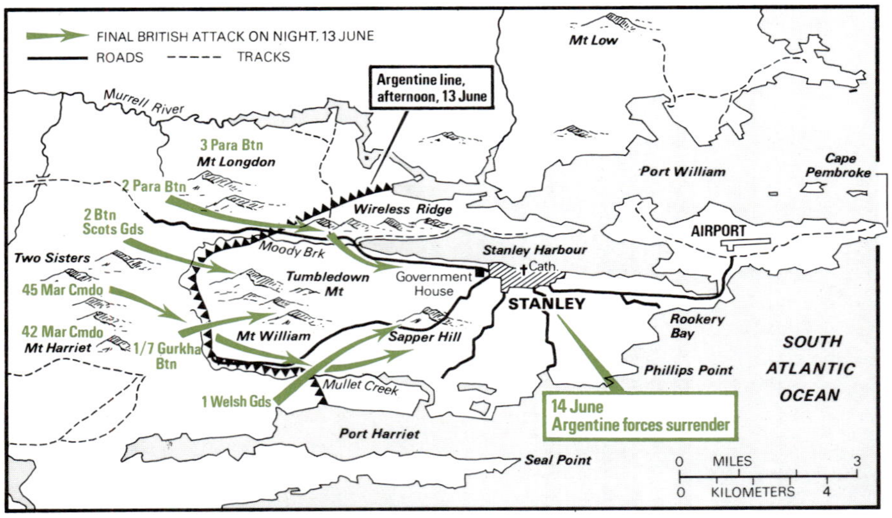

casualties were further increased when it was learnt that a land-based Exocet had hit the destroyer *Glamorgan*, engaged in providing naval gunfire support to the land forces, at 0235. Thirteen of her crew were killed.

5th Infantry Brigade should have pushed straight through to the next line of high ground, but poor weather and a shortage of helicopters forced a 24-hour delay. Late on 13 June the Scots Guards resumed the offensive with a silent approach towards Tumbledown, to the east of Two Sisters. They managed to reach the base of the mountain before being spotted, but then faced a barrage of defensive fire from Argentinian marines who had no intention of withdrawing. The ensuing battle was similar to that on Mount Longdon two nights before, with section firefights to dislodge snipers and machine-gun crews who pinned the Guardsmen down. It took six hours for men of the left flank company to reach the summit at the point of the bayonet. By dawn on 14 June the battalion had lost nine men dead and 43 wounded.

Meanwhile 2 Para to the north had captured Wireless Ridge in a totally different type of battle. Not wishing to repeat the attrition of Goose Green, they approached their objective at 2030 hours on 13 June behind a devastating concentration of firepower. Over 6000 rounds of artillery ammunition, supplemented by naval gunfire and 76mm shells from light tanks of the Blues and Royals, swamped the Argentinian positions, enabling the paras to seize the ridge at a cost of only three dead and eight wounded. It was the last piece of high ground to the north of Port Stanley. Further south, 1/7th Gurkhas exploited the success of the Scots Guards by taking Mount William, while the Welsh Guards (reinforced by men of 40 Commando from San Carlos) secured Sapper Hill, and it soon became apparent that the Argentinians had suffered enough. White flags began to appear among the Argentinian positions and General Menendez agreed to negotiate.

The surrender document was signed at 2100 hours on 14 June, ending a war which had lasted less than three months. In the process the British had lost 255 dead and 777 wounded, but had gained a notable victory. By comparison the Argentinians had lost over 1000 dead and 11,400 captured and had gained nothing.

Top left: Map of the advance on Port Stanley.

Left: A Royal Marine guards Argentinian prisoners, 14 June 1982.

Below left: Some of the 11,400 prisoners, on the waterfront at Port Stanley, June 1982.

Bottom left: Marines of 45 Commando enter Port Stanley, 14 June 1982.

Right: The surrender document.

Bottom right: HMS *Hermes* comes home to Portsmouth.

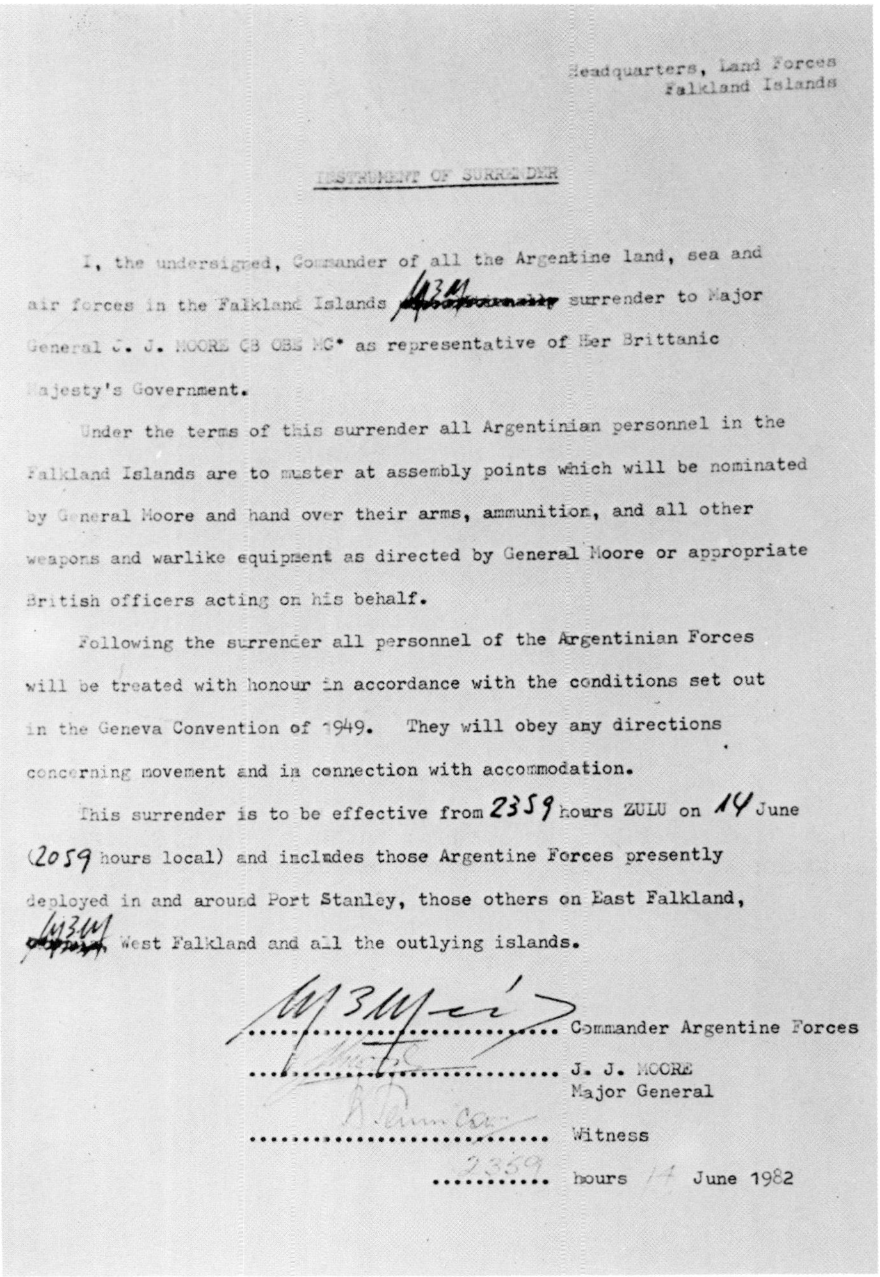

Headquarters, Land Forces
Falkland Islands

INSTRUMENT OF SURRENDER

I, the undersigned, Commander of all the Argentine land, sea and air forces in the Falkland Islands ~~unconditionally~~ surrender to Major General J. J. MOORE CB OBE MC* as representative of Her Brittanic Majesty's Government.

Under the terms of this surrender all Argentinian personnel in the Falkland Islands are to muster at assembly points which will be nominated by General Moore and hand over their arms, ammunition, and all other weapons and warlike equipment as directed by General Moore or appropriate British officers acting on his behalf.

Following the surrender all personnel of the Argentinian Forces will be treated with honour in accordance with the conditions set out in the Geneva Convention of 1949. They will obey any directions concerning movement and in connection with accommodation.

This surrender is to be effective from 2359 hours ZULU on 14 June (2059 hours local) and includes those Argentine Forces presently deployed in and around Port Stanley, those others on East Falkland, ~~and~~ West Falkland and all the outlying islands.

.... Commander Argentine Forces

.... J. J. MOORE
Major General

.... Witness

2359 hours 14 June 1982

XZ286

PROSPECTS FOR THE FUTURE

The liberation of the Falklands in 1982 was a remarkable achievement. At a political level it represented a degree of resolve virtually unprecedented in the post-1945 period, and this was strengthened by diplomatic moves which indicated that Britain, despite a relative decline in world power, still retained considerable influence. Of equal significance, the successful projection of military power into the vastness of the South Atlantic showed that Britain continued to deploy extremely effective armed forces. The creation and maintenance of the task force was a minor miracle of efficiency, flexibility and improvisation; the reoccupation of the Falklands in the face of an enemy garrison in prepared defensive positions, backed by air and naval units operating close to their home bases, was a tribute to the professionalism, bravery and expertise of armed forces which had suffered over 20 years of economic constraint and strategic uncertainty. Not that the outcome of the conflict was ever a foregone conclusion; however easy it may seem in retrospect to isolate the mistakes and misjudgements of an Argentinian junta desperate for prestige and popular acclaim, in the end the war was won through hard fighting and the application of superior military skills.

Yet the fact remains that the Falklands operation was an anachronism, displaying political and military responses which owed more to the traditions of colonial policing than to the new realities of European commitment. Operation 'Corporate' seemed to suggest that Britain was still dedicated to exerting her military influence on a global scale, in protection of far-flung overseas possessions, but by the early 1980s this was quite clearly not the case. As early as 1956 the Suez crisis and its outcome had shown that the idea of pursuing independent global policies in a world dominated by the superpowers was fraught with danger, particularly if the country was dependent upon one of those superpowers for strategic protection and economic support. This may not have been recognised immediately – Duncan Sandys' defence review of April 1957, with its attempt to disguise the problems of overstretch beneath a mantle of new technology certainly avoided the issue – but as economic pressures increased and the inevitability of decolonisation was accepted, changes were gradually introduced. The process began in the late 1960s with Secretary of State for Defence Denis Healey's announcement that military garrisons were to be withdrawn from east of Suez, and was taken one stage further in 1975 when his colleague and

Previous page: An RAF Nimrod long-range maritime airborne early warning aircraft, with distinctive nose and tail-mounted radar fit. The lack of early-warning aircraft with the Falklands Task Force in 1982 has led to a new emphasis on this capability.

Below: HMS *Boxer*, a 'stretched' Type 22 *Broadsword* class destroyer, armed with Exocet and Sea Wolf missile systems. Completed in 1983, *Boxer* is one of five new Type 22s currently on order for the Royal Navy.

successor Roy Mason committed Britain's main defence effort firmly to Europe. Financial problems persisted, reinforcing the need for such a shift to regional priority, and John Nott's defence review of June 1981 – *The Way Forward* – represented just one more move in a seemingly inexorable retraction of capability. By the time of the Falklands crisis, Britain's defence policy was concentrated almost entirely upon Europe, with only token forces earmarked for more global roles.

The fact that a war did, nonetheless, have to be fought 'outside the NATO area' in 1982 seemed to upset this trend of policy. The implications were clear: at a time when Britain retained residual global responsibilities, however small, a retraction of capability to the regional area of Europe was both premature and potentially dangerous. It was an argument which the government appeared to accept. In December 1982, as one of his last acts before retirement from office, Nott presented a new defence paper to Parliament, entitled *The Falklands Campaign: The Lessons*. Although principally a review of the campaign itself, this document did contain a section, titled 'The Future', in which a number of significant changes were announced.

In order to prevent a repetition of the recent crisis, a 4000-man military garrison, backed by appropriate air and naval units, was henceforth to be maintained in the Falklands, and various improvements – including the construction of a new airfield capable of handling long-haul jets – were to be made to the islands to render them easier to reinforce and defend. At the same time, 3rd Commando and 5th Infantry Brigades were to be augmented and retained specifically for non-NATO commitment in an emergency. More significantly perhaps, the naval reductions which had occupied such a central and controversial place in *The Way Forward* were to be effectively halted, with decisions to maintain three carriers and a destroyer/frigate fleet of 55 vessels, at least in the short term. *Fearless*, *Intrepid* and *Endurance* were all to be retained, *Invincible* was not to be sold and the losses of the Falklands war were to be replaced.

This looked like a return to a guaranteed global capability and was indeed applauded as such by the pro-naval lobby which had criticised *The Way Forward* in 1981, but it would be wrong to regard this as a firm pointer to the future so far as Britain's armed forces are concerned. Throughout his defence paper Nott made it crystal clear that the arguments of June

Above: RAF Harrier VTOL (vertical take-off and landing) aircraft streak over the countryside. The impressive performance of the Harrier in the Falklands War has led to increased export and domestic orders.

Below: A British soldier tests the newly-designed 5.56mm IWS (individual weapon system). More compact than the 7.62mm SLR, the IWS is designed to provide the next generation of small-arms for the British armed forces.

1981 still pertained. The main threat to British interests, he pointed out, continued to be posed by the Soviet Union, necessitating a European commitment as top priority. Furthermore, despite the implication that global capability had been permanently enhanced by the need to defend the Falklands, it was obvious that the changes of December 1982 would do nothing to solve and much to exacerbate the basic problem of finance.

In February 1983 the government presented advance public spending plans for the period up to 1986, and included in the mass of financial statistics was an estimation of the cost of the Falklands war and its aftermath. The figures make sobering reading, for although the bill for the 14-week conflict itself (£750 million) was to be met from a special Treasury contingency fund established to deal with such an emergency, all other expenses were to be absorbed within the annual defence budget. Most of these arose from the need to maintain the garrison on the Falklands together with its supply line back to Britain, something which, it was estimated, would cost about £232 million a year. As each flight from Britain to Port Stanley, via Ascension Island, was currently absorbing the staggering sum of £155,000, and at least 30 merchant ships were still being maintained on charter to carry more bulky cargoes, such figures were hardly surprising.

Nor was this the full extent of the problem, for the government's pledge to restore equipment lost in the Falklands conflict was estimated to require nearly £1000 million, spread over the next few years. The five RN/RFA vessels destroyed in the South Atlantic – two Type 42 destroyers (*Sheffield* and *Coventry*), two Type 21 frigates (*Ardent* and *Antelope*) and one logistic landing ship (*Sir Galahad*) – were all to be replaced, together with the Cunard container-ship *Atlantic Conveyor*, lost while under government requisition. In addition, many of the ships damaged during the war would have to be repaired and nearly all those involved in the task force, civilian as well as naval, would require extensive refits at the public expense. Taking into account also the cost of 10 Harriers and 24 helicopters, plus the wealth of less dramatic kit lost in Operation 'Corporate', the size of the overall bill for the war could be quickly appreciated. By 1985-86, it was estimated, something approaching £2000 million would need to have been found just to pay for the defence of the Falklands, without taking stock of any equipment changes resulting from the lessons of the recent war. Such items as Searchwater radar pods, attached to Sea King helicopters to provide airborne early warning to the fleet at sea, and Vulcan air-defence gun systems, added to some surface vessels to cover the deficiencies of certain SAMs, were needed straight away and had to be paid for from existing funds.

The financial impact of the Falklands operation was, therefore, quite substantial, particularly as it came at a time when the defence budget was already under considerable pressure. Despite government optimism and the occasional sign that the economic recession was easing, there was no escaping the fact that defence, in common with many other areas of public service, was costing more and more each year just to be maintained at prevailing levels. This was shown in July 1983 when the new Secretary of State for Defence, Michael Heseltine, presented his estimates for the financial year 1983-84. The total bill of £15,973 million represented a rise of almost £1500 million on the estimates of the previous year, and although this included £624 million for the Falklands garrison and loss replacements, it paid for no new weapons projects or increases to existing force levels. In other words, despite a hefty rise in cost, the armed forces were to all intents and purposes 'standing still', implying that the sorts of changes introduced by Nott in December 1982 could not be afforded. As Britain already spent more on defence in actual cash terms than any of her European allies, the additional and unforeseen burden of the Falklands was unlikely to be absorbed easily in the plans of a cost-cutting government.

But this was not the only consideration. By 1983 the Cabinet was firmly committed to the purchase of the American-designed Trident D5 SLBM (submarine-launched ballistic missile) system to replace Polaris as Britain's strategic nuclear deterrent and the estimated costs of this have continued to rise. The latest official figure is £7500 million, spread over the next 10-15 years, and it must be admitted that this seems a reasonable price to pay for strategic protection. But Trident represents only one of a whole range of new weapons needed to maintain the credibility of the armed forces in future years. The next generation of attack aircraft for the RAF has to be planned now if it is to enter service in the 1990s; the Army requires substantial numbers of the new Challenger MBT (main battle tank) and a programme of active research into its eventual replacement; the Navy is pressing for the next generation of surface ships; and all three services need the latest computers, radars and electronic devices if they are to operate effectively on a modern technological battlefield. Add to these the constant requirement to improve service pay and conditions if volunteer recruitment of a high standard is to be maintained, and the scope of the financial problem is clear.

All this suggests that any attempt to exploit the Falklands operation to gain a permanent reversal of Nott's strategy of June 1981 will not succeed. A strategic 'mix' of global and regional capabilities would be ideal, and it could be argued that Nott was aiming towards this in December 1982, but in the end the country cannot afford that luxury. Already there are signs that a final retraction from residual overseas commitments is taking place. Negotiations with China over the future status of Hong Kong are being actively pursued; the prime minister herself is talking openly of a military withdrawal from Belize; and, although it will take time to formulate, a new relationship with Argentina, designed to reduce the need for a large garrison on the Falklands, is likely to emerge. In short, the basic trends of *The Way Forward*, with their emphasis upon regional

Above: A Sea Harrier, armed with Sidewinder air-to-air missiles, shows its classic lines against a backdrop of broken cloud.

Right: HM Submarine *Revenge*, one of the four *Resolution* class SSBNs, each armed with 16 Polaris SLBMs, which currently comprise Britain's strategic nuclear deterrent. The replacement of the SSBNs and the adoption of the Trident D5 SLBM system, is likely to dominate the defence budget for the remainder of the 1980s.

ROYAL NAVY
250
N

commitments, will prevail, partly because Britain is now tied firmly to Europe in political, economic and military terms, and partly because the country would be hard-pressed financially to afford anything more ambitious. This does not mean that British forces will no longer serve outside Europe, but it does imply that any overseas involvement would have to take place either in close association with allied nations (as was the case in Lebanon) or under international agreements backed by the United Nations (as is the case in Cyprus). The era of independent military action beyond the NATO area should be well and truly over, and although the Falklands conflict showed that the armed forces were still capable of dealing with the unexpected, it was an aberration, the financial impact of which is likely to have long-term effects.

The period since 1945 has, therefore, seen a radical shift in defence priorities which the armed forces have had to absorb. In the process they have been called upon to fight a wide range of conventional operations and, as the record shows, they have responded well. As guardians of the empire, they stood firm against both external and internal enemies, preserving the status quo until the politicians authorised withdrawal, after which they supervised and aided the emergence of the new post-colonial states. At the same time they contributed to the defence of the West, joining the allied forces of NATO in creating and maintaining a credible and effective deterrent, and helped to preserve the integrity of Britain itself against the threat of terrorist attack. Problems were invariably experienced, but the fact that no campaign or operation since 1945 may be termed a military failure, indicates the level of professionalism and adaptability attained. The net result has been a wealth of experience, particularly in the difficult art of counter-insurgency, which few other armed forces in the world today can match. Presuming that financial problems do not become insuperable, the evidence of the last 40 years implies that Britain will continue to enjoy the benefits of efficient armed services. In this, she is extremely fortunate.

Above: A Tornado variable-geometry, all-weather, multi-role combat aircraft. Manufactured by Panavia – an international consortium from Britain, Italy and West Germany – the Tornado is designed to satisfy a wide range of air needs into the 1990s, although problems have been experienced and costs are high. This particular model is carrying wing-mounted fuel tanks and a centre-line weapons pod.

INDEX

Page numbers in italics refer to illustrations

Acknowledgements

The publishers would like to thank David Eldred who designed this book and Ron Watson who compiled the index. The publishers would also like to thank the agencies and individuals noted below for providing the pictures on the listed pages. Special mention should also be made of the Royal Navy Fleet Photographic Unit at Portsmouth and the Public Relations office at HQ UK Land Forces in Salisbury.

Picture credits

AP Worldwide Photos pp 50 (bottom), 51 (bottom), 100, 141 (bottom), 142 (bottom), 143 (bottom)
British Aerospace pp 115 (top), 120 (top), 182–83, 187 (top)
Crown Copyright pp 111 (both), 112 (top), 114 (bottom), 120 (bottom), 127 (top), 146–7 (all 3), 150 (bottom), 151 (both), 154–55 (all 4), 158–59, 160–61 (all 3), 167 (all 3), 168 (bottom), 170 (top), 171 (both), 172, 174–75 (all 5), 176–77 (all 5), 179, 178–79 (main pic), 180 (all 3), 181 (bottom), 187 (bottom)
Robert Hunt pp 81 (top), 91 (inset left), 98 (bottom), 101 (top), 103 (bottom), 104 (top), 105 (top right), 110, 112 (bottom), 114 (top), 130 (top), 131 (both), 135 (top and bottom left)
ImperialWar Museum pp 12, 13 (top), 21 (all 3), 22 (both), 23 (both), 24 (both), 25 (both), 26 (bottom), 28–29, 30 (both), 31, 32, 33 (both), 34–35 (all 3), 36–37 (all 4), 38, 39, 40–41, 42 (both), 43, 44–45 (all 3), 46–47 (both), 48–49, 50 (top), 51 (top), 52–53 (all 5), 54 (both), 55 (top left and bottom), 56 (both), 57 (top), 58 (both), 59 (top), 61, 74 (bottom), 75 (bottom), 83 (top), 84–85, 88–89 (all 3), 90–91 (main pic, inset left and right), 92–93 (all 3), 94–95 (all 4), 96–97 (all 4), 98 (top), 99, 102, 103 (top), 104–105 (bottom), 109 (top right), 113 (all 3), 115 (bottom), 116–17 (all 3), 118 (top), 121, 125 (inset), 126 (top), 136, 138–39 (all 3), 152 (top right), 153 (top), 156 (both), 162–63, 165 (left), 166 (right), 169, 173 (both), 181 (top), 188–89
Keystone Press pp 10–11, 13 (lower), 14–15 (main pic), 15 (top), 16, 17 (both), 18, 19, 20, 27 (both), 55 (top right), 57 (bottom), 59 (bottom), 60 (both), 62, 63 (both), 64–65 (all 3), 68 (both), 69 (all 3), 70–71 (both), 73 (both), 74 (top), 76 (both), 77, 78, 79 (both), 80, 81 (bottom), 83 (bottom), 86 (both), 87, 101 (bottom), 105 (top left), 109 (bottom and top left), 128–29, 130 (bottom), 132, 133, 135 (bottom right), 137 (both), 140 (both), 141 (top), 142–43 (top), 144–45, 149 (both), 150 (top), 153 (bottom)
MARS p 75 (top)
MOD pp 118 (centre), 118–19 (bottom), 122–23 (main pic), 152 (top left), 185 (top)
©**Richard Natkiel** (maps) pp 26, 39, 72, 110, 130, 136, 148, 170, 171, 177
PPL pp 122 (top), 123 (top)
Royal Ordnance Factories, Ministry of Defence, London pp 106–07, 108 (left), 185 (bottom)
Swan Hunter p166 (top)
C & S Taylor pp 126–27 (main pic), 164 (right and top), 168 (top), 178 (top)
Michael Taylor pp 124 (inset top two), 124–25 (main pic)
Westland Helicopters Ltd p 124 (inset bottom)
Jarrow Shipbuilders p 184